D0041032

How I Saved the World

How I Saved the World

JESSE WATTERS

BROADSIDE BOOKS
An Imprint of HarperCollins*Publishers*

HarperCollins books may be purchased for educational, business, or sales promotional use. For information, please email the Special Markets Department at SPsales@harpercollins.com.

Broadside Books™ and the Broadside logo are trademarks of HarperCollins Publishers.

FIRST EDITION

Library of Congress Cataloging-in-Publication Data
Names: Watters, Jesse, 1978– author.
Title: How I saved the world / Jesse Watters.
Description: First edition. | New York : Broadside Books, 2021. | Summary: "The host of the Fox News shows *Watters' World* and *The Five* lays out the only path forward for our nation—listening to him—in this funny, offbeat book, which echoes his irreverent voice."—Provided by publisher.
Identifiers: LCCN 2021014847 (print) | LCCN 2021014848 (ebook) | ISBN 9780063049086 (hardcover) | ISBN 9780063049147 (ebook)
Subjects: LCSH: Watters, Jesse, 1978– | Television journalists—United States— Biography. | United States—Politics and government—21st century.
Classification: LCC PN4874.W2945 A3 2021 (print) | LCC PN4874.W2945 (ebook) | DDC 070.92 [B]—dc23
LC record available at https://lccn.loc.gov/2021014847
LC ebook record available at https://lccn.loc.gov/2021014848

21 22 23 24 25 LSC 10 9 8 7 6 5 4 3 2 1

To Emma.
Timing is everything. I love you.

I'm Watters and this is my book.

CONTENTS

INTRODUCTION

I stepped onto the subway in midtown Manhattan and took a seat. Minding my business, I was sitting quietly, heading downtown to go home after work. At the next stop, a guy entered the car and sat down right next to me.

"Aren't you the guy from Fox?" he asked.

These conversations only go two ways. The guy either loves me or hates me. I sized him up: white male, maybe late twenties, early thirties, semiprofessional attire. It was a toss-up. Here we go.

"Yes," I responded.

His tone was accusatory. "You're the guy that . . ." as he tells me things I've said on the air. Except it wasn't me. He has me confused with another host on the channel. But he doesn't care when I tell him he has me pegged for the wrong dude. He's angry. It's guilt by association. Typically, in a situation like this, I walk away. However, I'm trapped on the subway, and he's sitting next to me, growing more animated now that he's come face-to-face with someone who symbolizes, in his mind, the destruction of the country. In fact, he tells me, "You're destroying the country."

Instead of staring straight ahead and ignoring him while he taunts me, I try a de-escalation tactic, and gently engage him in relaxed conversation. I crack a smile and banter slightly. This backfires. The guy only gets louder. People begin to notice.

"Aren't you Jesse Watters?" a young woman sitting across from me asks. "I'm a big fan. You're awesome."

"Thank you," I say. Subtly, I roll my eyes at her, conveying, *can you believe this guy next to me?*

The subway rolls on while the guy gets cockier. He's demanding to know my salary. Whatever I'm making is way too much, he barks, and whatever I'm paying in taxes isn't enough. Definitely a Bernie Bro.

The subway slows down into Union Square, and he stands up. This must be his stop. I see he's carrying a tallboy in a paper bag. He's been drinking, which explains a lot. At least he's leaving. But not before this . . .

A steady stream of beer hits my body. All over my jacket, tie, and lap. It must have been a wide-mouth because it soaked me strong and fast before I realized what happened. He'd stood over me and poured his beer on me as he left.

I stood up and walked toward him. He was still just inside the subway, standing nonchalantly in the crowd as everyone was getting off. With my left hand, I grabbed him by his shirt and quickly maneuvered him out of the car while I hit him with a short, straight right to the face. He reeled back, stumbling onto the subway platform while startled onlookers scrambled to get out of the way. I must have looked ridiculous. At this moment, I was a little bewildered by my lack of knockout power. Shouldn't he be lying on the ground? I also realized I'd left my bag on the subway and needed to make a decision. Ditch it and finish the fight on the platform, or dip back inside the subway and ride home with my belongings? The psycho was standing there, shocked, holding his face, glaring at me. I turned back inside the subway car and sat down next to my bag. People kept their distance from me, like I was some beast. Drenched in beer, I rode home, stunned at what had transpired. This must be why Greg Gutfeld insists on taking town cars home.

This isn't an isolated incident. In the span of just this last week, a man called me a "Nazi" in front of my children, another man screamed obscenities at me in front of *his own* children, and a college student confronted me for "ruining our democracy" while I was at the liquor store. "It's a republic," I replied, as I left with my bourbon.

Personally, it's unsettling when you're face-to-face with these people because they all have one thing in common. Unhinged rage. I've noticed oftentimes they're so angry that they're literally shaking. The flash of anger comes so quickly that they're unpredictable. It's like a switch goes off when they've identified me. It's mostly upper-middle-class white males in their twenties to forties. They're usually thin, pale, and wouldn't strike anyone as particularly threatening, until they snap. I'll leave the demographic analysis there, before I'm accused of reverse racism.

"Are you Jesse Watters?" they'll sometimes ask, or sometimes not. They'll just start screaming "racist!" or "scum!" at the top of their lungs in public. Occasionally, they feel it's their duty to warn people who I am. "That's Jesse Watters! He works for Fox! He's a traitor!" They'll yell like progressive Paul Reveres while I'm buying coffee, and make a huge commotion, confusing the strangers around us who've never heard of me or don't care, who just want to pay and leave without some maniac disturbing the peace. If a CNN anchor were in Starbucks, I doubt I'd start screaming bloody murder while they ordered. I'd probably do the right thing and pay for their coffee. Their fake news gives Fox so much free content for our shows it's the least I can do.

What is it about Fox News that drives the Left so absolutely crazy? The truth hurts. That's the easy answer. But it's deeper than that, and so am I. Or at least I'll pretend to be.

Liberals who hate Fox with a passion don't actually watch Fox. Instead, they consume edited, cherry-picked clips on *The Daily Show*, on Twitter, or on cable competitors. These clips are editorialized to demonize the Fox host and inflame the liberal viewer. Jokes are made to look serious. Liberal hosts explain that we mean something even worse than the actual words that we said. Fox hosts, like myself, are on air for hours and hours each week, all month, for years. Our commentary is fact based and contextual. A loyal viewer will see our personalities and senses of humor, our compassion, and insight over the hour and over the long haul. But clips of Fox hosts are edited tightly, and spun in the same way, to make us look bad or bigoted. If you were to cut and disseminate clips of Tom Brady throwing interceptions, fumbling, and yelling at his teammates . . . attaching headlines like "Tom Brady Sucks" or "Tom Brady is a terrible teammate," the people who only saw these clips, who didn't watch the whole game, would believe Tom Brady is a horrible quarterback. And yes, I just compared myself to Tom Brady. This isn't to say that I don't make mistakes on air, or occasionally misspeak, but the liberal media machine only accentuates the worst. You don't believe me? Google me. I'd hate me, too, if I only saw myself through a liberal media prism.

Competitors to Fox, which is just about the entire media establishment—including newspapers, social media, magazines, late-night TV—do their best to dehumanize Fox hosts. Rarely does a Fox host have a puff piece written about them; rarely is there a balanced spread in a magazine; almost never is there a friendly interview or commercially tasteful package produced. Many of those opportunities are denied to Fox hosts, but if they're given that kind of platform or exposure, it's a hostile hit job with aggressive, partisan attacks, and unflattering photography. This treatment marginalizes Fox hosts out of the mainstream and makes them enemies in the eyes of millions. Personally, I see other people in the media just as other people. I see them as politically misguided, but respect their political beliefs as authentic, just very different than mine, and that's okay. But Fox personalities aren't just deemed wrong, they're deemed evil. Once you're convinced another human being is evil, that gives you license to take them out, by any means necessary. Many on the far left truly believe that I'm evil, immoral, bigoted, and doing severe harm to the country. The media has radicalized them into hating me.* Therefore, they have every right to do whatever it takes to physically hurt me, get me fired,

---

* I'm such a victim.

and break me down to the point where I'm unable to speak freely and feed my family. And let's be honest, if I can't host a show, I can't put food on the table. That's how unskilled I am.

The media finds demonization more effective than debate. For decades, Republicans and Democrats duked it out on the issues. Public policy discussions were usually about real-world results of the implementation of political philosophy. No longer. While conservatives still try to debate ideas and persuade the public with logic, liberals have surrendered. Now Democrats label every Republican policy proposal as "racist," "mean," or "sexist." Not only is that policy evil, but the person proposing the policy is evil as well. If you support border security, something politicians from every country from the beginning of time have supported, including Democrats just a few years ago, you're a "bigot" who "hates" immigrants. If you don't want your daughters competing against boys in track and field, which has been the norm for centuries, you're "trans-phobic." Republicans were against a government takeover of health care when Hillary Clinton attempted it in the nineties, but Republican opposition to government-run health care only became "racist" when Obama attempted it in 2009. If you supported a robust War on Terror, you weren't just backing the best policies to keep the country safe, you must be "Islamophobic."

This is a cheap and lazy way to dodge dealing with issues of substance. If my intentions are evil and racist, then debating them is a waste of time. Liberals don't have to question their own assumptions, challenge their own beliefs, improve their own policies, or even examine the legality or results of policies.

If Republicans are evil, liberals must be good, and don't need to persuasively present their ideas, since they're deductively coming from an inherently good place. In fact, there's not even a need to give Republican ideas a platform. Why give a platform to hate? See how easy it is to create a paradigm to eliminate the opposition? We wouldn't elect a Nazi, approve ideas from a Nazi, or let a Nazi speak on TV, and if a Fox host is called a Nazi, or anyone who wears a MAGA hat is called a Nazi, why shouldn't we eliminate them? That's what Fox is up against, and so are millions of Americans who support conservative positions.

The reckless rhetoric deployed against Fox reveals how desperate the Left has become. Delegitimizing their opponents through mob tactics, race cards, and boycotts demonstrates how the Left has lost their intellectual rigor. Tax policy, foreign policy, gun policy, and immigration policy have been debated since the country's founding. It appears as if many liberals have given up. Watch Fox for a day and watch CNN or MSNBC. I guarantee there's more discussion of policy on Fox than both the other channels combined. Personality, character assassination, palace intrigue, and personnel drama dominate the day over there, especially during the Trump administration. Labeling your opponents evil, and then trying to censor and delegitimatize them, isn't a confident position. We're trying to communicate and persuade, while the other side is trying to intimidate and silence. This tells me they're insecure in their positions.

Insecurity is born from fear. Liberals fear what they don't understand. If you can't summarize the other side's position in a way they would accept, you're not ready to debate. Most liberals don't understand conservative positions at all. This is because they've never been exposed to conservative positions with an open mind. If they were exposed, they were exposed to conservative positions with a liberal spin. This phenomenon creates the hostility that you see manifested on the streets. Violence, suppression, and demonization are liberal psychological coping mechanisms when confronted by conservatism. The only thing that can alleviate this is more debate, more conversation, and more engagement between the two sides. Conservatives are forced to digest the liberal worldview in school, in corporate America, through Hollywood, and in social media. We deal with it. We tolerate it. Many liberals go through their entire lives in a warm, comfortable progressive cocoon. When they see a clip of a conservative on cable or hear President Trump speak, or heaven forbid Jesse Watters visits their campus, it rattles their fragile world to the core. A new generation of liberals has been bred without an ounce of resilience. Having never been intellectually provoked or had their worldview challenged, coming face-to-face with a Fox host on the street can spark the emotional response of a child. I often wonder how deeply unhappy and insecure these people are, to have them blame everything wrong in their lives on a cable news host. Perhaps their parents' lives were more fulfilling. They marched against the Vietnam War or for the civil rights movement. Their grandparents battled the Nazis, so maybe they're just looking to find meaning in a life that doesn't measure up to past generations. I'm happy to be the Left's punching bag, but besides my eyebrows, am I really that scary?

From a mass communications standpoint, Fox is the only thing standing in the Left's way of complete media domination. They're only happy with 100 percent control. Anything less than that needs to be discredited and destroyed. Liberalism is fundamentally about centralizing power and control, and Fox is a huge impediment to their media monopoly. Most businesses that had 95 percent of the market share would be ecstatic. Not liberals. They're furious with Fox for owning 5 percent. Combine print, cable, network news, and social media, and it's total liberal domination. Yet they're still not satisfied. They don't want competition at all. This is why Fox is such a threat. And when the Left is threatened, they lash out.

While the mob rages, my job is to stay the course. I'm extremely grateful for the platform that Fox has provided, and speaking not just for myself, but for millions of Americans, it is a special honor. When people see me on the street, many say "Jesse, thank you for speaking for me, thank you for saying what I've been thinking." I feel very connected to the American people, and when I speak from my heart, I hope I'm speaking from their heart, too. Getting information out to the audience that they haven't seen in the mainstream media is my goal every day. Telling the real story about the events that are unfolding is critical. Sharing my analysis, based on fact, is something I've learned from *The O'Reilly Factor* and will continue to share. If this makes enemies, I can live with that. Everything I say is based on true love for the country, and true love for all the citizens of the country.

Even though Fox is number one, I walk into the building feeling like the underdog. I've been physically attacked, have received death threats, and have had my personal information strewn all over the internet, but that's nothing compared to what some people in this country go through. There are those suffering right now who're having a *really* tough time. Workers being preyed upon, students being bullied, children being abused. Victims of injustice will always find a voice with me. All Americans want to be treated fairly. We want to work hard, be respected, get ahead in life, and find love. I'm a patriot above all else. Whatever is in the best interest for the people of this nation, I'm for it. The media will always be biased, and Washington will always be corrupt. Nothing is going to change that. I'm going to keep rolling the boulder up the hill every single day anyway because of the love I have for the American people. That's my inspiration. Telling the raw truth with a little flair so we all enjoy life in the United States just a little bit more.

Sometimes having fun with all this gets me in trouble, but it's not my fault liberals can't take a joke. By trying to "kill" conservatives, comedy is collateral damage. Lighten up, people. Not everything is an opportunity to cancel someone. There are a lot of things to mock besides rich white conservative men. That's why late-night jokes get applause instead of guffaws these days. They've trimmed down the comedy targets to such a small, safe space that the audience just claps to show approval. What the hell is that about?

Why can't liberals laugh at themselves? They take themselves too seriously. An MSNBC reporter stood in front of a Minneapolis building engulfed in flames this summer and declared the riot "mostly peaceful." That hysterical lack of self-awareness was topped by a CNN reporter who stood in front of a Texas border wall and announced that the wall didn't work. Why? Because he didn't see any illegals crossing over. What a head-scratcher. Donald Trump does a virtual stand-up routine at his rallies, material that is objectively funny no matter what your political persuasion, but the press can't bring themselves to crack a smile. Actually, the press fact-checks President Trump's jokes. News outlets have even threatened and investigated random people for posting satirical memes on social media when the liberal media is the butt of the joke. Facebook demonetized and censored a comedy website for posting an article playing off a Monty Python movie, headlined *Democrat Senator Demands Amy Coney Barrett Be Weighed Against a Duck to See if She Is a Witch.*

Liberals fear humor getting into the wrong hands. Jon Stewart was very effective during his *Daily Show* run by the way he hilariously characterized, ridiculed, and mocked conservatives. Those clips went viral and made fools of many politicians. The humor was able to move the political needle on issues, too. It was persuasive on a small scale. It wasn't always fair—comedy doesn't have to be—but it was fun. Fun for them, and funny for people with a sense of humor. But the minute you turn the jokes on liberals, they frown, censor, and cancel. Conservatives can't stereotype, use certain words, or go after certain people. Greta Thunberg is off-limits, but Barron Trump is fair game. Slander Melania Trump, but don't you dare crack a joke about Michelle Obama. Jokes about liberals are always "over the line," "misinterpreted," "racially tinged," or "sexist." Democrat comedians wear blackface and call Ivanka Trump the c-word—which isn't even comedy—and there are no repercussions.

My man-on-the-street segments were tame, playful, and illuminating presentations that somehow whipped liberals into an offended frenzy. Joking around on *The Five* or my weekend show is never mean-spirited. Half the time, I'm making jokes at my own expense. The other half is good, clean fun. Look even closer the next time you see a smirk on my face and a twinkle in my eye. We're all in on the joke together. If you can't laugh at yourself, you're boring. And being boring is truly the biggest insult.

I can laugh at "Cocaine Mitch" and John Boehner weeping. I can laugh at the Mooch fiasco. I can laugh at Trump trying to buy Greenland or ordering five thousand dollars' worth of fast food for the Clemson football team. Trump is comedy gold. I can laugh at all that, but liberals can't laugh at Hunter Biden, AOC, Beto O'Rourke (his arm movements), or the Seattle autonomous zone called CHOP? Not even a little giggle? Fifty different genders—fine, however many you want—but you're saying there's not anything remotely funny about that? Sleepy Joe hurting his foot while petting his dog. My sources told me that when Kamala Harris found out she said, "His foot? It was supposed to be his neck." See how easy it is? If Trump hurt his foot petting a dog, liberal late-night would be howling.

A politician would rather face traditional political attacks than face humorous ridicule. Therefore, liberals police humor going in their direction. The stakes are too high for them. Their life revolves around politics and power. Humor bridges the divide, whereas liberals' entire strategy is divide and conquer. Humor takes the edge off, but liberals need the edges sharp so they draw blood on contact. Conservatives who smile, mock, and laugh are too "likable." This cannot be allowed to happen. It's hard to demonize someone relatable and funny. The Right has evil intentions, therefore their jokes are "insensitive," "harmful," and "rude." And if liberals are the target of jokes, that means people will be laughing *at* them, and they may be forced to look inside themselves. Nothing is more terrifying for an insecure person. Walling yourself off from possibilities that challenge your small-mindedness is much easier. Better to be a victim or arrogantly align yourself with victims you claim to speak for but never really listen to. Cocooned off from conversations outside your social circle is safer than stepping outside and facing a world that doesn't fit your bias. Assuming the worst about the opposition makes smearing them feel righteous, when it's really just a cheap high.

You compete for approval from people who look down on you, and punch down on those you think are inferior, but behind it all your fear is that they're happier than you. The humorless hostility is the liberal's tell. Sleeping in that small apartment, longing for more money, but shaming those who earned it. They're only comfortable in their own class, all the while appropriating from the lower to gain acceptance in the higher.

They are dissatisfied with their clout while squeezing every last drop of it in front of people you barely know. They spew sophistry on social media, but won't debate face-to-face. They're unsure of who they are, but tell others that they're not good enough. I've traveled the country for years and have spoken to thousands of people. I know the type. The truth terrifies them. Humor is even scarier. If the Left could listen and laugh a little more, maybe they'd stop blaming Fox for their own failures. So lie down on the couch and relax. Watters will fix you right up.

Years ago, during spring break in Jamaica, someone must have accidentally spiked my tea with mushrooms. It wasn't anything like what I'd planned for the day. The sun was shining bright, and an intense light formed. In it, I saw an image of George Washington, Jesus, and an Indian chief. All of a sudden, I realized the light was coming from inside me. I had an epiphany. I was George, Jesus, and the chief reincarnated. It was at that moment I realized I was the chosen one. I have been to the mountaintop, my friends . . . and it was beautiful.

You can doubt the wisdom I found that day, but never doubt my belief in said wisdom.

People ask me all the time, "Jesse, when are you going to run for governor?" or "Jesse, why don't you run for president?" I'm sorry, but I can't take the pay cut, maybe later. For now, just read how I saved the world. You won't realize it's been saved until the very end. If you still don't get it, try some "tea."

How I Saved the World

CHAPTER ONE

How I Saved the Great Outdoors

People consider me the Teddy Roosevelt of Fox News. When I say "people," I mean me. I'm a conservationist who can live off the land . . . I just choose not to. I have a healthy respect for the environment. I have so much respect that I try to never go near it. I've weathered that storm and now appreciate modern technologies like air-conditioning. The phrase "central air" turns me on. A lot.

Roosevelt said, "There is a delight in the hardy life of the open. There are no words that can tell the hidden spirit of the wilderness." Well, I have lived the hardy life of the open, and have found the words.

I had just turned eighteen. It was the summer before I went off to college, and all I wanted to do was hang out at the pool, play Ping-Pong, and get into trouble with my friends. But my liberal parents had a different idea.

As I sat in the living room opening birthday presents, I kept wondering what the *big* present was in the corner. My parents *never* showered me with expensive presents. In our house, presents were seen as "materialistic." In fact, expensive presents were borderline "hedonistic." Plus, they cost money, and my parents were frugal. The other kids who got expensive presents from their parents were "spoiled." My parents had different "values." I only got presents on my birthday and Christmas. *Never* in between. If I really wanted something badly, I'd have to pay my dad back—in cash or in chores. Every time I opened a present, it was either a new book, an old book, or a turn-of-the-century farm tool that you'd find at a New England flea market. Dusty. Wooden. Always wooden. Some iron involved. A little rusty. Like a butter churner or a corkscrew. Extremely utilitarian. If I lived alone in a cabin with no electricity, my parents would be great gift givers. My mother would make a big deal about these presents, which she referred to as "family heirlooms." My mom would tell me how special this clay jug was to our ancestors. When I mentioned it smelled like gasoline, she announced that it was an "antique" that must be cherished and coveted. If I complained, my father would say, "You can't always get what you want, but if you try sometimes, you just might find you get what you need." Later on, I learned these were lyrics to a Rolling Stones song. Mick Jagger never wanted all that money, fame, and cocaine. He just needed it, I guess.

The worst presents my parents got me were "experiences." Things you can't touch, such as play tickets or museum passes. Every kid likes that, right? But the big box in the corner couldn't be that. It was too big. You have to pretend you don't see the *big* present sitting in the corner while you opened your *smaller* presents. Classic birthday-present-opening protocol. You can't stare at it. You can't even acknowledge it. You just open book after book after book, waiting for the big-ticket item in the corner. You have to act surprised when your parents hand you the *big* present, even though everyone in the room knew it was there the whole time.

"Oh my gosh! What is this!? I thought we were all finished!" Great performance by me.

I started tearing open the wrapping paper, then tearing open the box, getting closer and closer to the big eighteenth-birthday present. Finally, I see it. But confusion sets in.

"A duffle bag?"

"Happy Birthday, Jesse! We're sending you to NOLS."

"What's NOLS?" I asked. And why were they acting like luggage was so generous?

"It's the National Outdoor Leadership School. You're going rock climbing in Wyoming for the whole month of August!"

I felt something huge building in the pit of my stomach.

"It's like the Outward Bound trip in Oregon you went on last summer, except it's more of a survival school. You'll learn what it takes to be a leader. You leave in a few weeks! Aren't you excited!?"

I couldn't speak. This was an *experience*. The *worst kind of experience*. My parents had been sending me to these wilderness adventure camps every summer for the past five years. The last three in Wyoming, Oregon, and finally Tennessee (in the Smoky Mountains) were brutal. I hated them. They said it "builds character." It built me into a character, all right. A character on TV.

The Oregon Outward Bound trip the summer before had been a nightmare. I got off on the wrong foot with my counselor and it was downhill from there. It was probably my fault. He warned me that Class V whitewater rafting was serious. He warned me that we had to properly balance all the bodies by weight from bow to stern. The rapids were intense, and we could easily be launched overboard. I'd done some pretty hard-core whitewater canoeing and kayaking the summer before . . . so I was cocky. I was also falling in love. That first day in Oregon I'd met a girl. Lauren. She was now in my raft. I threw my new $200 wraparound Ray-Ban sunglasses on and smiled across the seat at her.

"Don't wear those sunglasses without croakies, Jesse!" my counselor Dan lectured. "You'll lose them in the water."

"I'll be fine Dan, don't worry." I didn't pack them. I didn't like *the look*. It didn't give off the I'd-rather-not-be-here-but-I'm-ready-for-love look.

We launched two rafts, seven in a raft. We're floating along. I'm sitting toward the back, behind Lauren, looking good in my new sunglasses. All of a sudden—boom!—I'm bounced in the air, off the raft, and into the water.

"We got a swimmer!!!" Dan yells. I sense Dan relished yelling this as I bobbed along with the cold current.

He guides the raft toward me and reaches his hand out to pull me in. But I see my Ray-Bans in the water. I can easily grab them first and hop back on the raft, so I take a few strokes upstream. Dan sees what I'm doing, but he has to teach me a lesson. Right before I grasp the glasses, he yanks me back into the raft empty-handed.

"What did I tell you!?" Dan screams at me. I'm soaking wet, and I've lost my new sunglasses. It's also a little embarrassing to go overboard in front of your soon-to-be girlfriend.

Dan looks smug. "Next time, *listen* to me, Jesse." I can tell he's happy I was thrown overboard and lost my sunglasses. He wanted me to lose them. Because they looked really good on me.

Dan hates me already. I'm very good at sensing when someone hates me. Everyone loves me, so when someone hates me, it's very easy to notice. Usually, adults love me the most. The older they are, the stronger the affection. Because I'm so polite and charming and respectful. So for this counselor to hate me this passionately, this early in the trip, was concerning.

My sophomore summer camp counselor loved me. Mostly because I didn't accuse him of being a Nazi. One of the other campers did. So I probably just looked good in comparison. This camper Jacob just flat-out didn't want to be there, and he took extreme measures to get out.

When I'd arrived at base camp that last summer, I began to wonder if this was a camp for "at-risk" youth. My parents had just dropped me off. I was unpacking my canvas Abercrombie & Fitch bag, lining up my new REI hiking boots and fleece vests—looking good as always—when two other kids arrived on a bus without their parents. They carried big garbage bags over their shoulders, the kind you raked leaves into. They plopped the garbage bags down and unpacked sneakers, some mesh shorts, and some sweatshirts. And knives. Interesting. I hadn't seen knives on the packing checklist we'd received in the mail. It was a two-week hiking trip through the Smoky Mountains of Tennessee. What were the knives for?

Within the first hour, a lightning storm forced us to scatter. We tossed any metals we were carrying and crouched facedown under trees. Chavez, the one with a knife, was crouching next to me. "I'm not getting rid of my blade," he whispered. "Me neither," I lied. I didn't have a blade, but I didn't want him to know I was unarmed. I *did* know that our chances of getting struck by lightning had just gone up. Big decision to make. Should I rat out Chavez for carrying a knife, so our chances of surviving the lightning storm would go down? Or does snitching on Chavez put me in greater danger later? I decided not to narc. Luckily, we survived the storm, and Chavez and I became friends.

We marched around carrying sixty-pound backpacks, almost got trapped spelunking through pitch-black caves (Chavez was a little hefty), and got stung by wasps. Jenny, a blonde with tattoos, broke her leg falling down a rocky trail. We had to build a stretcher out of tree limbs and carry her down a mountain to safety. She got medically evacuated by helicopter. A sad turn of events, but it gave Jacob an idea. Jacob wasn't enjoying the food, the wasps, or the slap-boxing fights with Chavez. He found inspiration in Jenny's tragedy. Jacob began fake-falling down the trails to injure himself.

"I just need to sprain my ankle, then I'm outta here," he confided in me. After a few "falls," our counselor was onto him and told him to knock it off. Our counselor, John, was a solid guy. Athlete, military background. His head was shaved. That gave Jacob another idea. Jacob was Jewish and started claiming John was "discriminating" against him. Jacob began calling John a Nazi. This went on for days. Jacob hurtling himself against the rocky ground, grabbing his ankle in pain, John inspecting his ankle, telling Jacob it wasn't sprained, and Jacob calling him a Nazi. Eventually Jacob wore John down. John hiked us miles out of the way until we found a cabin in a clearing. John and Jacob approached the cabin, made contact with the outside world somehow, and Jacob was taken back to base camp. His parents picked him up.

I'm sure Jacob and the camp settled their lawsuit, but I was thinking about filing a claim myself: child abuse based on malnourishment. The food on the trip was powder based. We just carried around sacks of powder. At meals, we'd put the powder bags atop boiling water, and the steam would expand the powder bags into bigger bags of cornmeal or mashed potatoes or whatever the powder was derived from. But my personal pot system was damaged. So my water never really came to a full boil. So my bag of powder never expanded into the bigger, warmer, fluffier bag of starch-like "meal" that everyone ate. It barely grew into anything, just a semi-warm ball of undercooked yeast. When I complained to John that everyone else had a large feast and I was stuck with a golf-ball-sized "dinner," he didn't care. "It still has the same amount of nutrients as everyone else's," he explained.

I starved in them thar hills. Was this a camp for disadvantaged youth *and* fat kids? Because *everyone* was hungry and losing weight. I was just the hungriest. As we walked the trails for hours every day, our entire conversation was about food. We all discussed in great detail our favorite meals: lasagna, fried chicken, bacon, tacos.

When the camp was over, my parents picked me up and said I looked "scary skinny." My mom asked what I wanted to eat. I said, "Shrimp." They say you are what you eat, I guess. After a long drive, we stopped for peel-and-eat shrimp in a basket. I sat down and started gorging myself. After a few shrimp, I threw up. Apparently, because I'd been eating golf-ball-sized meals in the mountains, my stomach had shrunk significantly. Did my parents see this as a sign? That perhaps maybe we should stop shipping me off to survival camps for underprivileged kids with emotional and/or eating disorders? No. It got more extreme.

Back to Outward Bound in Oregon's Cascade Mountains. In Oregon, we ate what we caught. Spearfishing is challenging. Due to the refraction, you can't stab the fish directly. It must be stabbed ahead of where it appears in the water. It's very frustrating. For a starving seventeen-year-old with zero spearfishing experience, it's torture. My counselor Dan was tormenting us. Outward Bound felt like Gitmo for privileged white kids. I was kept away from my family and yelled at, and we prayed five times a day. For food.

Do you know what a solo is? I wish I didn't. Your solo is when the counselor makes you survive in the wilderness alone for three days. Counselor Dan gave me three things: a book of matches, some rations, and a dirty look. Three days without any human contact. I missed Lauren. We'd really gotten closer after the sunglasses scandal. We paddled and hiked and stayed up late together. She was a great listener. She always nodded her head in agreement when I declared Dan hated me.

Our hiking teams had separated during our solos, so I wouldn't see Lauren for a while. So I wrote her a love poem. That took about twenty minutes. Then I practiced handstands. Another twenty minutes. I thought a lot about *why* my parents were doing this to me. They'd sent me to lacrosse camps and camps with sailing and tennis and wrestling. Camps I liked. But each summer, they'd gotten more extreme. Each summer, I played fewer sports at camp and went farther into the wilderness for longer periods of time. Was I being trained for a mission that I'd learn about later? Were my parents preppers? I had a lot of time to think about these things. I also thought a lot about mosquitoes. They were everywhere. The camp actually made you wear mosquito-netted helmets that tied around your entire head. Not one single inch of my skin was exposed. My skin was already sunburned because I didn't listen to Dan. He'd told me to wear sunscreen, but I wanted to be tan for Lauren. I probably stank from not showering for weeks, but I had a nice bronze going.

My friends got high that summer. So did I. Eleven thousand feet high. After the solo, we hiked to the top of Mount Hood. It was snow-capped, and we used pickaxes to climb higher. Just a normal summer day building character with a massive backpack on my shoulders and a pickax in my hand.

How did we go to the bathroom on a snowcapped mountain range? Good question. We found privacy and squatted. We didn't carry toilet paper because there was nowhere to dispose of it. So we wiped with what nature gave us. Atop this particular peak, nature gave us snow. Yes, we wiped with snow. In the woods, we wiped with leaves mostly. Sometimes stones. Or sticks. Anything with smooth surfaces. Occasionally pinecones. *With* the grain, never *against* the grain.

My face was now bright red. Not from fatigue, dehydration, or poop-snowball humiliation. Serious sunburn. That's when Dan whipped out some zinc oxide. The white gooey stuff. He ordered me to put it all over my face. I refused and only put it on my nose. I looked like a lifeguard from the early eighties. But at that elevation, the sun was reflecting off the snow and onto my face at "dangerous levels." When we'd descended, my entire face was scorched. Blisters were forming. Dan was furious. He said something about "second-degree burns," and I started getting anxious because we were supposed to reunite with our full team (Lauren!) the next day. Of course, Dan had to ruin my reunion. He forced me to put the zinc oxide all over my entire face, not just the nose. I looked like a total idiot. Like my face was covered in frosting. But it got worse. While I was hiking, mosquitoes started sticking to my face. Lots of them. So by the time we reunited with Lauren, she was shocked. I was a gooey-headed monster with dozens of black mosquitoes stuck to my once-beautiful face. Some of the mosquitoes were still alive and could be seen struggling to unstick themselves from my face. Other campers had thought it was funny and had thrown some small twigs onto my zinc oxide face. It was a game to them. Pieces of bark, small berries, anything that would stick. A medley of items dangled from my goopy face.

"What happened?" asked Lauren, keeping her distance.

"Don't worry, it's nothing major," I assured her. "It's just sun-burn. . . . Dan made me do it. He thinks I'll have permanent scarring if I don't put this stuff on. He's such a freak," I explained, with several squirming flies pasted to my face. Dan is the freak here, Lauren, let's remember that, baby.

"Oh, are you okay?" she asked, still firmly planted five yards apart from me.

"I'm fine! I wrote you a poem on my solo. Here." I handed her the poem. It was folded up. She looked down at it. Took it. Looked at me. Looked back down at the poem and looked back at me. She didn't open it. She just slid it into her pocket. I'm so glad she didn't read it in front of me. My balladry would have moved her to tears. We didn't want other campers to see our connection and be jealous. That would have been awkward. I'm so glad she wasn't making this awkward.

"Okay, I have to go, Jess. See ya later, I guess." She walked away. Except she didn't turn and walk. She kept facing me and walked back-ward slowly. Like she couldn't take her eyes off me. I could see this wasn't a positive development. Was she scared of getting too close? Maybe that was it. She wasn't ready to commit. Our love was too raw. That was definitely it. She was just scared. Either that or Dan totally sabotaged my look with his zinc oxide. "Medical emergency," my ass. Dan's probably one of those guys who think, "Well, if I'm not happy, then no one is going to be happy."

On the last day of Outward Bound, Dan lost his cool and yelled at me in front of the entire camp. Something about not listening. I don't remember. Which was weird because the same thing happened at NOLS.

We'd just finished rock climbing in the Grand Tetons, and we were back at NOLS base camp. Our flight home left the next morning. All of us were gathered in a room that evening for the final ceremony. Our counselor Peter was handing out manila envelopes. Our team was opening them and admiring their certificates of achievement. I opened my envelope, but there was nothing inside.

"Peter," I said. "Mine's empty." The room fell silent.

"That's right, Jesse. You failed."

Gasps were heard throughout the room.

"What are you talking about?" I stammered.

"Jesse, you did not fulfill the requirements necessary," explained Peter.

"That's bullshit and you know it," I said to Peter and stormed out of the room. Some of my friends followed me and consoled me outside. They all agreed it was total bullshit. I survived like everyone else, didn't I? We all left base camp and got drunk that night in town.

The next morning on the way to the airport, the head of the program handed me an envelope. I hopped in the shuttle bus and opened it. It was a report card explaining why my performance didn't meet the "standards" of the National Outdoor Leadership School. It was a total hatchet job. They said my lack of technical understanding "put other people's lives in danger," blah blah blah. Apparently, this was a very strict program, and they were watching my every move. They said I was "more concerned with working on my suntan" than on learning how to rock climb. They even quoted me. Apparently, during one difficult climb, I delayed the group, became flustered with my carabiner, and yelled, "I don't know what I'm doing! I have ropes coming out of my ass!" That was the only accurate line of the report card, though. Oh, and one more. The report said the only thing I did well was "dress appropriately." I read that line over and over again. I did look good out there. Never too hot, never too cold, always just right. My mom and I had gone to Patagonia and bought some really nice stuff before I left.*

When I got home, I forgot to destroy the evidence. My parents found the envelope in my luggage. They were pretty disappointed. I fought back hard against the smear job, arguing that it was about "the experience," not a stupid report card. I figured I'd use their own words against them. I even pointed out the part about me dressing appropriately and winked at my mom. She didn't appreciate it. Deep down, she knew her boy looked good out there.

My parents wanted to teach me that nature is better than what humans have created, and they ended up teaching me the opposite. I love the earth, but not as much as I love what we've done with the place.

Does AOC know anything about the environment? I doubt it. Has she ever hung her food from trees so bears can't eat it? Has she ever gone without washing her hair for thirty days? Maybe Bernie has, but she hasn't. Socialists can't survive in the woods. Only rugged individuals like me can. Frontiersmen like myself innovate our way out of the woods so we can live in Manhattan sky-rises.

All of the great advancements in human civilization over the last few hundred years resulted from capitalism and free enterprise. Individuals compete with each other to provide goods and services for others. We can travel, communicate, and produce products in a faster, safer, and more intelligent way because of one thing: *energy*. Entrepreneurs have unleashed an energy revolution that has raised the standard of living throughout the world. The human race is living longer, we're safer, we're wealthier, and we're better-looking than ever before. Too many liberals think this is all a big mistake, but they wouldn't feel that way if they still had to wipe with sticks.

Petroleum, natural gas, and coal make up 80 percent of American

---

* "You look good, you feel good. You feel good, you play good. You play good, they pay good."—Deion Sanders

energy consumption. Fossil fuel combos have made up 80 percent of the American portfolio since 1900. It hasn't changed in over a century, despite the massive spending on "green." Only 10 percent of our energy use comes from renewable energy sources like wind, solar, hydro, and wood . . . the rest is nuclear. I support renewable energy, but it's just a smidgen of the fuel that powers America. Not from lack of investment. It just doesn't do what other energy does. We can be clean *and* rational. Solar works well in the Southwest, hydro works well in the Northwest, and wind turbines work well in the plains, but let's be realistic. Banning fossil fuels is suicidal. If AOC wants to board a solar-powered airplane, be my guest. I feel much safer with jet fuel.

AOC wants to raise taxes to pay for her $100 *trillion* Green New Deal, which experts estimate will increase the average American household's costs by $70,000 or more. That may be ice cream money to people like Nancy Pelosi, but that's unaffordable for the rest of us. She says if we don't pay up, we're all going to die in twelve years. Give me all your money or you're dead? That's not a deal; that's a death threat.

The Green New Deal is a Trojan horse for socialism. Here's what's in it. You get a free house, free health care, free college . . . and if you don't want to work, you get free money. It gets rid of all oil and gas, gets rid of the internal combustion engine, gets rid of air travel, and aims to eliminate cow belching.* So you'll have no NASCAR, no airplanes, no motorboats, no gas grills, and no hamburgers on those grills. Also, every single building and home in the country goes under "green" construction. We'll go deaf from all the hammering! And every single project must be signed off on by indigenous peoples. So the Native Americans need to give their consent before we move forward. It concludes with this gem: "So the question isn't how we pay for it, but what we will do with our new shared prosperity." AOC thinks destroying the economy is going to make us all rich. She actually

---

* Cows make methane.

has an economics degree. If going green is going to create this big economic boom, why do we need guaranteed jobs and income? She wants to turn the United States green—but she's really turning them red—because we'll all be voting Republican for a generation.

"Experts" can't predict the weather this weekend in New York, so how can they predict the entire world temperature *ten* years from now? They can't. (But if they are right, the disastrous outcome they are predicting is that it will go up a few tenths of one degree in ten years.)

What's the difference between a fortune-teller and a climate expert? A fortune-teller knows they are guessing.

They predicted human starvation. The opposite happened. Now we're all fat.

They predicted people in cities would be forced to wear gas masks. Wrong. Only in Hong Kong.

They said there'd be no more sunlight; the entire earth would go dark. Obviously wrong. I have a great tan.

They predicted fish would suffocate. False. I had sushi for dinner last night.

They said the average life expectancy would drop to forty-two years old. I'd be dead. Many people would love that, but it's just not true.

They predicted we'd hit peak oil in the year 2000. Nope, just filled up my tank on the cheap.

They predicted we'd run out of gold. Have you seen Mar-a-Lago?

And famously, Al Gore predicted Antarctica would melt by 2014. I think it's still there, but I haven't checked.

All their consensuses keep changing. I've distrusted government scientists since the food pyramid. More like a food pyramid scheme. These so-called experts can't even tell me what food is healthy. What's healthy changes based on what industry lobbyist funds which study. When I grew up, carbs were good, then carbs were bad, now I'm hearing carbs are good again? Not cool, guys. Can we stick with carbs being good? Same with butter. I grew up on it. But then my mom switched to margarine. That gray tub of Country Crock took up prime real estate in Mom's fridge. But that turned out to be a crock. Now we dip our bread in olive oil? Because the Europeans do it, I suppose. Europe's never been wrong about anything, right?

I grew up on red meat, but apparently hamburgers are bad because too much red meat will kill you—and because raising cattle causes global warming? I read an article by Julie Lesnik, an anthropologist from Wayne State University, who says we should eat crickets instead of red meat. She argues crickets are a great source of protein, and we won't have enough meat for the growing population in thirty years. But AOC said we'll be dead in twelve years. If we're all going to die so soon, why can't we eat whatever we want?

Liberalism is based on guilt. Since America is inherently bad (slavery, genocide, patriarchy), liberals feel guilty and conflicted about our undeniable success. They process this through a system of blame: Capitalism causes climate change, and climate change creates hurricanes—and hurricanes are punishment for our sins. So it's our fault. This is literally how humans lived in ancient times. A hurricane? We need to sacrifice a virgin. An eclipse? The moon god is angry; let's fast for a week. These ancient polytheistic rituals are what modern-day global warming doomsayers practice. Today, liberals tells us we can stop the hurricanes if we just let them tell us how to live, what to drive, what to eat, and what brands to buy. It's the modern-day equivalent of ritualistic tribal sacrifice. We've made Mother Earth angry, feel bad about it, but absolve yourself by giving up your rib eye and your Tahoe. Consume less, but if you must, buy only the products we approve of (that so happen to be owned by liberals). Using guilt to exert power and control is the cornerstone of liberal psychology. Ultimately, they feel unnerved by the success of capitalism—a system liberal Democrats can't fully embrace because they can't fully control it—so global warming prevention gives liberals the justification and mechanisms to control capitalism. The Far Left doesn't like the fact that capitalism has delivered so much progress without their input. They need to restrain it and turn back the clock to make themselves feel relevant. Show me a control freak and I'll show you a liberal.

Liberals are jealous of capitalism because liberals are control freaks who can't stand a system that delivers the goods without their picking the winners and losers. So they deem capitalism dangerous for the planet, a threat to human existence, and only *liberals themselves* can reverse-engineer capitalism to save the world. If you just give them total power and all your money. See how this works? But by restraining capitalism, Democrats are taking us backward, so they have to glorify the rustic lifestyle and pat themselves on the back for living like a poor person.

AOC wants us all to grow our own food in community gardens. Have you ever met a New Yorker who looks like they have the time or patience or skills to harvest crops? We'd rather order takeout, not pull carrots out of the ground. Do you know how inefficient urban gardening is? These green liberals want us to live like the Amish. Horse and buggies and well water are carbon neutral, I guess. (Maybe someone should tell them the Amish all voted for Trump.) Some liberals are just cheap and can't afford bottled water. Some are poor and want to make themselves appear virtuous. Some are so rich they can afford solar paneling on their ski chalet. Either way, I think they're running out of things to protest. No more Vietnam War, no more civil rights revolution . . . we'll just protest the weather. That's how good things are in America. Because of capitalism.

Liberals never think things through. Nancy Pelosi is so worried about the environment but lets the homeless treat San Francisco like a toilet. New York City mayor Bill de Blasio wants to give driver's licenses to illegal immigrants, but don't more cars on the roads pollute and congest the city? The *New York Times* cuts down millions of trees each year to print their papers. Why not just go digital, guys?

The arrogance of these people. We want Liz Warren in charge of remaking our $19 trillion economy? What does she know about anything? She flipped a house once. So what? We're going to give her the keys to remodel the engine of the free world? Barack Obama claimed the Chevy Volt was the "car of the future." Now it's discontinued. Bernie Sanders can't do math, but his green agenda is going to magically add up? AOC says we should all move to higher ground. Great idea. Beach houses just got more affordable.

I want my showers to have the water pressure of a fire engine house. I want my dishwasher to take one hour, not two, and I want the warm, soft glow of incandescent lightbulbs on my face. As you recall, I had a bad sunburn once. I need all the help I can get.

CHAPTER TWO

How I Saved Hard Work

I attended Trinity College in Hartford, Connecticut. It's a small, lib-eral arts preppy party school with decent athletes. I found out quickly I wasn't "a decent athlete." The summer before I started there, I sent Trinity's head football coach my "highlight reel" from my senior sea-son. Big hits, diving catches, and a two-point conversion. Sadly, the tape was returned to me in the mail a month later without a response. Next, I tried out for the lacrosse team. But I was a little rusty and kept getting yelled at. Plus, practices started very early in the morning. I quit during the preseason. My father was a first-team all-American lacrosse player in college and a nationally ranked squash player. It was cold there in his shadow.

I'd been listening to a lot of Grateful Dead, so I started out as a philosophy major. Aristotle, Socrates, existentialism. Things were go-ing well until I got to Kant. What an ass. So I pivoted to history, and the rest was . . . history. One evening I passed out and woke up with C-SPAN blaring on TV. I was listening to the Senate floor speeches and realized the Republicans believed in the same things the Found-ing Fathers fought for: limited government and individual freedom. That was my "political awakening." I started listening to Rush Lim-baugh, reading Ann Coulter, and visiting the Drudge Report. When I came home from college to visit my parents, I made them listen to Rush during car rides. My dad could handle it, but it gave my mom

road rage. She swerved into oncoming traffic once during a mono-
logue about welfare reform. Limbaugh literally drives liberals crazy.

I had problems behind the wheel, too. The summer after my fresh-
man year, I threw a party at my parents' house. My dad ran a private
school in Long Island and lived in the headmaster's residence on campus. He was away in Maine with my mom. One thing led to another,
and I took some girls joyriding in my dad's car and did some dough-
nuts all over the football field. The next morning, the school's head
groundskeeper, Dick, woke me up at nine.

"What the hell happened here last night?!"

None of your business, I thought to myself. And who let you in? He
stormed into my bedroom and physically pulled me out of bed.

"Whoa! What are you doing!?" He didn't answer. He just led me
downstairs to the driveway in my boxer shorts.

"Look at this!" he screamed, pointing to the skid marks all over his
beautifully manicured fields.

I tried my best con job. "I don't remember, but I don't think I had
anything to do with this."

"Then what is *that*?!" He pointed to my dad's car, which was covered in mud and grass. I was busted.

"Oh wait, maybe I *did* do that," I admitted.

Dick was furious. "Come with me. You're an alcoholic. We're going
to a meeting."

"Wait! What!? I'm not an alcoholic! And I'm *not* going to a meeting. I have work." I had an internship at the New York Stock Exchange
that summer, which I was already late for.

"You're coming with me. You have a problem. Put some clothes on
and let's go." Dick was fifty and intimidating, and I was still drunk.
This was a bad situation, so I got changed and jumped into his truck.

Forty-five minutes later, I'm at an Alcoholics Anonymous meeting.
It's a public school classroom filled with drunks and drug addicts—
and me. Grown men are standing up and telling stories about how

they smoked crack during their lunch breaks and lost their life savings. Women are admitting they drive around doing errands, sipping vodka, and turning tricks. All of a sudden, it's my turn to stand up.

"I'm Jesse Watters, and I have a problem with alcohol." The whole room clapped loudly. That gave me a headache, but I powered through. I told the story about the joyriding and threw in some crazier details, so they thought I was really struggling. Finally, it was over. I felt sick. I excused myself from the meeting and found a bathroom. I sat there in the stall with my head between my legs. *Oh my God, this is rock bottom.* I'm in so much trouble with my parents, and maybe I have a drinking problem?

Suddenly, someone bursts into the bathroom. A very powerful man *kicks* down the *locked* door to my stall.

"What are you doing!?" he bellows. "Shooting up in there!?"

I'm sitting on the toilet, viscously hungover with my pants around my ankles. "No! I'm going to the bathroom, man!"

"Show me your hands!" the man yells, as if I'm hiding needles. I show him my hands. No heroin.

THAT was rock bottom.

I was convinced for a while I had a drinking problem, and didn't drink a drop my sophomore year. Eventually, I realized I was just an idiot, so I started back up again. Junior year, I studied abroad in the Netherlands. I know what you're thinking. And you're right. I was drawn to the museums filled with masterpieces from the golden age of Dutch realism. Also, the coffee shops. They have the best coffee there. I drank a lot of it.

When I was in college, I wanted to party, not protest. College kids today don't know how good they have it. When my parents were in college, they protested the draft and marched for civil rights. *Their* parents' generation stormed the beaches of Normandy. They made it possible for today's students to storm the beaches of spring break. The Greatest Generation saved the world from Hitler and kamikazes, while this generation is saving the world from offensive Halloween costumes and Ben Shapiro. I like Ben; he's sharp. But he's five foot five with a podcast. Is he really a threat?

Being constantly offended is turning college students back into children. Stroking a therapy llama in a safe space because Trump's election triggered PTSD isn't how you handle a loss. Neither is rioting against conservative speakers. Liberals can't debate, so instead, they seek to silence. Anything liberals disagree with, they label hate speech, and freak out about. Political correctness is the weapon the Left uses to shut us up. Don't fall for it.

Students at the University of Wyoming wanted to ban the school's mascot—the cowboy. Why? Because it may offend Indian students, and because cowboys weren't inclusive of cowgirls. So now cowboys *and* Indian mascots are offensive. Do you think British students who study at the University of Massachusetts are upset their mascot is the Minuteman? Are southerners angry about the New York Yankees? Are women unnerved over the University of South Carolina mascot? A gamecock? Well, maybe a little.

Students at Middlebury College wanted to ban Cinco de Mayo celebrations because serving burritos at the cafeteria might offend Hispanics. First, there's nothing offensive about a burrito. They're delicious. Second, are Italians offended if people eat pasta on Columbus Day? Of course not. In fact, *not* eating what an Italian serves you is offensive. Saying "no, thanks" to homemade manicotti is a declaration of war in some homes.

According to a study two years ago, 80 percent of Americans see political correctness as a problem. It was conducted by More in Common, an international research initiative. You'll never guess the groups who are most sick of it. Seventy-five percent of African Americans, 82 percent of Asian Americans, 87 percent of Hispanics, and a whopping 88 percent of American Indians feel political correctness is a bad thing. The study is fascinating, but there's more. The group that buys into the PC nonsense are rich, college-educated white liberals who identify themselves as atheists. These so-called progressive activists represent less than 10 percent of the population but "play an outsized role in political discourse." Mainly because they scream the loudest and populate the media. This study turns everything upside down. What are the lessons? Stop being offended on behalf of other people. Eighty percent of the time the groups you think you're offended for aren't even offended themselves. Also, being offended doesn't make you right, it just makes you offended. Being offended is a *feeling*. Taking offense is oftentimes a choice. Trump's travel ban offended people in the press. Journalists were offended on behalf of Muslims. They have the right. But on the merits, they were wrong. SCOTUS upheld the travel ban as constitutional. Just because something is offensive doesn't mean it's not constitutional.

I'm not an insensitive jerk. For instance, I'm for transgender bathrooms. If you want to build more bathrooms, good! I'm over forty now, and the only time I don't have to pee is when I'm already peeing. Plus, if there's a men's room, a women's room, and a transgender room, I'll always go in the transgender room. Because it'll be cleaner. Hardly anyone will ever go in there.

Colleges don't teach kids the one thing they need to know: If you want to succeed in life, you have to earn it. I didn't learn that in college, and I had to start from the bottom to really understand it.

I graduated from Trinity with a bachelor's degree in history. When people ask you, "What do you do with a history degree?" you're supposed to answer, "Anything I want to." At that time, I wanted to make money. Most of my friends were going into finance, so I thought, why not me? I landed a job in my hometown, Philadelphia. Rorer Asset Management. I was the youngest guy on the sales team. My nickname was "Spare" because whenever I called anyone in the office, the caller ID read "Spare." I assume they gave me a temporary spare phone used for interns.

I had no clue how the markets worked. But, boy, could I give a presentation. The sales associates had to deliver a fifteen-minute mock sales pitch to executives in the boardroom about the firm's investment strategy that summer. If you were good, you'd get promoted and make great money. I practiced the night before in the mirror and nailed the pitch. Flawless. The room applauded. But the executive sales consultant, Cus, was on to me. He said, "Great job, Jesse, but you have no idea what any of that means, do you?" He was right. I'd just memorized it. "What's relative value investing, Jesse?" I smiled like a dumb model. One single follow-up question like that would make the wheels fall off during a *real* presentation. He winked at me and told me to sit down. That afternoon he pulled me aside and said, "Jesse, you're a talented kid, but you clearly don't belong here." I was fired at the end of the summer. It turns out you have to have a basic grasp of arithmetic to handle millions of dollars of other people's money.

Surely I could handle other people's food, though. I got a job as a busboy at a hip restaurant in Old City, Philadelphia. Things didn't go as planned. The head chef quickly realized I had zero restaurant experience. I had to be trained to stack dishes on my forearms and pour water properly.

"You should have started at a diner before you came to a place like this," he muttered after I smudged his perfectly plated lamb chops.

I was the only white busboy. The rest were Mexican. The Democrats always said Mexicans do the jobs that Americans won't do. Maybe that's why we didn't talk much. Because I was taking the job, they were supposed to be taking from me. Or maybe because their English wasn't great. But it was probably because they had to keep sweeping up plates I dropped and shattered.

The hours weren't great. Working weekends wasn't my thing. I asked the manager for some vacation days. He pointed out that I only started a week ago, and it wasn't that kind of job. So I gave it another week and took off the next weekend. When I returned on Monday, I was fired. The restaurant didn't get the whole "work-life balance thing." I think I was just ahead of my time.

Fired from two jobs and desperate for cash, I applied for work at the Omni hotel. "You're a little overqualified to be a bellman," said the hotel manager, as he looked over my résumé. I was a little overdressed for the interview, too. Brooks Brothers button-down under a sweater and corduroy sport coat with loafers. I looked like a guy checking into the hotel, not the guy who checks you in. They always say, "Dress for the job you want, not the job you have." I didn't *want* a hotel job, and I didn't *have* a job at the time, and I didn't already own one of those little hats. Despite this, I was hired on the spot. I traded my corduroy sport coat for a gray bellhop blazer with shiny gold buttons. It had yellowish tassels dangling from the shoulder pads to match, accompanied by a dark-rimmed lobby hat. This was the Omni staff's "Fall/Winter" wardrobe. In the spring, the bellhops switched into their "Spring/Summer" style. This meant tan jackets with a wide-brimmed safari-style hat. I had to get a real job before spring. Tan doesn't go well with my complexion.

The first day, a pretty blonde pulls up to the hotel in a sports car. I head toward her to help her unload her luggage from the trunk. "Let me get that for you," I say, hitting her with my killer smile. "Why, thank you," she says, pulling her suitcase out. As she pulls it out, lingerie spills onto the curb. A pile of delicate silk and lace sits provocatively on the pavement. We make eye contact. Do I pick the G-string up for her? This wasn't in the bellhop handbook. "Oops! Let me get that!" She giggles and gathers it up, stuffing it into her bag. She must have done that on purpose, I thought. That's her move. She's so frisky. It wasn't an accident. Ball's in my court now. I stack her luggage on my rolling bellhop cart and maneuver it into the lobby. She checks in with the front desk, and the other bellman looks at me like, "You lucky dog."

"Right this way, follow me," I say, rolling her cart full of naughtiness into the elevator. When we arrive at her room, she invites me in, and I set her bags down by the entryway. "Thanks, Jesse," she says with a smile, handing me ten dollars. She'd read my nameplate, but it still felt extremely personal. "No, thank *you*," I reply, still standing in the doorway. Our eyes stay locked. Silence. I can feel the moment building. I make my move. "Is there anything else?" I ask slyly, giving her the green light. She looks at me, then looks me up and down and says, "No," and closes the door in my face. It was at that moment I realized I was wearing a bellman uniform. With a bellman hat. And this was not a porn movie.

Being a bellhop taught me a lot, not just about rejection. During my first week, I got outhustled by an older, cagier bellman, but I picked up the game quickly. I was younger, friendlier, faster, and more alert than the guys I worked alongside with. I was pulling in hundreds of dollars in tips a week—cash—by opening doors faster, identifying guests quicker, and valeting more expensive cars. NBA All-Star weekend and Valentine's Day were humongous paydays. It was all about outworking the other bellman and serving the needs of other people. That's what capitalism is.

My dad forced me to do manual labor growing up, so I understood the value of hard work. Mowing, raking, edging, planting, shoveling, clipping, trimming, weed-whacking, sweeping, washing, uprooting, chopping, stacking, painting, and so on. Today, I hold a microphone and gesticulate, so I still work with my hands, and I have a strong connection to others who do. It's been painful to watch the American manufacturing base be hollowed out. Since the China trade bill was signed in 2000, America lost nearly five million manufacturing jobs and 63,000 factories before Trump was elected. Over two hundred thousand manufacturing jobs were lost under the Obama-Biden administration, while 1.3 million jobs were outsourced abroad. Trump ran on bringing manufacturing jobs back to America, and he did. Before the pandemic hit, more than 400,000 manufacturing jobs were added during his term. Wages skyrocketed as well. Median household income jumped $5,000 in Trump's first three years. Adjusted for inflation, Americans were making record high wages. These gains blew away the measly raises Americans received under Obama-Biden. Incomes grew the fastest for working-class Americans, delivering a working-class boom. The poverty rate dropped to 10.5 percent, the lowest on record. The black poverty rate dropped below 20 percent for the first time ever. In his first three years, Trump's economy lifted nearly five million Americans out of poverty, the largest reduction in over fifty years. Industrial and trade policy, when directed strategically, with a dash of patriotism, can unleash a working-class renaissance and revive large swaths of the country.

But if you're on your feet all day, capitalism can hurt your back, so I decided I needed some relief.

I joined a gym, and there was a perk. Upon signing up, you could get a free chiropractic session. I peek into the chiropractor's office next to the front desk, and an attractive therapist is massaging someone. A perk indeed. The next day I'm getting ready for the gym, styling my hair, spraying some cologne on. Drakkar Noir, of course. I hit the gym and head straight for the chiropractor's office. But as I open the door, she's not there. Instead, it's a guy. A big guy. "Hey, my name's Brad. Come on in." Brad's jacked. He looks like Fabio. Within thirty seconds, my shirt's off, and I'm lying facedown on the table. Brad's hands are everywhere. Pressing and cinching, kneading, and bending. He suddenly takes my head and cups my chin, and jerk-twists it to the side. It sounds like microwaving popcorn. Pop, pop, pop! "Stand up," commands Brad. "Let me show you what I did." I stand up gingerly, and he points to a medical poster hanging on the wall. It's a guy with his spinal column highlighted. Nerve endings and vertebra . . . I don't feel so well. Everything goes black. Next thing I know, I wake up on the floor in Brad's arms. "Call 911!" Brad yells out to the front desk, loud enough for the whole gym to hear. Brad continues to cradle my head while a team of paramedics enters, puts me on a stretcher, and wheels me out. It's my first day at the gym, and I'm the fool being wheeled out of Brad's office by EMTs. Like an injured football player being carted off the field, I stick my arm in the air and give the gym a big thumbs-up. That's right, guys, I'll be back for the playoffs. I'm a warrior.

The ride to the ER in the ambulance is traumatizing. The nurse takes my blood and then loses it. She drops the vial on the floor of the ambulance, and it rolls around. She's on her hands and knees searching for it, but it keeps eluding her, like the antidote in the opening scene of *Indiana Jones and the Temple of Doom*. Finally, we arrive at the hospital. I dismount from the gurney and stroll into the ER. Guys are there with stab wounds, women have OD'd, and I'm in gym shorts feeling faint. Eventually, an emergency room physician sees me. I tell him about Brad, the popping sounds, and the scary poster. "What happened, Doc? What was my injury?"

The doctor says, "Mr. Watters, I think you sustained more of an *emotional* injury."

"Oh," I said, turning a little red. "Manipulation of the vertebra doesn't trigger loss of consciousness. Your relationship with Brad probably played a bigger role than anything else."

"My relationship? Doctor, I don't have a relationship with Brad," I tried to explain.

"Of course you don't, Mr. Watters," the doctor assured me. "By the way, what kind of cologne is that? Drakkar Noir?"

A few months later, I landed a *real* job in finance. My bellman buddies were amazed that the job came with a dental plan. Unfortunately, I never used it. I lasted less than a week. Cracking a risqué joke at orientation didn't go over well with Human Resources. They told me not to tell anyone about it. I told a secretary the next day. On the third day, I was fired. This was God's way of telling me to leave Philly. In one year, I'd been fired from three jobs and quit one. I couldn't go back to bellhopping. The seasons had changed, and they'd make me wear the tan safari attire.

I moved back in with my parents in New York and got a job in politics. The George Pataki for Governor reelection campaign was in full swing. The Republican governor put a judge on the ticket to run as his attorney general candidate. Her name was Judge Irizarry, but people called her Judge "Irregardless." Nobody on the Pataki campaign thought much of her since she'd get smoked by the incumbent Democrat attorney general running against her: Eliot Spitzer. His nickname was "the Steamroller." He was a hard-charging, ambitious dude, and my job was to take him down with opposition research. I wasn't very good at it because I missed the fact that he was sleeping with escorts up and down the East Coast. His new nickname became "Client Number 9" when a madame's little black book was released. But Spitzer trounced Judge Irizarry before the scandal erupted, and Pataki won reelection, and I was out of a job again. That's when Fox News hired me. The greatest decision they ever made. This time, I didn't crack any jokes in front of HR.

I started in the basement of Fox News. Literally. The only windows were Microsoft. I was like a cable news coal miner, working with my hands underground in the dark. The job was "Intake." A wall of TVs and tape decks recorded video footage that was fed in from all over the world. Once the feed was finished, someone popped the tape out of the deck and gave it to me. That's when my arts and crafts skills kicked in. I slapped sticky labels on the tapes, labeled them with a Sharpie, and logged them into the computer. Every thirty minutes a production assistant would visit my dark corner and take away my tapes. That was the only contact I had with the outside world during my day. That, and when I went to Wendy's for lunch. I wasn't making bellhop money anymore, Fox was paying me twelve dollars an hour, and the only tips I was getting were to "write neater." Those tips came from Candi, who sat next to me and dotted her *i*'s with a heart. Candi mentioned, "I was cute for a white boy." Mike sat to the other side of me and had gout. "Too many Spicy Chicken Sandwiches from Wendy's," he explained. As I wondered whether gout was contagious, the production assistant grabbed my stack of tapes. As she began to leave, I pulled her close and pleaded softly in her ear, "Take me with you." She smiled and walked away, but not before I noticed Candi staring daggers at me. So much workplace drama.

I was working freelance, no health insurance, Wednesdays to Sundays, 4 p.m. to midnight in a newsroom basement. There was nowhere to go but up. Thankfully, I heard *The O'Reilly Factor* had an opening. Surely there wouldn't be any workplace drama there! My résumé got into the right hands, and I had an interview scheduled with O'Reilly himself. Bill had a radio show at the time and "interviewed me" during a commercial break. The "interview" lasted two minutes. He popped out of the studio, sat down across from me, and looked at my résumé. I was a total mess at the time, but I looked great on paper: prestigious schools, finance internships, political campaign experience (I left out the multiple firings). But Bill wasn't interested in any of it.

"What's your father do?" he asked, cutting right to the chase. My résumé (and my killer suit) may have made it appear that my father was some Wall Street banker who pulled strings and got his entitled son the interview. I told Bill what my father did. Bill nodded and looked back down at my résumé. Dead silence. Bill didn't have any follow-up questions, it appeared. He just was looking down at my résumé. Did his mind wander back to his radio show and forget I was sitting there? More dead silence. Things were getting awkward, so I spoke up.

"Bill, I read your book; it was amazing!" All of a sudden, he perked up and looked directly at me.

"You seem like a smart kid; you start Monday." We shook hands, and Bill shot back inside the studio. Just like that, I was hired. But the next week I was nearly fired.

Monday was my first pitch meeting. It was like *American Idol*. Producers stood up in the middle of the newsroom and pitched ideas for the show in front of the judges. Except there was only one judge. Bill O'Reilly. And he was Simon Cowell. I hadn't really prepared for the pitch meeting and didn't understand the stakes. Producers were pitching stories, and Bill was shooting then down with gusto.

"No way! I'm trying to get ratings here. What else?"

"You don't know what you're talking about. Research it, and re-pitch it Thursday."

"Never in a million years. Next!"

Producers were dropping like flies. It was my turn. As I began to speak, Bill cut me off.

"Interns don't pitch! Next!"

The show's executive producer, David Tabacoff, jumped in. "Bill, this is Jesse Watters. He's not an intern. You just hired him as a production assistant." Bill thought he was interviewing an intern candidate when he hired me, I realized. That brief interview made more sense now.

"Okay, go! What do ya got!?" Bill bellowed.

I pitched and bombed. I mumbled something about New Hampshire separatists. Totally incoherent. Later that day, Tabacoff called me into his office.

"Bill doesn't think you're *articulate* enough to work in television," he explained. "You have two weeks to turn it around . . . or you're fired."

Not "articulate enough"? That was like telling Michael Jordan he couldn't score enough to play in the NBA. I'm not comparing myself to Jordan, but we're both the greatest of all time at what we do.* This was a pivotal moment. I stared into the abyss and buckled down. I refused to be fired *four* times in one year.

---

* Winning.

So much fake news is reported about Fox. I understand why. Winning drives people crazy. The channel has been number one for nineteen straight years. Number one in morning, daytime, and prime time. In the third quarter of 2020, for the first time in television history, a cable channel—Fox News—beat the networks (ABC, NBC, CBS) in prime time. Fox News beat *Dancing with the Stars*, *Big Brother*, and *The Voice*.

Fox is also "the most trusted" American news brand, as multiple surveys have shown. Our hosts are more talented, our commentary is more compelling, and our reporting/analysis is more fair. A big misconception is that the channel is a bunch of right-wingers. When I joined *The Factor*, half the staff were Democrats, including the line producer, the chief booker, and the two executive producers. Our news division is separate from our opinion shows. The hard news hours in daytime and at 6 p.m. are staffed by tireless producers and feature some of the best journalists and anchors in the business. During breaking news, political coverage, and natural disasters, the news division shines. Unlike our so-called competitors, our news division doesn't fall for hoaxes and make major errors in judgment.

We have a strong connection to the country and reflect what the country is feeling. Our hosts and contributors often disagree with each other about politics and policies, unlike some of the lemmings on other networks. Healthy, respectful debate and analysis are what we do best. Every single Fox News show books guests or has cohosts who debate and disagree, unlike CNN and MSNBC, which go hours and hours without a single dissenting viewpoint. Most of the people who hate Fox don't ever watch it; they just see out-of-context clips online. Maybe they're afraid to watch because they might like it.

Thanks to my tenacious work ethic, and fear of failure, I turned it around on *The Factor*. After two weeks of researching and fine-tuning pitches, I saved myself from being thrown out on the streets. But I made it onto the streets another way. During a pitch meeting, I told Bill about a judge in Alabama who'd given a child sex offender a sixty-day sentence.

"Okay, Watters, you're going to go down to Alabama and confront the judge."

Where's Alabama? I thought to myself. I'd never been south of the Mason-Dixon Line . . . except when I went to Disney World as a child.

CHAPTER THREE

How I Saved the Children

I was staked in the parking lot outside a county courthouse in Alabama with a freelance cameraman. It was 6 a.m. I sat in the driver's seat, the cameraman sat shotgun, and we waited for Judge Bush. A twenty-six-year-old man was convicted of sexually abusing a twelve-year-old black girl, and without any explanation, Judge Bush suspended all but sixty days of a ten-year jail sentence. It was a huge miscarriage of justice, and Bill wanted an explanation. I'd spoken to the girl's mother over the phone the night before, and she was heartbroken. Judge Bush refused to talk to our producers and appear on the show to justify his short sentence, so there I was, ready to stick a mic in his face and demand answers.

Before we'd finished our coffees, a black Lincoln town car with official plates pulled out of the courthouse garage and sped away. We were off to the races. I gunned the engine and took off behind him, trying not to tail him too tightly. The town car was ripping down the rolling roads of rural Alabama, and my heart was pounding with adrenaline. Where was he going? Is he trying to lose us? Thirty minutes later, the town car pulled into another local courthouse, and we caught a glimpse of the driver exiting the vehicle and walking into the main entrance.

"We got him now," I said to my cameraman. We parked opposite his vehicle and waited. "When he comes out of the courthouse, we jump out and nail him." We reviewed the picture of the judge in my file and scanned the door, ready for action.

Fifteen minutes later, the same man we'd tailed exited the courthouse and headed straight for the town car. "Let's go!" I said. The cameraman and I jumped out onto the parking lot pavement and moved toward him.

"Judge Bush, it's Jesse Watters with Fox News. Why did you give such a soft sentence in the child rape case last week?" I walked right up to him and stuck the mic right under his chin.

He looked at me and stopped dead in his tracks.

"I'm not Judge Bush."

Oh, no. I swallowed.

"I'm not Judge Bush. I'm a state trooper, but I'm going to tell Judge Bush you're looking for him." He even flashed his badge to rub it in.

It was my first ambush interview, and I'd ambushed the wrong guy. We walked meekly back to our car, sat down, and reviewed the photo I'd brought from New York to identify him. He was a dead ringer for the judge, but it wasn't him. The trooper would tip off the judge I was in town, and I'd lose the element of surprise. The judge could now take evasive measures and avoid me as long as he wanted. My cover was blown, so I only had one choice. I waited an hour and called the judge's office. I told his secretary I was in town looking for an interview. It was a long shot, but it was my only option. To my amazement, she called back and said the judge agreed to deliver an on-camera statement from outside his chambers. Incredible luck. I called Bill and explained the deal. Except I didn't tell him I blew the ambush. I was dumb, but I wasn't stupid.

"Okay, Watters, when the judge comes out, *yell at him*," Bill instructed. Yell at him? I was a polite, well-mannered young man. This was going to be hard for me.

"Right when he walks out, you let him have it."

That afternoon, we set the camera on a tripod outside of Judge Bush's chambers and waited for him to come out and deliver his statement. I stood behind the camera and worked myself up into a rage. I thought of the victim, her age, the mother's voice on the phone the night before, her anguish and confusion and most of all her helplessness. Suddenly, the judge appeared from his chambers wearing his robe. He sat down, put his glasses on, and began reading an explanation for his sentence. It was an emotionless prepared statement. That's when I unloaded on him.

"Judge Bush, what do you have to say to the victim's family?" The judge stopped midsentence. I was so nervous. My voice was screeching.

"Don't you believe in justice? Sixty days for child molestation!? Have you no shame?"

I peppered the judge with questions like this until he was totally rattled. He stopped reading his statement and scampered back inside his chambers. I felt rude but righteous. It was an emotional octave that I cultivated professionally for years to come.

His secretary came out, scowling at me, and handed me a copy of his statement. The statement didn't even address his rationale. It was fluff. It seemed to me like a corrupt situation.

The next night, Bill played the tape on the show, and it had a big impact. I was pretty pleased with myself, even though I had screwed up the ambush and hidden it from everyone. Nobody knew. Bill called me into his office after the show, and I expected a pat on the back. But that's not what happened.

"Good job down in Alabama," Bill said. "But your voice is too high-pitched for television." I guess my voice *was* a little high.

"If you want to make it in this business, you need a speech coach," Bill explained. His voice sounded like deep, rolling thunder. "Me? I never had that problem."

I left his office and walked back to my desk. Our executive producer, David Tabacoff, saw me leaving and asked what Bill had wanted.

I turned to Tabacoff and in my deepest, most masculine voice, said, "He told me, 'Good job in Alabama.'" Tabacoff looked at me, very confused, like, Why is this kid doing a James Earl Jones impression?

"Good night, Watters," he said. "And get some sleep. You sound like you're getting sick."

I woke the next morning feeling fine. One of my duties was screening and selecting viewer emails sent into the show. Viewers were very impressed with my performance, but they were a little confused about my name (and voice):

> Bill,
>
>   Your producer Jesse did an excellent job getting Judge Bush on tape. *Her* questions really made that judge squirm. *She* definitely deserves a raise.
>
> Mark Bowman
> Miami, FL

After reading dozens of emails that misgendered me, I needed to prove to the audience that this voice belonged to a man. An immature, frightened man, but a man, nonetheless. That moment came during the Jessica Lunsford case. A convicted sex offender, John Couey, had abducted a nine-year-old girl, repeatedly raped her in his trailer, and buried her alive in the Florida woods. Even sicker, though, was the fact that three other people were living in Couey's trailer while little Jessica was being raped. Couey was charged with a slew of counts including kidnapping, child rape, and murder. However, the three others living in the trailer weren't charged. Madie Secord, Dorothy Dixon, and Matt Dittrich told police they didn't witness anything. Bill called these three "the slugs." He couldn't believe that they didn't witness a child being raped repeatedly in a trailer the size of a school bus. Were they lying to police? If they knew, they could have saved Jessica's life by calling 911. This had become a national story, and soon I was on a plane to Florida with a mission: track down "the slugs."

I checked into a hotel in Homosassa, Florida. This was the backwoods of central Florida. Sixty dollars a night, and twenty dollars by the hour. Stains on the rug. Rust-colored water ran out of the bathroom faucet. One towel. All the rooms were on the ground level. You could hear the bed springs singing from outside. Breakfast was "included." Peel back the sealed foil top of your orange juice in a plastic cup and enjoy. Peel back the sealed foil top of your drenched, mixed fruit cup and enjoy that, too. Peel back the sealed foil top of your individual plastic cereal cup and pour your mini–milk carton in. Men of all ages, heads bowed, sitting around a picnic table inside a mosquito-netted tent in silence. The only sounds were hacking coughs, cereal slurping, and sealed tops peeling. It smelled like cigarettes and bad decisions. The slugs had to be close by.

Jessica Lunford's father met me in a McDonald's parking lot that afternoon. Mark Lunsford pulled up on a motorcycle all alone. Black metal band T-shirt with tattoos running down his arms, a mullet with wraparound sunglasses. It was a tough look, but I could see the pain and suffering in his glassy, hollow eyes and cracked, leathery face. He was distant and distrustful at first, but after we spoke for a little while he told me where to start looking for the slugs. Mark had been looking for them, too, and wanted to stick something besides a mic in their faces.

"They like to drink at Colonel Frog's," he told me. "It's a bar up a few miles north." Mark spit on the pavement. He was disgusted. I could tell his rage came partially from the fact that he hadn't been able to protect his daughter from being kidnapped. There was the potential of vengeful violence boiling beneath the surface.

"I'll let you know if I find them," I told Mark. "And, again, I'm so sorry."

He looked at me, said nothing, and roared out of the parking lot on his Harley. I now had a job to do. Go to the bar. It was a job I was familiar with.

Colonel Frog's was surrounded by swamp. The minute I walked in, I realized I was a tad overdressed. The nice, plaid button-down shirt wasn't a great idea. This was a jeans-and-wife-beater type of dress code. So I rolled up my sleeves, ordered a dollar draft, and posted up by the pool table. The slugs weren't there. But it was happy hour, so I stayed and waited. After about two hours of knocking back dollar drafts, I finally got the drop on the slugs. A guy I was playing pool with told me they'd scattered to different trailers after their police interviews. One of them was living in a trailer off the main road pretty close to my hotel. That was the break I needed.

I woke up the following morning a little groggy and met the crew. We wired up and drove over to the trailer park. Down a dusty road, we found a dilapidated trailer poking out of a wooded area. Trash was strewn about everywhere. The screens were busted out of the trailer windows. The rusty door was ajar. I knocked on the door, not knowing what would happen. Nothing. I knocked again.

"What the hell do you want!?" A man's face emerged from the window at the opposite end of the trailer. I'd woken him up. But it wasn't one of the slugs. I explained who I was looking for, and he gave me the goods.

"One of them lives about two miles up the road," the guy explained, shirtless, wiping sleep from his eyes. "When the road stops, make a right by the fence and her trailer is right there." This dude looked like he was in bad shape. Missing teeth, strung out on something, he lived in the same world as the slugs and wasn't trying to protect them at all. As I left, he warned me.

"Be careful, though. They have a nasty dog."

Good to know. Big dogs scared me. Before going to the address, I hopped in my rental and told the crew car to hang tight. I swung by a local Quickie-Mart and bought some Snausages. We regrouped and followed the guy's directions, but we hit a dead end. The road, if you could call it that, just stopped at a fence, with trees on either side. There was nowhere for the cars to drive, and the trailer wasn't anywhere in sight. Discouraged, I called back to New York and explained the predicament.

"The road just stops," I explained to my senior producer. "We'll have to leave our vehicles and search for the trailer on foot."

"Is the crew up for it?" my producer asked me.

"Not sure. They're a little *wet behind the ears*," explained the twenty-four-year-old rookie producer. The crew had at least ten to twenty years of experience on me, but I was trying to act macho to New York.

I hung up and walked back to the crew car.

"All right, boys, let's unload and bushwhack to the right of the fence and see if we find it."

The audio tech looked at me and said, "I dunno, Jesse. We're a little wet behind the ears."

My mic had been hot. The crew had heard my entire conversation from their car. This was so embarrassing. From that point forward, things were a little awkward with us. But I was an idiot. That, at least, was clear.

We got all our gear together and hung a right at the fence and started pushing our way across the property line through the trees. Then I heard the noise.

"Woof! Woof!"

Out of nowhere came a nasty German shepherd. I reached into my pocket and hurled a Snausage at the foot of the animal. The ferocious beast immediately calmed down and feasted on the little Scooby snack. The crew and I exhaled and kept moving. In a hundred yards or so we came to a clearing. A little trailer was sitting right where the guy described. I rolled up to the front door and started knocking. No one answered. Then my cameraman yelled, "There she is!"

It was Dorothy Dixon scampering around the backyard. She was a hideous woman. She looked like a crack fiend. I circled around and started lobbing questions.

"Dorothy! Why didn't you go to the police!? Dorothy, you could have saved Jessica's life!"

I hit her with another question as she was hobbling up her back steps, frantically trying to open the door. We'd gotten her on tape. Jackpot.

I high-fived the crew, and we hightailed it off her property. When we got back to the car, I called New York and told them the news. My phone rang back a few minutes later. It was David Tabacoff.

"Bill said nice work, Watters. He wants you in the A block tonight."

"He wants *me* on the show?" I asked. "Like, as a guest?"

Tabacoff said yes. "You need to get yourself to Tampa in two hours. Feed the tape up from a local studio and do the interview from there. We tape the show at five. Hustle."

"Got it," I responded, not really getting it at all. I was still hungover from knocking back drinks with the locals last night. Appearing on national TV in a few hours was the *second* reason I was going to get sick. Then another worry crossed my mind.

"What do I wear?"

"A jacket, a tie. Look professional," advised Tabacoff. I was wearing jeans and a T-shirt. I hadn't packed anything professional. The only button-down I'd packed was checkered and stank like smoke from the bar. I had two hours to get to Tampa, buy a jacket and tie, feed the tape to New York (whatever that meant), kill my hangover, and appear on national television for the first time.

"Guys! Give me the tape. I need to get to Tampa ASAP. Which

way is it?" Hopefully the crew knew. . . . These were the days before iPhones and GPS.

My audio tech looked me straight in the eye and said, "Not sure, Jesse. We're a little wet behind the ears."

Very funny, smart-ass.

I'm in Tampa two hours later at a local NPR affiliate. They fed the tape up to New York for me and tell me the only place close by that sells men's clothes is Walmart. So I hit Walmart and buy a white shirt, a blue blazer, and a red tie for the total price of seventy-five dollars. Back at the studio, a woman put makeup on me and sat me in a dark studio. I couldn't see a thing, not Bill, not myself, nothing. I just stared into the abyss and nursed a Gatorade until I was up. Bill ran my tape of Dorothy Dixon in his Talking Points Memo.

I was on with a Florida congresswoman, and Bill went to me first, off the top.

"So, Watters, describe how you tracked her down."

My mind went blank and I just talked. I described the hunt, the trailer, everything except the beers. Bill let me speak uninterrupted for a while, which was rare. He thanked me and let me go. Apparently I spoke clearly, passionately, and looked handsome. Later I'd realize those things were the key to TV success. Plus, the makeup helps hide the hangover. And with that, a "star" was born. Or at least someone who thought he was a star.

The O'Reilly Factor launched a national campaign against child sex offenders soon thereafter. We made it our mission for all fifty states to pass some version of "Jessica's Law," after the late Jessica Lunsford. Any person who sexually assaulted a child under the age of thirteen must serve a mandatory minimum twenty-five-year prison sentence. The tough sentence applied to first-time offenders and was *mandatory*, meaning the judge had no discretion. Child predators had a high rate of recidivism, continuing to prey on minors after being released from prison. Therefore, long sentences were necessary to protect children and prevent judges from giving slaps on the wrist. I was deployed like a heat-seeking missile across America to confront judges, politicians, and editors who were soft on child predators. These "ambush interviews" had a big impact. When our campaign ended, forty-five out of the fifty states had passed some version of "Jessica's Law." Thousands of children were safer. This is what I'm the most proud of in my professional career.

Years later I covered the Jeffrey Epstein saga with Jessica's Law in the back of my mind. Jeffrey Epstein, a shifty financier, amassed a mysterious fortune and managed to run an international underage sex-trafficking ring right under everyone's eyes. Local Palm Beach police officers built a solid case against Epstein, involving multiple counts of child rape and trafficking, including physical evidence and substantial testimony. But a Florida state attorney refused to bring trafficking charges and then squashed the case with a soft-pedaled grand jury. After it got kicked to the federal level, Epstein assembled a legal dream team and, with brilliant legal maneuvers and enormous pressure, scored a small-ball, single-count, secretive plea deal, allowing him to come and go from his jail cell as he pleased. Showering police departments, Ivy League schools, and hospitals with million-dollar donations, Epstein greased his way into almost untouchable levels of power. European socialite Ghislaine Maxwell escorted him into high society, while allegedly serving as a pimp, procuring teens for both of them to prey on. Modeling agencies were used as cover, and money made most of the problems go away. Epstein donated tens of thousands of dollars, mostly to Democrats, once claiming he was a founding member of the Clinton Global Initiative. Bill Clinton himself traveled on Epstein's private jet for several jaunts and was fingered by at least one witness as frolicking on Epstein's private island in the Caribbean. Clinton's former right-hand man Doug Band confessed the former president did indeed visit "pedophile island."

Billionaires, royals, politicians, and famous scientists associated with Epstein, while his penchant for underage girls was an open secret. Finally, after decades of abusing girls as young as twelve, Epstein was taken into custody and committed suicide in his cell before trial. Countless people, powerful ones, wanted him dead so he couldn't bargain and sing. Everyone immediately suspected foul play, since he had been taken off suicide watch, his cellmate had been transferred, substitute guards were on duty who fell asleep and fudged their paperwork, and shrieking was heard from the cell. Famed forensic pathologist Dr. Michael Baden determined the bones broken in Epstein's neck were more commonly associated with homicidal strangulation. How the feds had failed to protect the most high-value inmate in the entire US prison system was incomprehensible.

The feds have raided Epstein's properties from Palm Beach to the Virgin Islands to his New Mexico ranch to his Upper East Side town house. Epstein had safes, an array of computer systems, and all his properties wired with security footage. Meaning that if you were ever at an Epstein property, you were recorded. The feds have it all—the bookkeeping, computer files, photos, flight logs, phone numbers, surveillance footage—but nobody else has been charged, except his partner in crime, Maxwell. It looks more and more like a cleanup operation and less like a pursuit of justice. There are rumors Epstein was a notorious blackmail artist and even a foreign intelligence asset. This makes the lack of progress in bringing more indictments all the more suspicious.

A whistleblower from ABC News revealed that anchor Amy Robach had an Epstein exposé ready for air that would have rocked Prince Andrew *and* Bill Clinton . . . but ABC brass spiked the story. According to a leaked tape, ABC didn't want to do anything to jeopardize their access to the royal family, especially with the royal wedding coming up. A former ABC staffer suspected of leaking the tape was fired from her new gig at CBS, and Amy Robach released a statement that read like it was written under duress. ABC said the spiked story didn't meet its editorial standards. This was news to me, since after the Russia hoax and Kavanaugh, I didn't know ABC *had* editorial standards. Do the networks really care about female victims? Networks have spiked stories involving Harvey Weinstein and Juanita Broaddrick, but this was different. These victims were *children*. ABC had relentlessly covered illegal immigrant children housed in facilities at the border but turned a blind eye to children being repeatedly raped by powerful men?

ABC execs should be asking themselves one question: How many children were raped by Epstein in the three years after they spiked the story? Sadly, the rest of the media circled the wagons and barely covered it. Members of Congress wrote ABC, demanding answers, but nothing ever came of it. ABC is owned by Disney, a company that cherishes children, but did they decide to protect pedophiles for profit and power instead?

The country is hungry for laws to be applied equally. This is why many feel the system is rigged against them. There's justice for some, not for all. Politically connected people are protected while victims pick up the pieces. This two-tiered system of justice pits Americans against each other and destroys our faith in government. Liberal celebrities can fake hate crimes and skate, destroy evidence under subpoena if their last name is Clinton, or illegally spy on a political campaign and get rewarded with a multimillion-dollar book deal. But there's nothing more sinister than protecting predators who brutalize children.

When I sought justice with my ambush interviews, controversy followed. Each confrontation came with a combination of danger, drama, and, of course, hiccups. I wreaked havoc on Vermont for years. The state was very soft on child sex offenders. Our campaign began when the Vermont district judge Ed Cashman sentenced a sexual predator to just sixty days in jail. The sicko Mark Hulett had forced a girl to perform oral sex on him for four years, beginning when she was six. The entire country was outraged. Judge Cashman, a Republican, ignored our calls, so I caught up with him in his snow-covered driveway at the crack of dawn. He scurried inside quickly like a coward as I barked my questions. It was my first "driveway ambush," and it taught me a lot. Still determined, I called his house and urged him to face the music. I was budgeted to be in Vermont until the judge explained himself. Cashman agreed to talk to me off camera and invited me inside his house. I kept the camera rolling and my mic hot, so parts of our conversation in his living room were picked up. The judge rambled on about his judicial philosophy and sex-offender treatment. He was cut from the same cloth as George Soros, the liberal billionaire who funneled millions into "restorative justice" programs. These initiatives favored rehabilitation over punishment and had infected the minds of judges across America. It was clear that Cashman believed child sex predators could be treated and released quickly back into society. It was a dangerous belief system that harmed America's most innocent.

Afterward, I headed to the parents of the abused girl and spoke to them at the crime scene. Another trailer. I looked inside the bedroom where the rapes had occurred. It was difficult to see the stuffed animals strewn across the victim's bed. It really hit me hard how young she was. The family had trusted the perp, but he took advantage of their kindness. *The Factor* ratcheted up the pressure night after night, week after week, and then something unprecedented happened: Judge Cashman held a re-sentencing hearing . . . and re-sentenced the pervert to three years in prison. Judges almost never change their sentences, but sixty days for child rape was scandalously soft, and he upped it. Still not enough, but we claimed victory and kept pushing.

Another Vermont predator, Andrew James, raped a four-year-old boy and got off with no jail time. Judge David Howard sentenced James to probation and we were furious. After dodging our invitations for days, I staked out Judge Howard's house early in the morning. This time he had an attached garage. As the garage door swung open, I had to improvise. We tailed his car. Tailing targets would become my preferred way of doing business. Usually the targets would exit the vehicle in a public space and I'd have free rein to confront them. In this case, the judge parked at a recycling facility. He got out of the car and walked a good distance to dump his bottles. As he turned around, I was there with my cameraman.

WATTERS: Hey, Judge? Jesse Watters with the Fox News channel. How are you doing? Can I talk to you for a second?
DAVID HOWARD, VERMONT JUDGE: No.
WATTERS: That guy who sexually assaulted a four-year-old. You didn't give him any jail time. Can you explain that, sir?

He was a long way from his car, so I had a nice, clean stretch to confront him. I realized this was one of the main keys to ambushing villains. Pounce when they're in open space, away from their cars, or from structures I'm not allowed into. It began a cat-and-mouse game for me. Or like hunting. Preparing, strategizing, waiting, and then taking the shot.* When you ambush someone, you only get one take. You can't redo it. You have to approach it perfectly and speak flawlessly while remaining calm and thinking on your feet. Anything could happen during an ambush, and for me, just about everything did.

During Barack Obama's first presidential run, his association with a radical domestic terrorist named Bill Ayers became a big issue. Ayers founded a communist revolutionary group, the Weather Underground, which set off bombs throughout the country during the Vietnam era. Ayers himself set a bomb off at the Pentagon and showed no remorse, telling the *New York Times*, "I feel we didn't do enough."

---

* It's an analogy, libs, relax.

The Weather Underground was involved with the Black Liberation Army and sought the overthrow of the US government, which had designated them a "terrorist group." Ayers's organization raged all across Chicago for years, battling police in the streets and causing hundreds of thousands of dollars in property damage. Their guerrilla tactics ranged from graffiti to deadly bank heists to throwing Molotov cocktails through the windows of a judge's home. Ayers was an unrepentant radical who reemerged onto the scene in a dangerous way.

Barack Obama launched his political career at a fund-raiser in Ayers's Chicago home. Obama and Ayers were neighbors in Chicago and worked closely together. There were rumors that Ayers had ghost-written Obama's autobiography and questions swirled over their ideological kinship. This came on the heels of the revelation that Obama's longtime pastor, Reverend Jeremiah Wright, was an anti-American racial bomb thrower. Obama's radical past had not been vetted, so I was sent to Chicago to confront Bill Ayers.

The crew and I staked out Ayers's town house for three days until we saw movement. Finally, Ayers and his college-aged son emerged and hopped into their Volvo or VW station wagon, the preferred ride for retired radicals. We hit the ignition and softly tailed them to a supermarket parking lot. Whatever Ayers was buying, arugula or a pressure cooker, we were going to be right in his face. The cameraman and I hopped out and approached Ayers from behind as he entered the supermarket.

"Hey, Bill, it's Jesse Watters with Fox News, we have a few questions for you."

Ayers turned around, shocked. "I have nothing to say to you!" he screamed, and started running downstairs to the basement level of the store. I was right on his heels.

"Mr. Ayers, what's your relationship with Barack Obama?"

Ayers panicked and locked himself in a bathroom. I just stood outside and waited for him to come out. He soon realized that he'd just cornered himself and popped back out and sprinted back upstairs. As I followed him upstairs, his son grabbed my arm and tried to pull me away. I yanked free and kept up the pursuit. Now Ayers was back upstairs yelling for security.

"Bill, you bombed the Pentagon, are you ashamed of that?" His eyes went wide like a wild animal's. He spun around, got right in my face, and pointed at my chest. He was stammering a bunch of nonsense while I calmly held the mic to his frothing mouth. I thought to myself, "This is TV gold." Eventually the security guard arrived and escorted me out.

As we walked back to the car, I was jacked up. Pumping my fist, I turned to my cameraman and said, "We got him!"

"I didn't get it," said my cameraman sheepishly.

"What the hell do you mean 'you didn't get it'?" I asked him. "You mean the top? You got *some* of it, right?"

"When we first got out of the car, I thought I hit 'record' but I hit the wrong button."

"What the hell does that mean!" I started to sweat.

"I hit something and I couldn't get it back to the main menu. I was trying the whole time."

"So you're saying you didn't get *any* of that?" I asked.

"Nothing, I'm really sorry."

I tried to remain calm. Ayers was the hottest story in the media this week. The confrontation we'd just had was *wild*. It would be everywhere in the press. My bosses would love it. But I realized there was no "it." The ambush never "happened." If there was no video, it didn't exist. I laid into the cameraman hard. He deserved it. Total choke job. I'd heard about choke jobs like this in the business. They're heartbreaking.

I called my producer in New York and told him the bad news. The producer went ballistic. We came up with a two-pronged plan. Drive back to Ayers's house quickly and try getting him *again* when he returned with his groceries. And we would never say a word to O'Reilly about what happened. If Bill found out, he'd go on a rampage and demand everyone be fired, the cameraman, the Chicago bureau chief, everyone. As luck would have it, Ayers returned home with his groceries, and we sprang back into action. We had to re-create a reality that Ayers didn't know was lost. I approached his car and followed him to his front door.

JESSE WATTERS: How do you feel being the centerpiece in this presidential election?
BILL AYERS: All right.
WATTERS: What's your relationship with Barack Obama, Mr. Ayers? Did he write a blurb for your book and sit on a panel with you?
AYERS: This is my property. Would you please leave?
WATTERS: Mr. Ayers, do you want to take this opportunity to apologize for your terrorist acts? Mr. Ayers, don't you think it's time for some repentance? Do you still consider yourself an anarchist?

When O'Reilly heard that we got him, he was thrilled. If only he knew. I guess if he reads this book, he knows now.

The media didn't cover Barack Obama in 2008; the media worshipped him. In 2016, the media actually covered Hillary's campaign, her emails, her gaffes, her strategy, and her policies. When she lost, the media decided they covered Hillary too aggressively (yes, the media thought its coverage of a Democrat wasn't favorable enough). So in 2020, the media decided it wouldn't cover Biden at all. Historically, the media covers candidates when they misspeak or flip-flop, but not Biden. The former VP confused his wife with his sister and seemed to announce he was running for the Senate in Delaware. The media didn't touch it. Joe flip-flopped on fracking, declared he'd give illegal immigrants health insurance, said he wanted to do away with fossil fuels. Barely a chirp from the press. Biden stayed in his basement for long stretches of the campaign, hardly venturing outside his home state of Delaware, and went for a month at a time between taking questions from real reporters. The media rarely addressed hermit Joe, and when they did, hunkering down was described as "a winning strategy." Typically, newspapers will run long stories from "inside the campaign," detailing discussions over tactics, personnel drama, and policy fights. Not with Joe. The media didn't cover him, they covered up for him.

When allegations surfaced that his family was selling access to Biden while he was VP, that Joe was for sale, that the VP's office was a cash register, that kickbacks and shady loans were being set up and the Chinese communists were partners, the media blacked it out. Social media monopolies, which had donated millions to Joe's campaign, censored the story on their platforms. They called the story unverified, even though documents and eyewitness accounts implicated Joe Biden in his family's foreign dealmaking. A credible witness then came forward, Tony Bobulinski, and spoke to the FBI under penalty of perjury. He was a former Biden family business partner and former naval officer, who held a top security clearance. Very credible. On national TV, Bobulinski said Joe Biden was a liar. The former vice president had actually met with him in person twice about a deal with a Chinese communist energy company. Documents show a cut of the action was allegedly being set aside for "the big guy." Even worse, one of the Chinese executives at the company was arrested for bribery by the Southern District of New York, and was under a FISA warrant for suspected espionage. According to leaked emails, Hunter Biden represented him for a cool $1 million fee, before he was sentenced to three years in prison.

The Bidens stood accused of doing million-dollar deals with Chinese communist spies under FBI surveillance. This was the most credible and juiciest corruption allegation involving a US public official in decades. Biden was potentially compromised. But the story was labeled Russian disinformation, even though Joe Biden's family hadn't refuted a single specific fact. The media found themselves cornered, in a sense. Report on it and destroy their candidate or not report on it and destroy their credibility. They chose the latter, but by the election, both were destroyed.

CHAPTER FOUR

How I Saved Journalism

In the spring of 2006, some lacrosse players called an escort service to book strippers for a party. The service sent Kim Roberts and Crystal Mangum. The latter reportedly had mental health issues. She also had a rap sheet. She'd once stolen a taxi from a strip club and led police on a drunken high-speed chase. She'd even accused three men of gang-raping her before, but then backed away from the charges, supposedly out of fear for her safety.

Throwing crazy parties is a part of college, but calling an escort service that night was a huge mistake. The women showed up to a house off-campus to perform. Crystal was allegedly sloppy drunk and the guys weren't happy. She locked herself in the bathroom for a while, then barged out disheveled, screaming and insulting the players. Words were exchanged, the night was a bust, and most of the players left the party. Crystal and Kim left together in the same car but got into a fight. Crystal pulled over into a parking lot and tried to kick Kim out of the car. Police arrived and determined that Crystal was severely impaired. She was such a mess, police sent her to a substance abuse facility for a psychological evaluation. Once she arrived, she claimed she was gang-raped by a bunch of white guys. She was immediately rushed to the Duke Medical Center and evaluated. Nurses could find no physical evidence of rape.

That's when Durham district attorney Mike Nifong entered the picture. He launched a notoriously reckless investigation that destroyed everything and everyone it touched. Police rigged the photo lineups and showed Crystal pictures of *only* Duke lacrosse players, no fillers, violating their own policies. Even so, she was a complete disaster, fingering at least one person who wasn't even at the party. The three team captains, who lived at the off-campus house, offered to provide DNA samples and take lie detector tests very early in the investigation. Nifong refused their offers. Crystal's story kept changing, too. Her claims ranged from being groped not raped, to being raped by five guys, to being held up in the air and assaulted. Identities, times, and locations all changed. *60 Minutes* later reported she told *five* different versions of events. Her associate, Kim, told detectives that Crystal's story was a "crock." But law enforcement continued to railroad the students.

The first round of physical evidence came from the state crime lab: there wasn't any. *None* of the players' DNA was found inside the accuser. Nifong wouldn't back down. He submitted the samples a second time, this time sending them to a private lab. He cut a deal with the owner, who only released partial results. The boys were being framed. Nifong went public and convicted the lacrosse team on national television. He falsely implied the players were not cooperating with the investigation and suggested the rape was racially motivated.

Nifong arrested three players: David Evans, Collin Finnerty, and Reade Seligmann. They were slapped with a slew of charges ranging from first-degree rape to kidnapping. Seligmann had an electronic footprint putting him far away from the scene at the time: a time-stamped dorm entry when he'd swiped his key card, ATM and cell records, and a sworn affidavit from a taxi driver. Despite the airtight alibi, Nifong indicted him anyway. In what Seligmann's lawyer called an act of witness intimidation, the taxi driver was then arrested on a years-old shoplifting charge.

The heat was on. But it wasn't just coming from Nifong. The mixture of race, class, and sex was too intoxicating for the media to resist. Newspaper editorials condemned the players, insinuating something terrible happened that night, despite zero evidence that it did. The initial *New York Times* reporter assigned to the story had begun writing about the lack of evidence but was abruptly sacked. The replacement wrote more prosecution-friendly stories. The fix was in. Jesse Jackson and Al Sharpton got involved and the New Black Panthers held a rally in Durham. Deep racial animosity was being stoked throughout Durham County and the entire country. Campus protesters posted "wanted" pictures of the players and called for them to be "castrated." Even Duke itself sided with the stripper against its own students. Duke University president Richard Brodhead suspended the lacrosse team for the season and forced the head coach to resign. Eighty-eight Duke faculty members signed a letter—"What does a social disaster sound like?"—which excoriated a sexually violent and racist culture that the lacrosse team had apparently brought to the surface. All this blind hatred was happening while Nifong's case was crumbling. It was becoming clear to everyone that the facts were on the players' side, and they were getting hosed by a runaway prosecutor running a race-based reelection campaign. Bill assigned me to fly to Duke to confront some of the "Gang of 88" professors who convicted the kids. "While you're down there," Bill said, "pay Nifong a visit."

I'd played lacrosse and had been following the case closely. I spent Saturday knocking on professors' doors and getting the silent treatment. Sunday was the only chance I had for catching the DA. He'd done our show the first week the story broke but had been dodging us ever since the case unraveled. Nifong was a "big fish," and I wanted him badly.

Room service forgot to bring my breakfast Sunday morning. Not a great start. Gas station coffee on an empty stomach had me edgier than usual for a stakeout. Nifong's house was impressive, perched far up above the street on a significant hill. I didn't like how far I had to park my car from his house, and I was worried about the distance I had to cover when the time came to approach him.

After a few hours, that time came. "That's him!" I said aloud. There's a jolt of energy you get when your target shows his face. Nifong was moving around in front of his property with his dog. But good timing was critical. We were pretty far away in the car, and he was still close to his front door, so I decided to wait until Nifong wandered closer toward the street. The waiting was painful. You only get one shot at this. I decided to pull the trigger and approach him on his property. I gave the "go" sign to the crew and jogged up the Nifongs' front yard. Suddenly, Nifong turned around and went back inside. I'm now totally exposed in his yard. I'd whiffed. Trying to salvage the situation, I grabbed his newspaper and brought it all the way down to the end of his driveway. This way, when he came looking for it, he'd have to walk far from his house for a while to retrieve it and make himself vulnerable to me.

Moments later, sure enough, he went to fetch the paper with his dog. "Jesse Watters, Fox News!" I yelled, as he traveled far down to the end of his driveway. "Are you going to apologize to the Duke players?"

"Get off my property!" he shouted, walking toward the camera. Legally you have to leave the property once asked. But as I backed up, I leveled another question at him. "Do you feel bad about prosecuting these players?" Leaning down to grab his dog's collar, Nifong pointed his finger at me angrily and said, "I only discuss the Duke case in the courtroom!" It was an emotionally charged moment. I asked him what he felt about the Duke case now that it was falling apart, but he just walked his dog back up the driveway. It didn't register until then that I had gotten him on camera in his bathrobe and slippers. As serious as the legal circumstances were, I couldn't help but smile. Fox aired Nifong yelling at me in his jammies Monday night to big ratings. Almost every time we discussed Nifong on air, our director would play the exclusive b-roll of the disgraced DA in his robe rocking some serious bed head. He definitely deserved the humiliation.

Soon the North Carolina attorney general dropped all the charges against the lacrosse players. Nifong was disbarred for "dishonesty, fraud, deceit, and misrepresentation." He spent time in jail for criminal contempt due to his shenanigans with the private lab. The players received large financial settlements from Duke University but their reputations were still in tatters. Duke's relationship to the local community was forever tarnished. Nifong's lead detective committed suicide years later. The news media, the nutty professors, and the racial instigators never apologized. They just moved on to stoking the next controversy. The stripper was later stripped of her freedom. She was charged with arson and murder, for stabbing her boyfriend to death. Nifong left a wake of death and destruction in his crooked path of corruption. But lessons are never learned. Similar episodes continue to course through this country's veins. The Jussie Smollett fake hate crime, the Covington Boys smear, and the Kavanaugh rape allegation all contain similar ingredients of injustice: identity politics, hit jobs, rogue prosecutors, a rush to judgment, and character assassinations. Covering these stories closely, I always remember that Americans are presumed innocent, and you should reserve judgment until the facts come out. There are a lot of Mike Nifongs still running wild today.

Actor Jussie Smollett allegedly faked a hate crime and sucked the entire mainstream media into his web of lies. Anyone with a shred of common sense could smell a rat, but the press ran with the hoax because they desperately wanted it to be true.

White Trump supporters wearing MAGA hats in downtown Chicago in the middle of the night in below-freezing temperatures doused Smollett with bleach, beat him up, and slipped a noose around his neck? Oh, yeah, they also yelled, "This is MAGA country" . . . in Chicago. This occurred while Smollett was getting a Subway sandwich.

First of all, I doubt many Trump supporters watched the show *Empire* and would even recognize the actor. Second, Chicago isn't "MAGA country," and nobody talks like that. Third, Smollett doesn't strike you as a guy who eats at Subway. Smollett also left the noose around his neck to show police, then refused to hand over his phone to police during the course of the investigation. Yet Kamala Harris and Cory Booker and CNN and others spoke of the highly suspicious story as fact, blaming Trump's so-called racist rhetoric for inspiring the alleged hate crime. It all unraveled as police grew suspicious of Smollett. Their investigators claimed he had actually hired two black brothers to slap on red hats and stage a fake attack. It was all supposed to have been caught on a surveillance camera outside the Subway, but the camera was pointing the wrong way at the time. America dodged a bullet. The video of the staged attack would have gone viral, riots would have resulted, and untold damage would have occurred. Smollett eventually walked away with a slap on the wrist after framing sixty million Trump supporters as racist and forcing the entire Chicago Police Department to divert their attention from real crimes.

The Covington Boys hoax was another perfect storm of knee-jerk partisan media outlets falsely framing an innocent citizen. Students from Covington Catholic High School in Kentucky traveled to DC on a class trip to participate in the March for Life. While congregating at the Lincoln Memorial, the Black Hebrew Israelites, an anti-white hate group, began verbally harassing the students. A radical Native American ex-con and political activist who many media outlets falsely claimed served in Vietnam walked into the group of students and banged a drum, getting in their faces. One student, Nick Sandmann, remained respectful and stood silently while the older activist seemed intent on provoking a response. A deceptively edited clip flew across the internet while media personalities and news sites piled on, accusing MAGA-hat-wearing Nick Sandmann of harassing an elderly indigenous person of color and hurling racist epithets. In just a few hours, Nick was the face of white supremacy in Donald Trump's America, taunting minorities with a smirk dripping of white privilege. Liberal media personalities threatened the minor with violence, salivating for a chance to punch him in the face. The entire media war machine unleashed a multifront cyberbullying attack on the teen until additional video revealed he was completely innocent. Nick had the last laugh. While details remain confidential, Nick Sandmann worked out a deal with the *Washington Post* and CNN for what many believe was an eight-figure settlement. Journalists, whose job it is to get both sides, follow the facts, and report accurately, disgraced their profession and pounced on a child to score points against a president they despise. They cost their companies millions of dollars. Character assassination is costly. But until victims like Nick continue to fight back, you'll be presumed guilty until proven innocent.

Judge Kavanaugh learned that the hard way. He fought back and prevailed, but the cost to the country, the court, and his family was severe. Brett Kavanaugh has a pristine reputation in professional circles and in his personal life. A champion of female clerks, a father to two girls, and a volunteer at soup kitchens on the weekends, the judge was a man of character and integrity. Until a malicious smear nearly knocked out his nomination to the highest court. Christine Blasey Ford accused Kavanaugh of pushing her down on a bed and grinding on her at a high school party more than thirty years before. Only she and Bret know what happened. I'm in no position to cross-examine her experiences, and she has my deepest sympathy if a crime occurred, but if she had brought a legal complaint against Kavanaugh in 2018, no prosecutor would have even taken the case. Ford didn't remember exactly when the incident happened, whose house it happened at, or how she got home that night. She never mentioned it to anyone at the time, and everyone she said was at this alleged party swore they had no recollection of the party ever happening. She had no physical or circumstantial evidence and no eyewitnesses or corroborating witnesses. The last-minute maneuvering by Senate Democrat Dianne Feinstein appeared to be a sandbag attempt. Her lawyers, recommended by Feinstein, were highly partisan Democrat attorneys. In the desperation to "Bork" Judge Kavanaugh, additional flimsy allegations were tacked on. Women appeared out of nowhere to accuse Kavanaugh of ridiculous behavior from high school. Shakedown artist and fraudster extraordinaire Michael Avenatti trotted out sketchy females claiming Kavanaugh participated in booze- and drug-fueled gang rapes. Network news aired these insane, unfounded allegations gleefully. Then accusers began to recant their tales. Perhaps Brett was just at the gang rapes but didn't participate in them, or maybe she heard from a friend that there were parties like this in high school. You get the idea. Donald Trump stuck by Kavanaugh, and so did Senate Republicans. Kavanaugh kept his chin up and blasted the disgraceful tactics at his hearing, proclaiming his innocence. We haven't heard from Dr. Ford afterward or the other women who came forward with tales of drunken orgies. Poof, they're gone.

There are a lot of Mike Nifongs still running wild today. Sometimes they take the form of journalists, maybe actors, perhaps even Senate Democrats. These snipers come in all shapes and sizes, but the dizzying speed of attack and the destruction of due process are always the same. Never give in to it. And when you see someone under attack, from an ally or an enemy, follow the facts, because everyone in America is presumed innocent.

Occasionally, I was deployed to send a message to our competitors. Fox News was, and still is, very protective of the soldiers who sacrifice everything to keep our country safe. As the Iraq War went sideways, certain pundits on other networks crossed a line, attacking American troops instead of American policy. William Arkin, an NBC military analyst, wrote a column in the *Washington Post* calling our brave soldiers "mercenaries," who had no right to voice their opinions. Arkin also labeled American service members "naive" spoiled brats. Questioning the patriotism, intelligence, and integrity of innocent American forces during wartime was unacceptable. Our CEO at the time, Roger Ailes, was disgusted by Arkin's comments, as was O'Reilly. NBC News even issued a statement saying Arkin's opinion did not reflect the opinion of the network. As usually was the case, Arkin refused to defend his comments on television. After several attempts to seek comment, I was dispatched to confront him face-to-face.

Arkin lived in Vermont, outside the small town of Manchester. The refined, rustic inn where I stayed was certainly an upgrade over the swampy motel in Florida. The in-house restaurant was highly rated, and a delicious chef-selected cheese plate awaited me at check-in. The brie was as soft as the state was on sex offenders. After my hungover debut on national TV, I never liked to drink the night before a shoot, so I ordered a Shirley Temple and ate alone. As I became more recognizable, ordering a Shirley Temple out loud in a crowd became very embarrassing. So much so that I would have to whisper to the waiter. Luckily, the place was empty that night, and only the staff judged me. But at least I was crisp the next day.

At 6 a.m., the crew and I were staked outside of Arkin's charming Vermont home, replete with the customary red barn garage covered with snow. It was around 30 degrees, so we waited with the engine running and the heat cranked up. And we waited. And waited. For hours and hours. Viewers only see the thirty or so seconds of action of the ambush interview. What usually precedes that is hours and hours and hours of sitting in a car with a camera crew. You're listening to Howard Stern, Limbaugh, or music on the radio. Many times, it's a crew you've never used before, so you're making small talk with perfect strangers, swapping stories and game-planning your attack strategy: What if he leaves on foot? Do you think that's his wife's car? Should we park on the other end of the street? The logistics in Arkin's case were clear. The garage barn was basically attached to the house, so we were probably going to tail him if he drove away.

After an eight-hour stakeout, we finally saw movement. The barn door opened from the inside, and Arkin's Volvo station wagon pulled out. The libs definitely love their Volvos. We tailed his car for a few minutes, waiting for him to pull into a local shop or pub. But that's not what happened. The Volvo headed toward an on-ramp for a busy thruway and suddenly we were going 70 mph. Where the hell was Arkin going? Twenty minutes passed, then forty minutes, then an hour. Arkin was still driving, and we were running out of gas. Soon we'd crossed state lines and were entering Massachusetts. We only had a little gas left and were extremely close to having to call off the pursuit when the Volvo hit an exit and slowly pulled into a fast-food parking lot. Finally, we had him. As I jumped out of the car, I realized something. Arkin had his kids with him. He was loading his young children's ski gear into their friends' family's vehicle that had met them there. There's a code to these ambushes. I don't like to do it when the kids are around. It's like an assassin's creed. But there was nothing I could do at that point, so I went in for it.

WATTERS: Bill Arkin, how are you doing? Fox News. How's it going? Mr. Arkin, can we talk to you about some of the comments you made?

ARKIN: Can you leave me alone for just a . . .

WATTERS: Actually, no, we'd like to talk to you for a second. How could you say what you said? I mean, don't you think it was really hurtful and harmful to the military families, to the soldiers serving in Iraq? Let's address this. I mean, you called these people "mercenaries." They're serving in harm's way in Iraq and you called them mercenaries, sir. Let's address this. You also said they were "pawns" and "naive." How could you say that?

ARKIN: Can you give me a business card?

WATTERS: I'll go get you the business card.

ARKIN: I don't believe you're with Fox News. Go get me one and then I'll talk to you.

WATTERS: Well, I'm—are you calling me a liar? Mr. Arkin, you said the soldiers.

ARKIN: *(Inaudible).*

WATTERS: All right, thank you very much. You said that the soldiers should be grateful . . .

ARKIN: I told you I wanted a card.

WATTERS: You said that they should be grateful that people aren't spitting on them.

I had to annihilate him in front of his children. His children were outside the car and watched as their father took it on the chin. I didn't like doing it, kinda felt like I needed a shower afterward, but it had to be done. Arkin was way out of line and needed to answer for his vile comments. His business card shtick was just a deflection. You can't fall for that in the moment. People will try anything to deflect from their conduct, and create a diversion or an excuse for not taking ownership. I've seen all sorts of tactics like this in the heat of the moment; saying they'll sit down for an interview if you'd just kindly contact their assistant, pretending not to know what I'm talking about, asking me to wait and they'll "be right back." Don't fall for it. After filling up the tank, the crew and I chewed over the ambush on the hour-and-a-half drive back to Vermont.

The next day, Fox rightly decided to pixilate the faces of Arkin's children when we aired the piece. We had standards at Fox. But NBC didn't. Their channel's 8 p.m. host, Keith Olbermann, began going on nightly jihads against the personal lives and family members of Fox hosts. This was all taking place as the Iraq War had completely enraged and divided America. The country was reaching a boiling point. Soon I would be thrust into a proxy war between parent companies. At the time, I didn't realize how serious it was.

George W. Bush had slapped sanctions on the Iranians during the Iraq War because the regime was directly, and indirectly, waging a deadly campaign against US forces in Iraq. Sources had told Fox that General Electric was skirting those sanctions, was selling airplane parts that the Iranians were then using to manufacture IEDs. These IEDs were sent across the border and used by Iranian-backed militias in Iraq. Hundreds of American men and women were being injured and killed by these Iranian-made IEDs. GE claimed it had stopped taking orders from Iran in 2005, but some GE investors were accusing GE of profiting from the murder of Americans. At the time, GE owned NBC News and MSNBC, two outlets disparaging American soldiers. It was decided that the General Electric CEO, Jeffrey Immelt, a Republican, had to be held to account. We discovered that Immelt would be attending an energy conference in Calgary.

Like an agent under diplomatic cover, I boarded a plane to Canada on a secret mission. Another producer accompanied me. Dan Bank was a few years younger than I was and just as gung ho. We were advised not to disclose the truth behind our trip. General Electric was an international conglomerate, and Calgary was in the midst of an oil boom. GE was instrumental in pulling energy out of the black tar sands, and billions of dollars were at stake. We didn't want anyone in Canada getting wind of our assignment. Dan Bank, twenty-three years old and wearing the only suit he owned, went a little overboard and nearly didn't make it into the country. When a Canadian customs official asked him why he was traveling to Canada, Bank went into 007 character and said just one word: "Consulting." That apparently raised some red flags because of Bank's age, attire, and demeanor. Customs officials detained him for an additional thirty minutes. I'd said, "I'm a news producer covering the energy sector," and breezed right through.

But Bank's squirminess nearly cost me my sidekick. Eventually they let Bank in, and we drove to Calgary ready to complete the mission.

Calgary at the time was like the Wild West. The city was surrounded by tundra and oil rigs. Men from all over the world were there to make millions. Downtown was mostly old-world hotels and dark steakhouses. The streets were cold and empty, and the ratio of men to women was around 80:20. We decided to have lunch at a clubby, underground restaurant and met a man who gave us the goods on Immelt. Ruddy Balzac (not his real name), a wildcat investment banker in his mid-thirties, recognized me, and we struck up a conversation at the bar. With a scotch for him and a Shirley Temple for me, we found out that Immelt was actually the guest of honor at this event. A team of Japanese investors were in town to lavish praise (and money) on General Electric as they sought profits in the oil sands. Ruddy knew people attending and informed us there would be no media availability. It was a banquet. This completely upended our battle plan. We thanked Ruddy, exchanged business cards, and headed toward the banquet not knowing how we'd have access to the guest of honor.

We arrived at an ornate hotel and were escorted upstairs to a ballroom by our "media handler." The woman had a light load because we were the only media "covering" the event. This was more of an undercover ambush, so we didn't book a cameraman. The woman thought I was a print reporter covering Calgary's booming energy business. Little did she know Dan Bank was carrying a handheld mini-DV camera in his pocket. These were the days before iPhone cameras. Our handler led us into this beautifully appointed, high-ceilinged ballroom packed with tables of well-dressed Japanese businessmen. Dan and I stood in the back of the room, as we were instructed, and I laid eyes on Immelt. Clearly, there was no Q&A availability, and clearly, I wasn't allowed to go anywhere near the guest of honor. Eventually Immelt took to a podium, receiving an award and warm applause. He delivered a few remarks.

Dan and I were pinned up against the back wall making nervous eye contact at each other. We were so obvious that we spooked our handler. She began to realize we were up to something, and she positioned herself right next to me. Maybe it was because I wasn't taking notes or didn't have an audio recorder, but the jig was up. I had to make my move. Right as Immelt returned to his seat, I shot into the room like a receiver off the line of scrimmage. Dodging between tables, I zeroed in on Immelt. I felt the hand of my handler grab my bicep, but I wrenched free and launched into attack mode.

"Jeffrey Immelt, I'm Jesse Watters with Fox News. Why are you selling airplane parts to Iran that are being used as IEDs to kill Americans in Iraq?"

A huge commotion erupted throughout the room. I was being pushed and pulled by security and handlers. Immelt looked stunned, with a nervous smile across his face. I rolled another line or two out at him, but I was pushed away. It was a huge victory for us, and a huge humiliation for Jeffrey and GE. They didn't know Bank had the whole thing on tape as they whisked us out of the banquet, scolding us along the way.

That night we celebrated and ate out with our new intelligence asset, Ruddy Balzac. It was one of the finest meals I'd ever eaten at that young age. Several bottles of wine were consumed as we toasted our operation. We thanked Ruddy afterward and he insisted he drop us off at our hotel. Not thinking, we accepted, and hopped into his brand-new sports car. Right away, Bank and I realized this was a bad idea. Ruddy Balzac was toasted. He was all over the road. It was 1 a.m. and the streets were empty. He was racing around the city like it was his private track. We cleared a small bridge going at least 80 mph in the center of town and Ruddy tried to rip a tight left turn.

The car completely loses control and he starts to skid. I'm in shotgun and Bank's in the back. We brace for impact and boom! Balzac smashes the Jag around a telephone pole. We all get out of the car. I'm shaking and look at the damage. The car is totaled. Ruddy kicks it and curses, then just chalks it up to a wild night. "I'll get another one next week, haha." Bank and I laugh but we know we should both be dead.

There wasn't one police officer; no cars, no pedestrians. The coast was clear. Ruddy called himself a taxi, said goodbye nonchalantly, and left us alone in Calgary standing next to his totaled luxury car. Dan and I looked at each other and started speed-walking back to our hotel before anyone arrived at the scene. A block before our hotel, we passed a car full of people.

"What are you boys in the mood for?" asked a young girl in the passenger seat of the parked sedan. We looked through the open window. It was a car full of girls, maybe nineteen, smoking cigarettes and listening to music. Dan said, "Heading home, what are you guys up to?"

As we looked closer, we noticed the girl had a full leg cast on. Like from her ankle to her upper thigh. She winked at us and smiled. She was a prostitute. We'd heard about the scene in Calgary, single men looking to get rich, the nightlife. But this was warped.

"What happened to your leg?" I asked, kind of curious.

"It's nothing, I'm fine. Where's your hotel?"

Dan and I looked at each other. Looked back at the broken-legged teenage prostitute trying to pick us up after our brush with death. It was just like Iraq. Behind enemy lines, mission accomplished, heading back to base, nearly dead, getting propositioned by foreign hookers. We were just like the real heroes. Better not press our luck.

"We have to call it a night," we said, turning to walk away.

"What do you boys do anyway?" she asked, still trying to reel us in.

Dan and I paused, then replied at the same time. "Consultants."

Immelt stayed in our crosshairs over the years. MSNBC became more and more disgusting while the parent company made no effort to rein in the filth. There was a whiff of corruption in the air, too, as Barack Obama became president. After all, wouldn't it be in GE's interest to have NBC go easy on the new president, so that they could make sure new stimulus and fat federal contracts would flow to the corporation? Sure enough, not only did NBC go soft on Obama, but the network and its cable sister began labeling any criticism of the first black president racist. Left-wing firebrand Janeane Garofalo appeared on MSNBC and scorched the newly formed Tea Party as "racist" "tea-bagging rednecks" who didn't really care about bailouts, socialism, and spending. What really motivated these protesters, she claimed, was "hating a black man." The MSNBC host didn't even push back once, letting the despicable hate spew on the GE-owned network. Immelt had refused to take any responsibility for his hate-filled profit center and was dodging our interview requests.

It just so happened that GE had a shareholder meeting in Erie, Pennsylvania, around the corner, and I was a GE shareholder. My grandmother had gifted me some GE stock as a teenager. This allowed me to attend the shareholder meeting legitimately.

GE was a blue-chip company, an iconic corporate brand that designed and built things that had powered America for decades. I wasn't qualified to shine Immelt's shoes. But I was a rascal. I had been training my whole life for corporate espionage. Back-of-the-classroom hijinks, capture the flag, and ambush interviews had prepared me for this moment. I linked up with an actual activist investor, Tom Borelli, at breakfast before the shareholder meeting. GE's green initiatives were costing the company money. GE had also set up a cap-and-trade venture to capitalize on the Obama administration's quest to tax carbon, an extremely lucrative possibility for GE if that passed Congress. Borelli basically saw MSNBC's left-wing assault on the Tea Party as GE's PR strategy to win federal cash from the global warming alarmists in the Obama administration. Together we hatched a plan. Recording devices were strictly prohibited from the meeting. We would be screened, wanded, and patted down upon entry. So Tom's associate would do our dirty work. We stashed a tiny audio recorder in her purse since she wouldn't receive the level of attention I would. I was known to GE brass at that point. The plan worked. All three of us entered the enormous auditorium separately, no hiccups, and converged to sit next to each other near one of the microphones used for shareholder questions.

The place was packed. Several thousand shareholders filled the room, from retirees, to union reps, to Wall Street types. The GE stock price had stalled since Jack Welch retired as CEO, the dividends weren't rolling in like they used to, and the Great Recession was putting a lot of pressure on core company assets. Let's just say it wasn't a friendly crowd. But Immelt and his team delivered an upbeat and polished presentation, patting themselves on the back and assuring the shareholders that GE was in great shape. Listening to him speak, I thought, this man is brilliant. He was confident, eloquent, and razor-sharp. Much of what he said went over my head. Which was why I'd been fired from both of my jobs in financial services. But Immelt was on *my* turf today. The undercover shareholder ambush activist was in the building. The presentation ended, and Immelt stood onstage and opened the meeting up for shareholder questions. After a few investors spoke their minds, it was my shot. I glanced at Borelli. He signaled the recorder was hot. So I stood up to the mic and addressed the CEO in front of thousands.

WATTERS: Last week on MSNBC Janeane Garofalo said that Americans who were attending Tea Parties and protesting high taxes and government spending were racist rednecks. She was not challenged by the anchor on MSNBC. Are you okay with that, and do you consider that a form of hate speech, sir? *(audience applause)*

IMMELT: Again, we have not censored MSNBC. Again, my own personal beliefs aside, I believe that MSNBC has some standards that they follow, and that's what you are seeing. *(audience booing)*

WATTERS: With all due respect, this is the kind of hate that MSNBC traffics on a regular basis. Are you comfortable with this? And do you think this hurts the GE brand? *(audience applause)*

IMMELT: Again, we're in the network business. We are in the MSNBC business. We compete with Fox News, CNN, and others. Again, I don't censor what they do or what they say despite the fact that I might disagree with some of it or most of it, some of the time. *(audience groans)*

WATTERS: So do you condemn those statements, Mr. Immelt?

IMMELT: Yes, sir—next question. Microphone number two.

The crowd was with me. Boos and applause erupted as I spoke. Immelt tried his best to distance himself from MSNBC, but he failed. Parent companies have a fiduciary responsibility to police their brands. While interfering in a news division is frowned upon, venomous and corrupt propaganda shouldn't be tolerated at such a level. They cut my mic as Immelt became cornered and moved on to the next question across the room. I decided to leave immediately, assuming I'd be escorted out, and was followed by multiple GE officials as I left. Afterward, I met Borelli in the parking lot, and we checked the tape. He'd captured it all. We shook hands. I called Fox to report. Before we even aired the footage that night, news of my confrontation broke on the *Hollywood Reporter* and swept across the internet. We decided to capitalize on the buzz and posted audio on our new Fox Nation website. Drudge picked it up and made it his lede story. *"GE shareholders outraged over MSNBC bias; Microphone cut off."* This was a big moment for me because then CEO Roger Ailes had just launched the Fox Nation website and named me managing editor. The GE story made a big splash and generated massive traffic with our debut Drudge link, setting the site on a strong course the first month.

Immelt had thin skin. Reports surfaced that Immelt was so outraged by what happened at the shareholder meeting that he ordered a ban on the *Hollywood Reporter*'s parent company, Nielsen, tapping NBC's Jeff Zucker as the point man to freeze out Nielsen's media and advertising arms. GE denied that Immelt had anything to do with the reprisal, but it was amusing to watch the dominoes fall after an escapade like that. I'd become quite the troublemaker. It's what I was good at. Instigating drama.

In middle school, I would whisper to my friend Dan at the lunch table, "Hey, Dan, Dave says he can kick your ass."

Dan would shoot back, "No he can't."

Then I would whisper to Dave, "Hey, Dave, Dan said you couldn't kick his ass if you tried."

"Bull crap," Dan shot back. And the trash talk started and Dan and Dave squared off in the locker room after school. It was a legendary rumble. They fought to a draw, even though Dave landed cleaner shots. This happened around the time when Dan and Dave battled each other in the Olympic decathlon in 1992. I billed it as such in the locker room. The white Don King. Now I was getting paid to instigate corporate fights in a bigger ring.

CHAPTER FIVE

How I Saved Prime Time

The Fox Nation website was a valuable piece of our arsenal. I'd been aggregating a large variety of stories, videos, and headlines for *The Factor* each morning. They'd be sent to senior producers who would pitch them to Bill on the 9:30 a.m. call. But after the call, I was left with dozens of great links just sitting on my computer unseen. Twitter wasn't much of a thing yet. The only game in town was Drudge and a few other conservative blogs. So I met with our VPs and they pitched the idea for Fox Nation to CEO Roger Ailes. The idea was to have a Fox News digital aggregation space that was fair and balanced, had a sharp point of view, and included a comment section for our audience to participate. Ailes approved the idea and invested resources in it. I was included in several meetings with him and was captivated. He had the authoritative air of a legendary executive, mixed with the relaxed wit of your grandfather after a bourbon. In total command of the boardroom, he'd run the meeting like a conductor, eliciting performance updates, regaling us with hilarious tales, pivoting back to business, and then treating us to gossipy punch lines.

Ailes was from a small town in Ohio and had risen to the top of the game in Manhattan, exercising great power over the country's political landscape and news industry. But he was instinctively anchored in Ohio and mocked the pretentious culture of the elite media. ("Donny Deutsch looks like the kind of guy who drives back from the

Hamptons in loafers without socks" . . . "Rachel Maddow is smart, but she looks like a thumb"). Ailes exuded bedrock American heritage— the whiff of another era—and he appreciated what our country had accomplished and trusted the character of the people to continue on the right course.

I'm keenly aware of what Roger Ailes was accused of during his exit from Fox. This was a confusing time for many of us who admired the man. Many, including me, were deeply disturbed by the nature of the allegations and distressed by the cloud of impropriety. Roger was so successful at running Fox, and so generous to so many people, processing whatever personal faults he had can be difficult.

Roger gave O'Reilly a shot and O'Reilly gave me a shot. I'm eternally grateful to both men. Bill's departure from Fox was extremely controversial and stunning. The swiftness of it left me shocked. If anyone was hurt they have my deepest sympathies. The MeToo era was long overdue, and exploded after being suppressed for decades. As someone who covered it closely, the movement ripped through all industries like a hurricane. People on both sides of the aisle, upon reflection, admit that the guilty, the innocent, and the in between were taken out, sometimes without due process. Some withstood true accusations, and others wilted under false ones . . . while many got what they deserved.

Bill is the greatest television broadcaster I've observed in my career. His raw authenticity, powerful delivery, and concise, honest presentation dominated and defined cable news for nearly two decades. Witnessing *The Factor* firsthand was a gift. I'm forever thankful for Bill's guidance during this period. He's extremely competitive, insightful, and talented. A perfectionist, Bill constantly honed his craft and reinvented the show during transitioning news cycles. The audience, and for that matter, America, was always number one. Like Ailes's, Bill's news analysis and commentary always centered on "the folks." *The Factor* was always dialed into the emotion of the day. Whether it was gas prices, crime, or far-left politicians, Bill focused the show on how the news impacted "Main Street." Our presentation was enjoyably digestible because it was presented as a story, with characters good and bad, duking it out for right and wrong. Broadcasts that were too wonky or passionless couldn't compete. Bill made the news personal to the audience. It was relatable; even if it involved strange players hundreds of miles away, he made it familiar. Villains and heroes tangled on *The Factor* for years while story lines ebbed and flowed across different administrations. Liberal zealots, "bad judges," and phony celebrities cascaded into the 8 p.m. hour, always confronted by forces of good, defending what was righteous and honorable about America and the American family. The show was a bulwark against insane ideologies and a crusader for justice, especially for those who weren't strong enough to defend themselves. I truly miss the show and am proud of having played a small part in all that it accomplished. Bill and I don't see eye to eye on everything. We're different in a lot of ways. But we're very similar in our sense of justice, fairness, and patriotism. I'm honored to have worked on *The O'Reilly Factor*. I learned much of what I know about field producing, editorial, and hosting from Bill and his team. Hopefully, I haven't left anything out, or his next book will be called "Killing Watters."

With Ailes's strong backing, we launched Fox Nation at the beginning of the Obama administration, and I was named managing editor.

For someone who ran a website, I'm terrified of Twitter. I don't really tweet. The whole platform is a scandal embryo. Doing live TV all week is enough of a tightrope. Plus, I have enough self-awareness to see how delicious my cancellation would be to the left. And how it wouldn't take much for them to pounce. Merely missing a comma could mangle a tweet and make it appear controversial. The value of risk reduction is something that comes with age. Therefore, I only tweet the video clips of my on-air commentary. If I said something on air, and wasn't fired, it's probably safe for Twitter. But as a news source, Twitter is unmatched. No longer do you need to visit individual sites anymore; you can curate your own Twitter feed with pundits, reporters, and news sites you prefer. All conservative voices or all liberal voices, or a glorious mix. But while Twitter is helpful to news consumers, the platform can warp your perception of what's real.

A Pew study found Twitter users are younger, wealthier, and more Democrat-leaning than the average American. They're also more sensitive to perceived racial and gender discrimination, and they are more permissive toward immigration. Most people on Twitter don't even tweet. Ten percent of users make up 80 percent of the tweets. This small but loud crew tends to be mostly politically active women. Do you see what I'm getting at here? The topics of conversation on Twitter are largely driven by younger, more affluent, politically active liberal women. This group tends to overlap with members of the media who have a very powerful influence on the political debate in America. An echo chamber of group-think has radicalized a swath of Democrats, who have considerable influence in the Democrat-Media matrix, and the results have been detrimental to national Democrat Party politics and the American worker as a whole.

It is no wonder why the national Democrat Party has lost its electoral touch with white working-class Americans without a college degree. This demographic was traditionally the backbone of the modern Democrat Party. They became Reagan Democrats in the 1980s, switched back to Clinton in the 1990s, went for Bush after 9/11, and came home to Obama in 2008. However, Obama's coalition was so broad, he blew them off during reelection and relied on blacks, Hispanics, single women, college students, and college-educated whites. The white working-class vote was up for grabs in 2016, and Donald Trump stormed in and won their vote handily, sweeping across the Rust Belt and busting down the Democrat blue wall. Issues such as immigration, trade, and wages mobilized this group for Donald Trump. These core issues were not touched upon heavily by national Democrats.

Instead, the party focused on identity politics: gender, race, and sexual orientation. Those are legitimate issues but not central issues that drive turnout in a national election. In addition, Trump's political incorrectness and unapologetic patriotism were deemed "offensive" to Twitter influencers and media elite. The backlash increased his popularity with this critical voting group. They spoke his language, and his personality created a bond. So, in a twist of fate, Twitter brought people of similar thought together, yet separated them further from the population at large.

The more Twitter that Democrat politicians and media personalities reinforced each other's collective bias, the more they drifted away from the constituency that unlocks the key to the White House. Democrats recognize this but appear conflicted about recapturing this voting bloc. Rather, they're obsessed with re-creating the Obama rainbow coalition. But this new coalition isn't materializing at a fast-enough pace because of immigration patterns and small but significant changes in the black and Hispanic vote in favor of Republicans. And, let's be honest, Obama was a uniquely talented and historical political figure who turned out a different electorate.

Democrats are now caught waiting for demographic changes to establish permanent political dominance, while yearning for a younger and more progressive base, but still needing to remain competitive with more traditional, values-oriented white working-class Americans in the battleground states. Twitter has exacerbated this dilemma. It's why the media misses the mark on Trump's popularity and continues to get caught off guard by Republican electoral success.

Fox had my back when I kicked up dust in the field. As I said, I'm a shy, polite boy, but sometimes I had no other choice but to bend the rules. Our cause was always just. After the election of Donald Trump in 2016, liberals' heads exploded. Far-left Hampshire College in Amherst, Massachusetts, actually lowered the American flag on campus. According to the Department of Veterans Affairs, it's appropriate to

fly the flag at half-staff "when the whole nation is in mourning" . . .
not when liberals lose an election. Traditionally, flags are lowered
by order of the president to mark the death of a significant historical
leader like a former president or a pope . . . or to recognize a deadly
tragedy like a mass shooting or a terror attack. Lowering the flag is
not a political action . . . it's always been a move to unify the country
in times of national mourning, and to show reverence and respect for
a lost hero.

Trump hadn't killed Clinton, only her candidacy, so when Hampshire College lowered the flag, Massachusetts veterans and American
patriots weren't happy. But then things took a dark turn. In a shocking
scene, students removed the flag and burned it on Veterans Day. Protests exploded around Amherst. Thousands of flag-waving veterans
descended on the scene, and the mood on campus grew tense. Instead
of healing the community and hoisting the flag back up, Hampshire
College president Jonathan Lash decided to not fly the American flag
at all. "We hope this will enable us to instead focus our efforts on
addressing racist, misogynistic, Islamophobic, anti-immigrant, anti-
Semitic, and anti-LGBTQ rhetoric and behaviors," Lash stated. Most
of America thought Lash was a lunatic. As protests intensified, Lash
mounted more defenses of his flag policy, calling American society
"deeply complicit" in "fostering hatred," and condemning "the ris-
ing Islamophobia all around us." Hampshire College was a hotbed for
social justice warriors, who responded to Trump's election by cancel-
ing classes and meditating. Lash even played the race card, lamenting
"the reality of how much people of color are forced to deal with others' ignorance, micro-aggressions, and overt oppression and violence
every day."

Lash was becoming a national joke, and Hampshire College represented the early symptoms of Trump Derangement Syndrome: wan-
ton destruction, flagrant disrespect, ignorance of history, and general
foolishness. *The Factor* reached out to Lash in an attempt to better

understand his spaz attack, but our requests were ignored. That's when I was dispatched to the commonwealth to investigate the lonely flagpole.

Amherst, Massachusetts, is a sanctuary city. It flies the flag of the United Nations above town hall. The town council voted to impeach Bush for war crimes, and it was ground zero for a high school rendition of *The Vagina Monologues*. That should tell all you need to know about the city. But like most radical left enclaves, the working men and women of the town are normal people. Diners are great places to find regular opinions, so I chatted with folks over bacon and eggs. They told me Amherst exists in a "leftist, alternative universe," where disrespect is "rampant." The thousands of people who were protesting felt "violated," and were "disappointed" at how "insensitive" the flag-burning students were. President Lash had reached out to veterans in an attempt to quiet the storm, but it had backfired when he droned on about social justice and hadn't even apologized. Lash was viewed as a failed leader in the community. That's when I decided to visit campus, to start the healing.

Hampshire College is a small, private, New England liberal arts college that doesn't give grades. You can pick your own major, or you can design your own major entirely. Classes offered include "Reinventing the Toilet" and "Buddhist Economics." As tempted as I was to sit in on a class, I set out to locate President Lash. My producer entered his office posing as a student and smoked out some details from his secretary. We discovered when he was leaving, figured out where he'd parked, and waited. It was getting dark and started to rain. Then suddenly his car lights came on, and he began backing out of his spot. Of course, it was a Volvo. Game on. We followed him from campus, and my heart started beating hard. We had no idea where he was going, but we'd have to jump out and get him whatever place he stopped. That place happened to be his garage. As he pulled in, I had to make a call. Enter his garage or fail. I couldn't fail. The country was counting on me to defend the flag, so I hopped out and entered his dark garage as he opened the door.

WATTERS: Hey, President Lash. How are you? Jesse Watters with *The O'Reilly Factor*, Fox News Channel, good to see you.

JONATHAN LASH, PRESIDENT, HAMPSHIRE COLLEGE: Not good to see you.

WATTERS: Well, now that I have you here, why did you remove the American flag from campus?

LASH: Nice to meet you.

WATTERS: Don't you realize the whole country is laughing at you right now? *(I put my foot in his door so he couldn't close it.)*

LASH: Come on. Get your foot out of my door.

WATTERS: President Lash, why did you remove the flag?

LASH: I don't want to talk to you about it.

WATTERS: Don't you think you owe it to the veterans to explain yourself?

LASH: I don't want to talk to you about it. Would you please remove your foot from my door?

WATTERS: You made a lot of people very upset. I think you owe the country an explanation.

LASH: You are giving speeches.

I couldn't be any more aggressive or I'd lose my moral high ground, so I removed my foot from his door. He slammed it shut, and I bolted out of there before he could close the garage door and trap me inside. That had almost happened once in Colorado, where a target had nearly closed her garage door on me. Then you're locked inside their property while they call the police. You can't let them turn the tables like that on you.

But Lash did call the police. Fox got word that a police report had been filed against me. Trespassing. The Amherst Police Department wanted a word with me. They had my rental car's make and model, too. Luckily, I flew the coop. I was staying at a hotel in a different county and arrived there without incident. I was advised to leave Massachusetts immediately because there might be a warrant out on me. That must have made me the only Fox reporter "at large" besides Geraldo Rivera at the time. But before I left the state, I stopped in Boston to hit on *The Factor*. Bill commended me for being "polite" with the president, whom he called a "coward," before predicting Hampshire College was "done." He was right. A few days after my ambush, Lash buckled and raised the flag back up. It was a big victory for America. The college, sadly, never recovered from their mistake. Lash resigned less than a year later, and the school is struggling to survive as enrollment plummeted. Everyone learned a lesson. Especially me. I now never speed in Massachusetts. That warrant might still be active.

Not every confrontation goes according to plan. Sometimes you get thrown a curveball. There was a case in Florida where a career criminal shot a cop. But he never should have been out on the street. The killer, Michael Phillips, was a Nazi. He had nineteen arrests and a violent history, including armed burglary, battering his girlfriend, and aggravated assault with a deadly weapon. While out on bail, he was booked on an assault charge. Prosecutors sought no bail, but Judge Manuel Lopez let him out with easy bail. Days later, Phillips murdered a black Florida police officer, Ronald Harrison, ambush-style. This never should have happened. Judge Lopez, appointed by Jeb Bush, refused to answer our calls. Instead, he put out a press release with no information.

So I went to Hillsborough County, Florida, to confront him.

We staked out his courthouse until we saw him slip into his car. But our tail was too light and he lost us in traffic. It was the first time I'd lost a tail and I was furious. By the way he was driving, it looked like he was trying to shake us. We figured he might be heading home, so we went straight there. The GPS took us down a long and narrow, wood-lined dirt driveway. When we arrived at this house, nobody was home. Our SUV was just sitting there a half mile onto his land in an untenable position. An idea then dawned on me. We'd drive the SUV halfway back up his driveway and wait for him to come home. The driveway was so narrow, when he arrived, he wouldn't be able to drive around us. He'd have to stop. Unless he threw it in reverse, we could hop out and nail him. It worked. Sure enough, he pulled into his driveway and our vehicles met nose to nose. The crew and I sprang into action while he sat in the driver's seat.

JESSE WATTERS: Hey, Judge, why did you give Michael Phillips such a low bail? Judge, you have an obligation to talk to us here. You're a public official. Why was the bail so low?

MANUEL LOPEZ, FLORIDA CIRCUIT JUDGE: I'm not going to answer any more questions about this case right now. I've already given my statement to the media. And I'm not going to collaborate any more on this.

WATTERS: Well, a lot of people are saying that your statement was insufficient.

LOPEZ: That is the public's right to reach that opinion. I've given the only statement I'm going to give, sir. Can I make it any clearer than that? Anything else you'd like to say? I'm not going to respond to your comment.

WATTERS: Do you feel bad about what happened?

LOPEZ: What do you think, sir? I'm a father with three children. I deal with people on a daily basis. How do you think I feel about Sergeant Phillips and his family?

WATTERS: Sergeant Harrison?

LOPEZ: Excuse me, Sergeant Harrison and his family. How do you think I feel about that poor man and his family?

WATTERS: Well, I don't know. Why don't you tell me?

LOPEZ: I'm not going to elaborate on it any further. Thank you.

WATTERS: Why was the bail so low? The guy had nineteen arrests. Burglary, battery, witness tampering, drug possession; it was a mile long. The guy was obviously a violent criminal with no respect for law enforcement. Wasn't there a red flag? Do you want to come on *The O'Reilly Factor*?

LOPEZ: Absolutely not.

The judge had gotten the name of the slain officer wrong. He did show sympathy for the officer's family, but it was a sad slip of the tongue. As I walked back to the SUV and loaded in the gear, I realized something. The judge wasn't backing out. He wasn't letting us leave his property. I hopped back outside and told him to back up, but he wouldn't budge.

Judge Lopez called 911 on me. He told the switchboard that a Fox crew was trespassing, and he was detaining us until a squad car arrived. The judge's vehicle had us pinned back on his property unable to escape. This would be a tough spot for me to wiggle out of when the police arrived. I banged on his window a few times, but he sat in the car with his arms crossed.

Finally, after an awkward twenty minutes, a police unit showed up. First order of business was to separate us and take statements. In order to do that, the officer asked that Judge Lopez back up and let me leave his property. Score. Out on the main road, I explained to the officer that I had merely been seeking a comment from the judge on why he released a "cop killer." I emphasized the phrase "cop killer" several times during my story and could tell the officer was well aware of the tragic case. I explained that once I realized the judge wasn't home, I turned around, but the judge pinned me onto his property and refused to let me leave. (I left out the part about lying in wait.) The officer was clearly on my side; this judge was no friend of law enforcement. He wrote me a "warning" for trespassing and told me not to do it again or I'd be charged. There wasn't even a fine or a court appearance required.

Few things are more important than safe streets. Without public safety, society plunges into vigilantism, mob violence, and financial ruin. America teetered on the brink in the summer of 2020. After the death of George Floyd in Minneapolis, protesters surged onto the streets. The outpouring of emotion was aimed at rectifying the perceived injustice in our system. As a white man in America, whose parents provided him with a good education and financial stability, I'll acknowledge a certain privilege. This is something I accept as a reality, but not something I feel guilty about. But all Americans, no matter our background, should strive for equality in the eyes of the law. Many of our countrymen don't feel that, based on their own experiences. So how do we improve that experience? The answer is not "defund the police."

What began as a righteous, peaceful movement protesting a sickening instance of police brutality quickly morphed into a divisive wave of destruction. Riots and looting racked up close to $2 billion in damages, while over thirty fatalities ensued, most of which, in a sad twist, were black Americans. Small businesses, owned by people of all backgrounds, were hardest hit. Already suffering from the pandemic lockdowns, small business owners in our inner cities saw their life's work looted or forced to board up and file for bankruptcy. Democrat mayors and governors allowed the chaos to rage, pulling back their police departments and refusing to allow the National Guard to quell the violence. Far-left DAs dropped charges, and with a wink and a nod turned loose troublemakers without consequences. Whether it was to politically hurt President Trump or because they didn't want to aggressively put down left-wing violence, we'll never know, but the damage was done. Gun sales skyrocketed, property values plummeted, and homicides spiked as America witnessed its most violent summer since the Rodney King riots in 1992.

Dozens of city councils voted to "defund the police," after activists screamed the slogan. Surveys across the political spectrum showed citizens of all races strongly against defunding the police, but the hardleft political class in major metropolitan areas were tone deaf. Defunding police actually harmed black Americans more than any other demographic. Smaller, poorly financed police departments result in slower 911 response times, more gang activity, fewer detectives, and higher crime rates. Even Al Sharpton piped up and explained that defunding the police was crazy. But activists, night after night, clashed with innocent officers, spitting in their faces, hurling projectiles, and torching patrol cars. The lack of support from politicians triggered a wave of early retirements.

The media poured gasoline on the fire. Toggling between not covering the riots or spinning them as "peaceful protests," the press blamed President Trump for the violence, as if these were *his* supporters looting and lighting fires. More incidents involving police were exploited in the most irresponsible way possible to further enflame the streets. Suspects who assaulted police, reached for knives, or shot tasers at officers were treated as innocent victims. No matter how many drugs were in someone's system, or how many felonies they had, or if they were involved in a life-and-death struggle, even mentioning the full scope of the situation was frowned upon in the media. Deceptive video clips were released without providing the full picture, inciting public anger, and demonizing the boys in blue. In many quarters, merely mentioning the phrase "blue lives matter" was deemed racist.

When Republicans initiated a bipartisan police reform bill, Democrats turned their backs, keeping the issue alive for the election instead of solving the problem. Police reform is a critical issue that should be addressed. Mandatory body cameras, expanded use of tasers, eliminating no-knock warrants, and more robust internal affairs departments should all be on the table. Discipline for officers shouldn't be meted out by arbitrators handpicked by the police union. Departments should never be used as revenue collectors, aggressively pulling people over just to write tickets and hand out fines to prop up debt-ridden cities. But it takes two to tango. If you give an officer respect, he'll give it back. Compliance is key. In a high-crime area, when you're pulled over, police will ask you to step out of the car, show your hands, and get down on the ground. As emasculating as this is, it's done to protect the lives of officers who don't know if a suspect is armed or has felony warrants. Honesty, compliance, civility, and respect go both ways during police stops. Foot pursuits and resisting and assaulting a police officer can lead to unexpected and sometimes deadly outcomes.

Most of the violence plaguing our inner cities is drug and gang related. America's drug appetite is humongous, and the cash flow for illegal narcotics is extremely tempting for ambitious young men who believe their other economic and educational options in life are limited. Latin cartels flood the streets with large quantities of pure product, and inner-city gangs handle the street distribution and compete for territory. The business is all cash, and the competition is bloody. The pandemic squeezed drug profits and exacerbated the violence. Gang shootings claim so many innocent victims because, in urban warfare, there are so many innocent bystanders at such close proximity, stray bullets have a higher percentage rate of finding a body. Therefore, a strong police presence in these neighborhoods is necessary to interdict shipments, serve warrants, get illegal guns off the streets, arrest violent offenders, solve murders, and respond quickly to 911 calls. Defunding the police only makes the murder rate go higher. The police hostility in the political-media arena accelerates crime because it kills proactive policing. Officers pull back. They're less likely to patrol on foot, knock on doors, and make traffic stops when they fear the system doesn't have their backs and their badges will be stripped over a routine stop. In turn, criminals take advantage of the power vacuum. They're more likely to carry illegal guns, take more chances, and resist arrest. Welcome to the death spiral.

Democrats ignored the violence all summer until polling told them they were getting hammered. Trump had been blaring a law-and-order message, backing police departments and insisting radical Democrats allow in the National Guard. His poll numbers in the battlegrounds jumped, and Joe Biden eventually pivoted. But it was too late. Democrats owned the "defund the police" brand, and many House Democrats blame their 2020 losses on this poisonous movement.

Here's some valuable wisdom for people (or perps) who find themselves on *my* radar. Avoid me at all costs. If I'm ambushing you, there's no way you'll look good. I'm a trained assassin with tricks up my sleeve. You need your own bag of tricks. I'm retired from the ambush game, but if you've triggered controversy, a younger version of me could be staking you out, ready to pounce. Or the paparazzi. Or if you're a Republican, the entire news media. So here's how to put your best foot forward. *Don't* put *any* foot forward. Don't leave your house, if that's possible. Work remotely. I know where you live. I know where you work. You're easy to find. I'm self-aware enough to know how invasive this sounds, but I'm giving you advice. I'm a respectful gentleman, but most reporters are extremely aggressive, self-righteous, and confrontational. They'll get physical if they have to. They know the law, and they know the gray area. Plus, they've been given an assignment and have a deadline every single day. They're paid bloodhounds. Again, this isn't me; it's everyone else. I'm different.

So if you're in the middle of a media firestorm, look out the window in the morning. Are there any random cars parked outside? Like an SUV or a van? Could be me. Couldn't hurt to call the police and report a suspicious vehicle in the neighborhood. A squad car will be dispatched to make contact with me. Call the police back and ask why the car was there. Maybe the police will tell you why, maybe they won't, because it depends on the conversation I had with the officer.

Remember that officers are almost always on my side. Because Fox supports law enforcement, and because I'm a great guy.*

Make yourself a big breakfast and brew some coffee, because it's going to be a long day. You're going to need your energy. If it's a waiting game, I'll win. I'll have the budget to be in town until I get you. I've ordered a pizza delivered to a stakeout. Waiting all day is easy for me. I'm a patient man. I survived for months in the wilderness wiping with sticks. Listening to the radio in an air-conditioned car is a luxury to me. The only way to outlast me is to wait all day until I need to have dinner. Once my car leaves, drive to a hotel and spend the night. Call your neighbors the next day and have them report back on the whereabouts of my vehicle. But your neighbors are probably fans of mine, so good luck.

If you absolutely need to go to work, bring a rabbit's foot. There are certainly things that can work in your favor. An attached garage is your biggest asset. Is it *you* that's pulling out of the garage? Or is it your spouse? Or your son? I'll have to tail the car and try to find out. If you're smart, send your wife out first as a decoy. I'll follow her until I realize it's her, and you can zip away in your second car, leaving me in the dust. It's hard for me to admit it, but that may have happened to me once, and I tip my hat to the guy who pulled it off. He'll remain nameless because I'm still bitter about it and don't want to give him the credit he deserves.

Don't answer your phone, either. If you pick it up, I'll know you're home. Once I know you're home, that's all I need to design a stakeout. Sometimes a spouse will answer the phone and unwittingly reveal valuable intelligence. "Oh, he's at the office and won't be back until after six p.m. . . . who may I ask is calling?" Click. Thanks, lady. Just make sure you and your spouse are on the same page. Trust me, I know that's asking a lot.

---

* And charming.

Walking your dog is asking for it. I know the dog has to go out, but have someone else walk it. I annihilated a Colorado state legislator while he walked his cocker spaniel. The barking in the background was annoying, but it just added to the real-life drama. Scooby Snacks weren't necessary since the mutt was on a leash.

Garbage days are great days to ambush someone at home. During a stakeout in Missouri, we arrived at a judge's home moments after the garbage collection. The judge's trash cans sat empty in the middle of his driveway. I crept up and quietly dragged the trash cans *all the way* down to the end of the driveway and placed them nearly forty yards from his front door. Each second is valuable during an ambush because I can lob a question about every ten yards. Sure enough, the judge came out to retrieve his empty trash cans and had to walk an extra long time, giving me ample time to confront him about his soft sentence.

If you leave for work during a swirl of controversy, don't stop for breakfast. Judge Torrence from Missouri had to have his McMuffin. After giving a sex offender probation, the judge stopped at McDonald's. Little did he know I was right behind him. Put the mic right in his face while he waited for his breakfast meal. Nowhere to run, nowhere to hide. Should have taken the drive-through that day.

Another judge, this one from Florida, failed to punish a pervert who preyed on a developmentally disabled boy. The sicko was back in the neighborhood, terrifying the community again. Judge Padgett was pulled out of retirement to handle the case and botched it. He then made the mistake of stopping at a 7-Eleven one morning while the heat was on him. Convenience store ambushes are always fun because the look in the cashier's eye is priceless. He rings up Slim Jims and a soda while a TV crew peppers his customer. It's the most excitement he's seen at work since the last robbery attempt. I followed the judge outside. He was the same judge who went light on Debra Lafave's sentence, the bleach-blond teacher who slept with one of her middle school students. I used a trick I learned from a *Factor* producer. As

Judge Padgett got into his car, I positioned my body inside the car door so he couldn't close it. "I'm going to hurt you if you don't move your leg," he threatened. The target is unable to close the door and leave, buying you more time to question him, and creating a dramatic scene. "The victim is scared. You owe that family an apology," I said as he slammed the door and sped off. The cashier had come outside to watch the scene unfold. As the cameraman turned around, the clerk waved at the camera and said, "Hi, Mom," and went back to work.

Your best shot is leaving from an attached home garage and pulling into a secure office garage, no stops in between. This foils me every time. Not everyone has the luxury of a secure garage at work, though. Some targets are sitting ducks in their own office buildings. One of the greatest advantages reporters have is that state capitol buildings are public property. Any yahoo and reporter (same thing) can waltz into these gorgeous buildings and confront politicians in the hallways. Or in the cafeteria. That's what I did with Vermont Democratic state senator Bill Lippert. In the state of Vermont, you could rape a young child and serve only five years in prison. For raping a little boy or girl! Vermont was one of the only states in the union not to pass some version of Jessica's Law. In fact, Senator Lippert had bottled up the sex offender bill in his committee for years. But as Vermont children were being brutalized, Lippert and his liberal pals found the time to pass a bill for transgender people. It's not that the transgender bill wasn't legitimate, everyone deserves equal protection. It was that Lippert's *priority* was to protect the transgendered from being discriminated against, instead of protecting the children from being sexually assaulted. Big difference. So my cameraman and I surprised Lippert and his fellow progressives in the statehouse cafeteria during breakfast.

JESSE WATTERS: I'm Jesse Waters with *The O'Reilly Factor*. Nice to meet you.
LIPPERT: Really, really lovely to meet you.

WATTERS: Great. Quick question for you, why did you pass that transgender bill and kill Jessica's Law?

LIPPERT: I beg your pardon?

WATTERS: Why did you pass that transgender identity bill and kill Jessica's Law?

UNIDENTIFIED FEMALE: What is this?

LIPPERT: People don't know what you're talking about.

WATTERS: That transgender identity bill that you guys just passed. Just seems like those priorities are a little strange.

LIPPERT: I passed an antidiscrimination bill to protect transgender people in Vermont. And I'm proud of that. What's your problem?

WATTERS: What about Jessica's Law? It seems like the priorities are a little out of whack. . . .

UNIDENTIFIED MALE: Who are you with?

WATTERS: I'm with *The O'Reilly Factor* with the Fox News Channel.

UNIDENTIFIED FEMALE: Go home! Go home! Go home!

WATTERS: Mr. Lippert, it just seems like these priorities are a little strange considering the fact that you're not protecting the children.

LIPPERT: Welcome to Vermont.

WATTERS: Why aren't you protecting the children against child rapists? Instead, you're passing bills that protect transsexual rights?

LIPPERT: You're disgusting. You people don't even begin to know what the truth is. Yesterday we passed a strong bill against sexual predators. If you start with getting your facts straight for once, it would be a refreshing change.

WATTERS: What about twenty-five-year mandatory minimum for child rape?

LIPPERT: We have the strongest laws in the country against sexual predators.

Lippert was lying and lost his cool. All hell broke loose. His face turned red, and his eyes bulged out of their sockets. But since his crew was there, he got brave and began to stand up and point fingers at me. This is exactly what guys like me want. We *want* you to go nuts. And that's what happened. His radical associates swarmed the cameraman. Some little nut job of a woman was chasing Jimmy, my cameraman, around the cafeteria, grabbing his jean jacket and hitting his lens with a rolled-up newspaper. The group was chanting something and trying to get physical with me. It was like the reject lunch table rebellion and we captured every second of it on tape. Just the kind of crazy content we were looking for.

What we didn't expect was to be accused of homophobia. A rag, the *Rutland Herald*, ran an editorial accusing us of gay-baiting. "So why would Fox News ambush Bill Lippert, one of the most respected members of the legislature? The answer is as simple as it is unsettling. Lippert is gay. Bigots like Bill O'Reilly have the right to free speech but Vermonters also have the right and responsibility to stand up to intolerance. Go home, indeed, Mr. O'Reilly. Hate has no place in Vermont." The truth is, I didn't know Lippert was gay. Why would I even care? I don't. Am I supposed to know who a small-time state politician likes to sleep with? Was the fact that he was eating egg whites for breakfast supposed to give it away?* This happened time and time again; when Fox would crusade against injustice, the media would collude with the corrupt liberal politicians and call us bigots. So we fought back and asked our audience to contact the publisher directly. We put his email and phone number and business address on the screen and asked people to be polite, of course. We may be straight, but we do have manners.

Of course, a year later, a little girl named Brooke Bennett was sexually assaulted, murdered, and buried in a hole near Braintree, Vermont. *Then* Lippert declared passing a harsher law his top priority.

The best way to handle me, if you can't hide from me, is to go

---

* Personally, I like the yolk, but I don't judge.

mute. The former CEO of Merrill Lynch handled me better than anyone. If only he was any good at his real job. CNBC described Stan O'Neal as "one of the worst CEOs of all time." A true villain of Wall Street, O'Neal golfed while Merrill loaded up with subprime mortgages. Described as the kind of boss who "never walked the trading floor," O'Neal was out walking courses all over Long Island, Westchester, and Connecticut. As his company posted the biggest quarterly loss in Merrill history, $8 billion, Stan O'Neal was posting really low scores, playing nearly two dozen rounds of golf in two months, including three rounds at three different clubs on just one day. A single-digit handicap didn't help him to save the company. The market crashed, layoffs hit, millions of Americans lost everything, and Stan tried to sell the company behind the board's back. He was forced into retiring, but not before leaving with a $161.5 million severance package. This was on top of the nearly $100 million in compensation he earned the year before. Americans, who lost their jobs, homes, and retirement savings, were disgusted and appalled. The *New York Times* called O'Neal one of the "feckless dolts" who helped precipitate the financial crisis.

Fox sent me to track down the dolt who made out like a bandit while America cratered. Dying to find him on the golf course, I drove up to his home course. O'Neal's tasteful country estate bordered the Waccabuc Country Club in Westchester County, New York. After poking around the pro shop, I discovered his usual tee time. But I decided there was no way I could bring cameras on the grounds, so I staked out his Upper East Side residence the next morning instead. Lo and behold, at 6:30 a.m., Stan strode past his doorman out onto the sidewalk with his clubs. I sprang on him.

JESSE WATTERS: Hey, Stan, Jesse Watters with Fox News. How are you?

O'NEAL: *(silence, walking)*

WATTERS: Millions of people lost millions of dollars at Merrill Lynch. You pulled a lot of money out of there and didn't do a very good job. How do you feel about that?

O'NEAL: *(silence, walking)*

WATTERS: You know a lot of people trusted you. Mr. O'Neal, you don't have anything to say?

O'NEAL: *(silence)*

WATTERS: You had a $161.5 million golden parachute. You don't have anything to say to any of the shareholders or any of the investors, any of the employees? To the rest of the country? Do you feel bad about what happened at all?

O'NEAL: *(silently puts his golf bag in his Mercedes and leaves)*

It was a perfectly executed perp walk. Corporate executives often undergo expensive rounds of media training for all sorts of things press related. O'Neal aced the ambush test. Show no emotion, say nothing, and leave as quickly as possible. You look guilty, but so what? We already know you're guilty. You don't *feel* guilty, though, because your great-great-grandchildren are set for life. But flawless performance. Don't give me anything to work with. What you say can be used against you in the court of public opinion.

CHAPTER SIX

How I Saved the Internet

Rosie O'Donnell understands the game well. When we met, she showed me how it's done, even though I got what I wanted out of her. ABC parted ways with Rosie in 2007 after a wild run on *The View*. She was a liberal lightning rod, declaring "radical Christianity is just as threatening as radical Islam," and suggesting US soldiers were terrorists. Her constant feuding with Donald Trump and on-air sparring with Elisabeth Hasselbeck burnished her brand as a media pugilist, but she made a huge mistake when she implied 9/11 was an inside job.

"I do believe that it's the first time in history that fire has ever melted steel. I do believe that it defies physics that World Trade Center tower 7—building 7, which collapsed in on itself—it is impossible for a building to fall the way it fell without explosives being involved. World Trade Center 7. World Trade [Center] 1 and 2 got hit by planes—7, miraculously, the first time in history, steel was melted by fire. It is physically impossible." She continued: "To say that we don't know that it imploded, that it was an implosion and a demolition, is beyond ignorant. Look at the films, get a physics expert here [on the show] from Yale, from Harvard, pick the school—[the collapse] defies reason."

When Hasselbeck threw her a lifeline and asked Rosie who she thought was responsible for the building's collapse, she said she didn't know. Purdue University, *Popular Mechanics*, a federal scientific study, and firefighters themselves all debunked Rosie's conspiracy theory.

Nine/eleven victims' family members were upset by this, as were service members who felt she was giving aid and comfort to the enemy. She'd been avoiding coming on *The Factor* to explain herself . . . until we visited her at a book signing in Huntington, Long Island, where I was living at the time.

I'd moseyed up to people at book signings before: Barack Obama, Howard Dean, and Jane Fonda. It takes a different approach. You can't roll in with a large camera crew. It needs to be low-profile. The move is to bring another producer who shoots the confrontation with a tiny handheld camera (this was pre-iPhone).

A *Factor* producer, a nice, funny liberal guy who worked pretty hard and went to happy hour with the staff . . . went loco one day and started leaking to Gawker while still working at Fox. His role as a mole was short-lived. He got smoked out in less than forty-eight hours. He'd left his digital footprints all over the company's system. A VP called me into her office during the investigation and asked if I thought this producer was the mole. I told her, "No way, he would never do that." Later that afternoon Fox busted him. Way to go, Agent Watters. In my defense, he was the first twentysomething to have a midlife crisis, so forgive me for not seeing that coming.

After he was canned, the Mole wrote a book. Here's how he described me: "sarcastic to the point where I decided it was a miracle he'd never been punched in the face; but he was still oddly likable." Honestly, I totally agree with that assessment. He continued: "[Watters's] ideology didn't consume him—which made him so good at ambushing liberals . . . he was able to approach them with an 'aren't we all having a good time demeanor'—treating the ambush as an amusing lark and making for much better television." Again, can't argue with it. The Mole has my number.

So the Mole and I roll up to the Rosie book signing at Book Revue in Huntington. We're waiting, holding our copies of *Celebrity Detox*, chatting in line with fans, and this woman asks us, "So how long have you two been together?" It dawned on me that two dudes standing in line together with five hundred women to meet Rosie O'Donnell might look a little gay.* While the Mole explained we were straight, I couldn't help but be a little offended, because if I *was* gay, I'd like to think I could do better than the Mole. I was clearly out of his league. Being gay was a great cover, though, so I shushed my producer and tried to hold his hand. The Mole, confused, rejected my fake advances. We waited in awkward silence for an hour until Rosie was right in front of us. I looked at the Mole. He hung behind, kept the small camera low and inconspicuous, and signaled he was rolling. Rosie was sitting, signing, and surrounded by an entourage of publicists and security. That's when I approached with a big smile.

JESSE WATTERS: I'm with Bill O'Reilly.

O'DONNELL: No, you are not. What do you mean you are with them?

WATTERS: I work with Bill. He wants to know why you will not come on the show? It seems like you had such a good time last time you were on. You're always invited.

O'DONNELL: Is your name Bill or Jesse?

WATTERS: This is for Bill O'Reilly.

O'DONNELL: Oh my God. Is that what you do? You go around to book signings.

WATTERS: No, we want to meet you. We want you to come on the show.

O'DONNELL: He knows how to find me, the guy.

WATTERS: We've called you a hundred times.

O'DONNELL: I do not want you to call me. If Bill wants me, he should tell me himself. He is a big boy. He is a grown-up.

WATTERS: So you're saying if he calls you, you are going to come on the show?

---

* Not that there's anything wrong with that.

(Security starts laying hands on the Mole)

O'DONNELL: Hey, this is Bill O'Reilly's camera crew, but don't throw them out because it makes it all worse when he puts it on the Bill O'Reilly No Spin Zone.

WATTERS: Rosie, he wants to know if you regret saying that 9/11 was an inside job?

(The mood suddenly changes)

O'DONNELL: I did not say that. He is quoting the wrong people.

UNIDENTIFIED MALE: Okay. That is enough. Thank you.

(The Mole and I begin to be corralled)

WATTERS: Weren't you trying to imply that Building 7 . . .

UNIDENTIFIED MALE: Thank you. That's enough. Sir. Enough.

The Mole and I are physically escorted out by security, while Rosie leads the crowd in a triumphant chant. The manager tells me I'm banned for life. (Hopefully he forgets my face when I sign *this* book there.) Rosie understood that lunging at the camera and grappling with the man filming is exactly what I want. She didn't play into it. She played along with me nicely until I hit her where it hurt. I left laughing with a signed copy of her book. Not to be outdone, she actually had her team filming the signing, so before we aired our footage, she leaked *her* footage to *Access Hollywood* and dished her spin to "Page Six" that she'd been confronted by "khaki-clad henchmen."

On her blog she said, "BO [bleep]wipes showed up. Cocky young white men. They were bullied out not soon enuf4 my liking." Weird that she played the race card, but how did she know we weren't cocky, young white *gay* men? Rosie obviously knew the Mole wasn't my type. Not that I have a type, of course, but hypothetically.

Once we started confronting the media, things reached another level. The media has the thinnest skin of any industry. Especially the print media. So when we turned the cameras on them, it got ugly. It started innocently enough, but escalated over the years to full-blown media warfare, and I found myself in the trenches.

O'Reilly was invited to speak at a fund-raiser for the It Happened to Alexa Foundation, a charity established to support rape victims. In 1999, Alexa Branchini was viciously raped in her Boston University dorm room by Abdelmajid Akouk, a Moroccan national. The attacker was sentenced to forty years, but his defense attorneys made the trial very long, very painful, and very expensive. Her parents took on massive expenses, relocating to Boston for a month. "Our family could not imagine Alexa having to go through the ordeal of a trial alone. Going back to the crime scene, reliving the ordeal in order to prepare for trial, then actually being in the courtroom with the rapist who assaulted her," said her father, Tom Branchini. "We wondered about other rape victims whose families were not able to afford the trip and planned the foundation to help ease the financial burden other families face while supporting their loved one through a criminal trial."

O'Reilly accepted the foundation's invitation to speak in Palm Beach, Florida, free of charge, so all the money raised would go toward rape victims. Unfortunately, Fox's enemies politicized the charitable event, setting off a chain reaction that caused a lot of problems for a lot of people. It was the very definition of what we called "the smear pipeline." The cyber-leeches at Media Matters cut a clip out of context, left-wing blogs picked it up, and MSNBC pushed the polluted propaganda onto the airwaves to damage us. Media Matters splashed a three-year-old clip of Bill on their site. The clip made it look like Bill said a rape victim was asking for it. As usual, when you listen to the clip in its entirety, it tells a completely different story. Michelle Malkin and O'Reilly were discussing Jennifer Moore, a young girl who'd been kidnapped, raped, and murdered by two random thugs in Manhattan at 2 a.m. While reporting the story on his radio show, Bill summarized a news report describing what the eighteen-year-old was wearing and how much she'd had to drink. Malkin and O'Reilly then pivoted to a larger conversation about how alcohol impairs the brain's ability to function, specifically what alcohol had done to Mel Gibson's career. Media Matters clipped out the context and made Bill appear to say women who dress and behave like Jennifer Moore should expect to be raped. The line of attack was not only deceptive, but ignored the fact that *The Factor* had done more for crime victims than almost any other show on television.

Word got out that Bill was speaking for the It Happened to Alexa Foundation, and the Left launched a takedown attempt. Liberal blogger Amanda Terkel packaged the out-of-context Media Matters clip into a slanted post for ThinkProgress, a low-rent site run by Hillary Clinton's hit man at the Center for American Progress, John Podesta. MSNBC host Keith Olbermann sucked up the garbage and pushed out a petition targeting the Alexa Foundation. It was another slimeball move by NBC president Jeff Zucker to smear Fox News personalities because they couldn't compete in the ratings race. But a rape victims' group was just collateral damage for NBC News.

The Alexa Foundation was inundated by hostile Fox haters after the petition was promoted on the internet and airwaves. The protest movement was intense, and Ellen Augello, the executive director of the It Happened to Alexa Foundation, was forced to respond:

We of course were thrilled to have someone of Mr. O'Reilly's stature offer to speak at our event. The fact that he has agreed to do so at no cost, so that all of the proceeds of the event can be used for the victims we serve, is very generous. Instead of receiving support from groups who believe themselves to be progressive and enlightened, we have been besieged by KO followers who, for whatever misguided reason, feel as though it is their duty to tell everyone they come into contact with not to support us. Although we are a national foundation, we are staffed by one full-time employee and one part-time employee, both of whom are quite modestly paid. Almost all of the funding coming into the Foundation goes directly to the victims we serve. So I ask you, who are these zealots truly hurting?

I attended the Florida fund-raiser. The group was forced to arrange security for the event due to the large number of threats generated by ThinkProgress and MSNBC. Thousands of dollars were raised for crime victims, and everyone was grateful for Bill's participation, but the foundation was saddened and shell-shocked by the negative partisan publicity. Crime victim advocate Wendy Murphy was there, too, and said Alexa herself was suffering. Alexa was so distraught by the protest that she couldn't eat or sleep. She had to quit her job. Her parents were incredibly hurt by this, especially on the heels of their daughter being raped at knifepoint not that long before. The Alexa Foundation isn't political. They don't ask rape victims who they voted for or what cable network they watch.

Soon after, we contacted the Center for American Progress about their employee's irresponsible posting, which helped trigger all this madness. No response. Therefore, O'Reilly asked me to personally catch up with the post's author, Amanda Terkel, in DC. I flew down to the capital, was scooped up by my cameraman, and tracked her down. We spotted her leaving her apartment complex with a guy and hop in a small car. We pursued in our SUV and realized she was going out of town when she hit the highway headed south. Well over an hour later, she arrived at a small inn off the main street of a little Virginia town in horse country. She emerged after checking in, and I confronted her on the sidewalk.

JESSE WATTERS: You wrote a blog about Bill O'Reilly going to speak for this great function, this charity group. And you attacked him personally, and you attacked the foundation, and you brought a lot of pain and suffering to this group. What's your reaction?

AMANDA TERKEL: What I remember writing was highlighting a comment that Bill O'Reilly had said, and that's what I remember doing. I don't remember attacking the foundation.

WATTERS: What did Bill O'Reilly say?

TERKEL: I can't remember exactly what he had said, because it was awhile ago. But I remember it was something having to do with the way he had talked about a rape victim in a derogatory way that seemed to place the blame for the rape on the victim.

WATTERS: Did you actually ever hear "The Radio Factor" segment in question?

TERKEL: Yes.

WATTERS: You did hear it?

TERKEL: There's audio online.

WATTERS: So what was the Mel Gibson component to Bill's analysis?

TERKEL: I don't believe I highlighted the Mel Gibson component.

WATTERS: Do you know what the Mel Gibson component was?

TERKEL: No.

WATTERS: Why not?

TERKEL: Because I didn't highlight it.

WATTERS: Because you didn't hear it, did you? Because you're just dishonest.

TERKEL: I listened to the portion that I highlighted.

WATTERS: You didn't hear the entire thing. You don't know the context, and you owe everybody an apology, because you brought a lot of pain and suffering to this rape victim and this foundation and her family.

Terkel couldn't process the pain she'd caused Alexa and the charity. It's best to leave charities out of political smear campaigns, especially ones helping crime victims. I'm sure she learned from her mistake as she grew up. Immediately after the ambush, though, ThinkProgress and the Center for American Progress launched an ad boycott against Fox News. Terkel alleges that our tactics were sexist, and she was a bullying victim. For years *The Factor* had tracked down and confronted men and women of all ages, of all races, of all political persuasions and professions, but Terkel played the victim card. She didn't handle it well. Apparently, the entire liberal media felt sorry for her, and suddenly Jesse Watters became notorious. Which couldn't be farther from the truth. I'm the nicest guy you'll ever meet. People are saying all the time, to know me is to love me. In any case, the tables turned, and the hunter became the hunted.

My mom called me one day very concerned. The *New York Times* had written about me. My mom worships the *Times*. She believes you should only be in the paper twice—when you get married and when you die. I wasn't dead and the *Times* had rejected my wedding announcement two years earlier. So, Mom was a little worried. "Gotcha TV: Crews Stalk Bill O'Reilly's Targets" was an attempt to discredit our ambush interviews by labeling liberal targets off-limits. You see, only the mainstream media is allowed to stake out people's homes, surprise them with camera crews, and ask confrontational questions. Network news can camp outside Scooter Libby's house, chase Republican senators down the street, and stick mics in Andrew Breitbart's face while blistering him with hostile questions, but Fox News is somehow excluded from this decades-old journalistic tactic?

The *New York Times* wrote, "Mr. O'Reilly's young producers have confronted in the past three years . . . more than 50 people. . . . The Fox News producer responsible for most of the ambush interviews, Jesse Watters, refused repeated interview requests." I did? The *Times* should have tried a little harder and tracked me down on the streets. I guess that wasn't their style. Instead, they cut and pasted a line from my blog. "If they don't come to us, we'll go to them." Isn't that what reporters do? The *New York Times* doesn't decide where Fox points our cameras and what questions we ask. The paper botched my photo, too. They used a picture of my colleague, Dan Bank, and called him Jesse Watters. The *Times* really didn't want my picture in print, I guess. First, the wedding announcement rejection and then this. Why should I care that a paper that hates me doesn't publish my wedding announcement when they publish my liberal sister's wedding announcement and my liberal parents' wedding announcement? Perhaps the *Times* didn't have room to feature a Fox News producer whose submission was riddled with run-on sentences. Again, I'm not upset by this.

The *Times* wrote that our ambush targets had shifted from corrupt public officials to "political and personal opponents" of O'Reilly. Among them, "Amanda Terkel, a managing editor at the liberal Web site ThinkProgress.org, was interviewed about a protest she helped organize against Mr. O'Reilly. Ms. Terkel's case generated immense attention on the internet last month partly because she called it an incident of stalking and harassment." Leave it to the left to slap scary legal terminology on a journalistic technique that *they've* perfected once it's turned around on them. Terkel played the victim card and the media circled the wagons around her. I politely asked her a question on a public sidewalk and left after a minute. I could have been a lot tougher. The *Times* described one incident this way: "When the subjects don't answer—at least not to the satisfaction of Mr. Watters—the questions become more provocative and emotional. Last summer Mr. Watters asked Governor Jim Douglas of Vermont about that state's criminal statutes and asked, 'About how many dead girls are we going to tolerate here?'" Notice how the *Times* leaves out that Douglas was a *Republican* governor. You'll also notice these are the types of questions mainstream media reporters ask Republicans all the time. This very question was asked about the Iraq War and the coronavirus pandemic. Sure, it's an emotionally loaded and leading question, but so what?

After the *Times* hit piece, I became a target, and got a taste of the Jesse Watters treatment. I definitely had it coming. But it made me realize how good I was at my job. And how bad the media was at theirs.

I got to work one day—as I usually did at the time—around 6:30 a.m. Being in to work early helped me get a jump start on Fox Nation. An anchor who usually never emailed me forwarded a link from Gawker saying, "They're looking for you." I clicked the link to see a picture of a strange guy standing outside my apartment building in Manhasset. The post was titled, "Ambushing Bill O'Reilly's Ambusher." Apparently, this Gawker editor had arrived at my place to ambush me at 6 a.m. Luckily, I'd left for the train around 5:30 a.m., and he missed me. You have to wake up pretty early in the morning to pull one over on me. To his credit, 6 a.m. was commendable. There was no way for him to know I was that hardworking. I definitely didn't give off that vibe.

Gawker was the slimiest website in America. They trafficked in sleaze, gossip, and militant leftism. The blog outed gay people they didn't like, published private information that put people in danger, and violated copyright laws for fun. They published hacked emails— almost exclusively of conservatives—and made enemies everywhere. It would have been nice to have a right-wing version of Gawker, but, alas, one can only dream. Eventually Gawker posted a sex tape of Hulk Hogan and was sued into bankruptcy. Couldn't happen to nicer people.

The Gawker guy sporting a creepy goatee and a beige blazer was waving at me in front of my apartment, satirically chronicling his ambush attempt in real time. "Watters, as you may have read, likes to sneak up on people without warning and ask them questions so that O'Reilly can air video of his enemies looking aggrieved and flustered," he wrote. My ambushes of Terkel and Arkin and Immelt were highlighted, along with my infamous line, "If they don't come to us, we'll go to them." They'd called me the day before to ask for an interview, but, as was company policy, I transferred the call to media relations. Media relations had declined the request. "So, we decided to track him down and ask him about his ambush interview tactics face-to-face," explained Gawker.

> If we find him, we'll post the video as soon as we can. If we don't, we'll keep trying, and for that we'll need your help. What do you know about Jesse Watters? Did you go to college with him? Do you ride the train with him? Do you work at the Starbucks where he buys his coffee? Let us know. We'll get you started: If you see him, snap a camera phone picture and send it to us. Or better yet, ask him why he stalks and ambushes people that his boss disagrees with, and tell us what he says. Two years ago, during an on-air celebration of Watters' ambushes, O'Reilly had this to say about his young charge: "Jesse Watters, everybody. He's becoming a big star all over the world." Let's make that happen.
>
> —*Gawker*

By comically live-blogging the ambush, Gawker blew their cover and was forced to crowdsource. No tips came in from Starbucks or the train. Nobody in Manhasset read Gawker, number one, and number two, I wasn't that famous. But the attention I was getting for being controversial enough to ambush was certainly helping my star rise. Thank you, Gawker. This was useful during my contract renegotiations. I owe you.

Gawker botched their first attempt and whined about it in a follow-up post. They called my refusing to answer their questions "an act of pure weeniness."

> We thought we had a good chance of finding him leaving his house for the office this morning, but not everyone can be a stalker extraordinaire like Watters. Our team learned some valuable lessons: 1) a stakeout's best done on an empty bladder and 2) be sure to

cover all possible exits. (If he's not still at home, we think he either slipped out when John and Richard went to the loo, or walked out a back way to the nearby train station.) Rookie mistakes happen. And, Jesse, your taunts only make us more determined. In the meantime, we'll be making a careful study of the master at work.

—*Gawker*

"My taunts" were actually from a fake Twitter account that Gawker fell for. I don't tweet anything but *Watters' World* clips because I don't need to give people an additional reason to fire me.

Gawker took another shot at me a month later. Another whiff. Not that easy, is it? In "Ambushing Fox's Ambusher, Part Two," the Gawker editor discovered I'd moved out of the Manhasset apartment and bought a house in Huntington, New York. He congratulated me for "moving up in the world" and announced he spent some time "hanging out in the new 'hood.'"

We met some of your neighbors, Jesse—they are lovely people (we mean that in earnest), and we don't blame them in the least for calling the cops on us because they were creeped out by two blogger-looking dudes hanging out on their street all day. Did any of your targets' neighbors ever call the cops on you when you stalked and ambushed them, Jesse? The officer who questioned us while we were parked outside your house was very friendly and didn't try to run us off, and we're curious about your experience. We should compare notes! Especially because the other cop that detained us yesterday pointed his gun at us. Did that ever happen to you? Don't worry—in the end it all worked out. He was a big fan of your work, and he found it pretty funny that we were trying to ambush you. He wished us luck.

—*Gawker*

No. I've never had a gun pointed at me. At least not during a stake-out. I have to hand it to Gawker, though: The transparent attempts to ambush me were an amusing stunt. The editor was a good writer, and he made me laugh. He also made me feel much more important than I really was. Not everyone had fake paparazzi on their tail. This generated some gossip in my new neighborhood. The guy who just moved in has police pointing guns on reporters outside his home. For the next few years my neighbors would text me whenever a suspicious vehicle pulled into the cul-de-sac. We had our own neighborhood watch going, except we weren't looking for burglars, we were looking for bloggers.

I confronted the Gawker guy once outside the Fox News building during this whole episode, and he wasn't as charming and eloquent as he was in print. Most likely trying to ascertain my commuting schedule, he was lurking outside our headquarters after the show taped, but made the mistake of not carrying his camera. I recognized him and whipped my camera out and started recording his face. "Aren't you that Gawker guy?" I asked. He panicked and slinked into a taxi. Weird dude in person. But then again, he worked for Gawker.

After three months of being hunted, Gawker finally got me. Well, he barely got me. I left through my side door on a Saturday morning to go to Home Depot and got ten yards down my driveway when the editor jumped out of nowhere. By that time, I was already in my car, so I just hit reverse and drove off. He said hello or something; I can't recall. It was over in five seconds. I was totally caught off guard, but I smiled and waved while I left him in the dust. If he was a pro, like me, he would have tailed me and nailed me at Home Depot. There would have been an ugly scene in the paint supply section.

But the Gawker ambush really made me reflect on what I was doing as a producer. Was I a hypocrite for dodging the ambush attempt? Did I have an obligation to talk after expecting that obligation from others? Were my tactics below the belt? Was I seeking drama instead of answers? Just kidding. None of those questions crossed my mind. I know exactly how the media operates. Gawker got some clicks and cash out of me; that's fine. But Gawker lost the game. They knew it, too. This is media warfare. The country is at stake. This isn't a business to get lost in self-reflection and self-doubt. You make enemies when you get close to the truth. Deal with it. There are usually two sides to everything. Find the line and stand *on* the line and fight for what you think is right. I never stressed out when I was called a soulless hypocrite, a cheap takedown artist, or a vile yes-man. Half the country loved me; I must be doing something right. Plus, I loved me. Don't they say that's the most important thing?

After the last episode, Gawker wrote, "We finally met Bill O'Reilly's stalker-producer Jesse Watters on Saturday. It was a fleeting and civil encounter—jovial, even—but ultimately unsatisfying." The editor claims he really wanted to ask me questions but in the same breath writes, "Why would he just sit there and let himself be attacked? So he drove away, like a coward." That's the point that Gawker misses. The way the ambush goes is entirely up to the person being ambushed. The target can stop and talk, argue and scream, run and hide, or just stay silent and leave. Fox and Gawker or any media company has every right to seek answers from individuals, and those individuals have every right to answer or not answer those questions, in whatever manner they see fit. I handled Gawker like a total pro, slipping away in silence. I didn't have to stand there and take it on the chin in my own driveway. Gawker knew the better man won, and threw in the towel.

Though we'd still love to actually ask Jesse questions about why he does what he does, and how he does it, we're done with the 4 a.m. wake-up calls to drive out to Long Island and sit on his house. We've made our point. But that doesn't mean Jesse shouldn't have to answer for what he does. So if you ever happen to run into him—maybe on the streets of downtown Huntington, N.Y., or on the Long

Island Railroad into Manhattan from Huntington, or around the
News Corp. building at Sixth Avenue and 48th St. in Manhattan,
or near his parents' summer home in Pemaquid, Maine—don't be
afraid to politely and calmly walk up to him and ask him why he
stalks people. Let us know what he says.
—*Gawker*

In a way, I'm glad I was targeted. The feeling that races through
your veins when an antagonist pops out of nowhere with a camera is
intense. If you don't control it, the feeling can overwhelm you. But
true champions have the ability to recognize the situation immediately, slow things down, and take control of the action. True champions like Tom Brady, Wayne Gretzky, and myself can slow things
down in the moment and see things before they happen. The Gawker
rallying cry inspired a few copycats, and it wasn't long before the Left
really got me. But when they got me, I got them back. Kind of.

CHAPTER SEVEN

How I Saved DC Nightlife

Fox used to send me down to CPAC in Washington, DC, every spring. The Conversative Political Action Conference is an annual gathering of grassroots conservative activists who spend a few days at a DC hotel attending seminars and networking. Radio hosts, pundits, and politicians give speeches, sell books, and mingle with the crowds. Today you'll encounter people like Charlie Kirk, Glenn Beck, and Dan Bongino. Trump will speak and bring down the house. The CPAC scene has changed a lot over the years.

I covered CPAC during the Obama presidency, and there was a fresh, swashbuckling insurgency afoot. This was the renaissance of conservative internet entrepreneurs. Breitbart, Hotair, Townhall, CNSNews, Drudge was where the action was. Ann Coulter was a star. The Tea Party had begun. We all felt like renegades—like the party was being reborn with a younger, more aggressive attitude—and the GOP establishment, the media, and the Democrats were all taking notice. It was a sea of coalescing factions—from libertarians, to hawks, to bloggers, to fiscal and social conservatives, to taking on Islamofascism, the mainstream media, RINOs, environmentalist wackos, and the radical Obama agenda. Andrew Breitbart was the leader of a merry-prankster crew of upstart conservatives, and he was the life of the CPAC party. Breitbart was a whirling dervish of energy, zigzagging all over the conference corridors, giving impromptu interviews, debuting films, and screaming at counterprotesters outside until he was red in the face. The man was a relentless attack dog, constantly on offense against the Left, never giving any ground, and hitting them where it hurt.

But whenever CPAC launched, left-wing media reporters would get credentialed, roam around, and try discrediting the conservative movement. In addition to the usual suspects—*Politico*, the *Washington Post*, the *Times*—the dark underbelly of the liberal media would show up: ThinkProgress, Media Matters, Gawker, Newshounds. These character assassins would take photos, conduct sly interviews, and portray CPAC participants in an unflattering light, essentially as radical racists, Islamophobic rubes, or merely right-wing hacks. One afternoon in 2011, they found *this* "right-wing hack" strolling solo through CPAC. Media Matters, the George Soros–funded anti-Fox operation, had just released a story, purportedly from a so-called anonymous "Fox News Insider," who claimed Fox is a propaganda machine that "makes stuff up."

Out of the blue, some young, pudgy dude approached me and started filming me with his camera phone. My first instinct was: Where are the exits? I had a room booked at the hotel, so I needed an escape plan. I was on an upstairs level, far away from the elevator bank, and I realized this young punk was going to have a good long run at me. But after I sized him up, and saw how ridiculous he looked with his little camera phone, I decided to turn the tables on him. It was then that I decided, as a trained ambush specialist, to critique his technique. You know, offer some sage advice to the wannabe. So I put a smile on my face and casually turned the tables on him while I made my way to the elevators.

TP: Hey, Jesse Watters?
WATTERS: What's up?
TP: Jesse Watters?

WATTERS: Who are you?

TP: I'm Ben Armbruster from ThinkProgress.org.

WATTERS: Oh, what's up, buddy? How you doing?

TP: I just wanted to ask you a quick question.

WATTERS: Is this an ambush? Listen, this is not how you do an ambush, man.

TP: Why not?

WATTERS: You got to have a real camera first of all.

TP: This is real. It works.

WATTERS: If you're going to do like, a real ambush, you got to get a crew. You got to get a sound guy. You're not—

TP: Why what's the—

WATTERS: You're just kind of, a little JV.

TP: Oh yeah?

WATTERS: Yeah. I got to teach you some things, all right?

TP: Yeah, I mean I never made the varsity team in high school so I don't really know what it's like.

WATTERS: It looks like it. It looks like you're a little JV.

TP: So I wanted to ask you, there was a report out a couple days ago about a Fox News insider saying that Fox News just makes stuff up and is a propaganda outfit for the GOP. I was wondering what you think about that.

WATTERS: Well first of all, when you do these things, you kind of got to like, start, you know, "Hey how you doing?" You know, "What's your name?"

TP: Well, so what do you think about it?

WATTERS: . . . introduce yourself. You know, usually when I do these things, I say, "Hi, Jesse Watters . . ."

TP: I did introduce myself.

WATTERS: ". . . I'm with Fox News. Nice to meet you." Like, a smile usually helps at first to kind of like break the ice.

TP: Uh huh.

WATTERS: A little tip.

TP: So what do you think about that, that story?

WATTERS: Um, the other thing is when you approach someone with a camera phone? It's just kind of weak.

TP: Yeah?

WATTERS: You know what I mean? It's just kind of weak.

TP: So you don't have any comment on that story? Do you not have a comment on it? Do you think that Fox News just makes stuff up?

WATTERS: Bro. You're doing it with a camera phone, bro.

TP: Well answer the question. Yes or no? Do you think Fox News makes stuff up? Yes or no?

WATTERS: Do I think Fox makes stuff up?

TP: Yeah.

WATTERS: That's your question?

TP: Yeah.

WATTERS: You know, another little piece of advice when you're doing these ambushes or whatever. The question is very important. And I just don't think you're really bringing it with that question. I think you need to go back—

TP: So yes or no?

WATTERS: —and try again. Come back with like a more hard-hitting question. Maybe not like a yes-or-no question. Usually when I do ambushes I try not to ask yes-or-no questions—

TP: It was a Fox insider that said that Fox is a propaganda outfit—

WATTERS: —just the person to kind of just say, yes or no, you want to like draw them out a little bit.

TP: I just want to get your response to that. Do you have no response? I guess that's a "yes," you have no response. Right?

WATTERS: Watch my blazer, bro.

TP: Do you have no response? Where's your camera guy? Where's your camera guy?

WATTERS: Where's your camera guy?

TP: Let's go get him. So no?

WATTERS: Do you want to repeat the question?

TP: Do you have an answer or no?

WATTERS: Do you want to repeat the question?

TP: A Fox insider said that Fox—

WATTERS: Bro, I'm kidding around. I heard the question. I'm just messing with you, man. [Looking into the camera] How you doing? What's up, ThinkProgress?

TP: So no.

WATTERS: Your hand's shaking. You look a little nervous with that thing.

TP: I'm not nervous.

WATTERS: Why are you like fumbling with your words? The other thing is when you do these ambush interviews you really got to, like, practice beforehand.

TP: Mhmm. All right, well, I guess that's a no, then, huh.

WATTERS: See you later.

The elevator closed and I was clear. I called Fox and let them know ThinkProgress got me, and explained how I handled it. The footage soon posted and I came off okay. The "watch my blazer, bro" line went viral and *The Factor* ran the whole clip the next night. It was a learning experience in the sense that I realized how to handle oppositional media. You have the ability to totally control the conversation. This is a lesson for everyone who does TV. Answer their questions how *you* want. You're under no obligation to directly answer their nasty questions. Feel free to interview them. Talk about what *you* want to talk about. It takes a certain dexterity and discipline, but it's better than being suckered into a losing debate. Run out the clock, ridicule your opponent, dismiss the premise of the question, and never let them touch the blazer. The blazer is sacred.

Years later, the Think Progress/Jesse Watters saga came full circle at the 2016 White House Correspondents' Association Dinner. They call the annual dinner "Nerd Prom" because for one night, liberal journalists get to wear black tie, give themselves awards, and mingle with celebrities. The media executives fly the celebrities out to DC for free, where they walk the red carpet and listen to a hired comedian roast the press and the president. A-list comedians who emceed over the years have included Bob Hope, Merv Griffin, Richard Pryor, George Carlin, Jay Leno, and Jon Stewart. The sitting president then roasts the press (and himself) while the C-SPAN cameras pan the crowd of drunk celebrities, senators, and anchors laughing hysterically. Money is raised for the White House Correspondents' Association, which awards scholarships, and everyone wakes up the next morning hungover, feeling good about themselves, with a story about seeing Sinbad in the bathroom (or someone as random as Sinbad).

I shot the WHCAD red carpet for Fox in 2013 before I attended the dinner, armed with a very simple question: "Is there bias in the media?" The answer is obviously yes, but it was amusing watching Hollywood and the elite media wiggle. I approached it with my usual laid-back disarming charm, so it went smooth as butter.

Norah O'Donnell gracefully blew me off with the old "hi and goodbye" routine. Left-wing writer Jonathan Alter asserted, quite angrily, that my question was "just dumb." CBS president and CEO Les Moonves said there was bias "on both sides" in the media and, when pressed by me, refused to admit the media tilted left. Les was in denial about a lot of things. Years later, he was blindsided by the MeToo movement and lost his job. After I told Tracey Morgan the media leans left, he told me it leaned right. Al Roker smoothly dodged, saying, "The Weather Channel goes right down the middle." When I asked Claire Danes about media bias, she froze. Lucky for her, Bob Schieffer of CBS jumped in to say he was "biased toward Claire," which got a laugh and saved her. Bradley Whitford, the *West Wing* actor, was game, admitting there were two sides to every story. Matthew

Perry glided by me like a pro saying, "There's bias everywhere," before being whisked away by handlers. Hayden Panettiere sarcastically said there was no bias at all, while rolling her eyes acknowledging the massive bias. She'd later go on to marry Russian heavyweight champ Wladimir Klitschko, so according to the Left's standards, this may have been Russian disinformation.

Chris Matthews, Piers Morgan, and *Duck Dynasty* star Willie Robertson stopped by for some friendly banter. Even Olivia Munn made her way over, then admitted she had no clue who I was. I gave her a pass on the innocent slight. Most people still don't know who I am.

Conan O'Brien kicked off the festivities: "It's an honor to share this stage with the president," he said at the top. "When you think about it, the president and I are a lot alike. We both went to Harvard. We both have two children, and we both told Joe Biden we didn't have extra tickets for tonight's event." The late-night star continued: "I have a question, and I think some of you also have this question," he said. "It's been several months since you were reelected, sir, so I'm curious, why are you still sending everyone five emails a day asking for more money? You won. Do you have a gambling problem we don't know about?"

Conan killed. As I scanned the room I realized the *bigger* stars had avoided the red carpet (or slipped past me). Michael Douglas, Sofia Vergara, Steven Spielberg, and Scarlett Johansson were scattered among the tables, eagerly awaiting their favorite president. Finally, "Hail to the Chief" played as POTUS took over the dinner. He was starting his second term, and his comedy writers were on point: "These days, I look in the mirror, I have to admit: I'm not the strapping young Muslim socialist I used to be." (The crowd roared in laughter.)

"Yet I still make rookie mistakes. Out in California, we're at a fund-raiser. I happen to mention that Kamala Harris is the best-looking attorney general in the country. I got in trouble when I got back home—who knew Eric Holder was so sensitive?" Referencing the recent controversy involving Jay-Z going to Cuba, Obama cracked, "I've got ninety-nine problems and now Jay-Z is one." The president's delivery was perfect, everyone was drunk, and despite what haters say about "nerd prom," if you ever get invited, definitely go. It's a once-in-a-lifetime opportunity. In my case, I wish it *was* just once, because the second time I went, "nerd prom" turned into "Revenge of the Nerds."

Everything began swimmingly. I was invited to the dinner, but, of course, Fox had me shoot the red carpet beforehand. Gotta work to eat, I guess. It was spring 2016, and I was a little more established, so red carpet walkers knew what they were getting into when they swung by my position. Not everyone, though. DJ Khaled stopped by, chatted, and took a picture with me. He was frantically informed afterward by a liberal flak, "Don't you know he *hates* Obama!?"

Newt Gingrich set the scene perfectly, explaining to me, "This is the 'I love me night' for Washington. And they manage to wrangle Hollywood into deciding they love Washington, too." And Hollywood did show up big for Barack Obama's final White House Correspondents' Association Dinner, although not every celebrity wanted to rap with me. Will Smith wouldn't answer "Who is going to win in November?" If he had answered, he probably would have been wrong. I asked Gabrielle Union if she'd leave the country if Trump were elected. "No. Somebody needs to stay and fight." And fight they did. Jeff Goldblum praised Bernie Sanders as an "intelligent," "heartfelt," and "wonderful man." I'll give him heartfelt. Aretha Franklin was the only celebrity who admitted she was "excited for Hillary." Neve Campbell got the best of me, although I set her up perfectly, when I shared my thoughts on her performance with Denise Richards in *Wild Things*. "My favorite all-time movie scene was when you had that lesbian kiss in the pool," I remarked gratuitously, throwing one right the middle of the plate. Neve nodded gamely, retorting, "I'm not surprised." Home run.

I had jocular exchanges with Jake Tapper, Joy Behar, Van Jones, and Chris Matthews because you catch more flies with honey than you do vinegar. When White House press secretary Josh Earnest approached, I asked, "What is the biggest lie that you ever told on the White House podium?" He smiled and claimed, "I have never told a lie on the White House podium." I immediately started laughing and clapped back, "Now, I know you are lying." Then the Trump sons showed up, and I asked Eric, "Who would win in a fight, you or Don?" Eric touted his height advantage, but as I'd learn later in the night, the tale of the tape didn't dictate the outcome.

We wrapped the carpet up and headed inside for cocktails. Fox's Sandra Smith and Kennedy were with me floating around when we heard the CBS room had great hors d'oeuvres. It was a private event within the hotel, but Kennedy walked right up to the velvet rope expecting to breeze through. A young woman, fresh out of college, stopped her and asked who she was. "I'm Kennedy," she announced. The woman looked down at her guest list and said, "Ah, okay, *Anthony* Kennedy?" We all looked at each other, and stood up a bit straighter since we were in the presence of a Supreme Court justice. "Yes . . . and they're with me," said Kennedy confidently. She grabbed Sandra and my arms and escorted us inside, where we stocked up on shrimp cocktail and complimented Kennedy on her judicial temperament.

The main ballroom was packed. You get pressed up against the most random people while mingling toward your table. I asked Bernie Sanders for a selfie, and Don Lemon asked Kimberly Guilfoyle and me for a selfie. Probably for the same ironic reasons. Soon thereafter, President Obama spoke, and as usual, his timing and delivery were flawless. Obviously, it helps to have the most gifted joke writers in entertainment crafting your speech. After ribbing Hillary and Sanders, Obama turned his sights on Donald Trump. "The Republican establishment is incredulous that he's the likely nominee. Shocking!" Obama said. "They say Donald lacks the foreign policy experience to be president. But in fairness, he has spent years meeting with leaders

from around the world: Ms. Sweden, Ms. Argentina, Ms. Azerbaijan."
You had to laugh.

"And there's one area where Donald's experience could be invaluable. That's closing Guantanamo," said Obama. "Because Trump knows a thing or two about running waterfront properties into the ground." The room exploded in laughter.

"Eight years ago I was a young man, full of idealism and vigor. And look at me now: I am gray and grizzled, and just counting down the days till my death panel." More laughter. The president finished by thanking the press for its diligent work the last eight years (kissing his ass), and dropped the mic to a standing ovation.

The night went downhill from there. Larry Wilmore, an African American comedian on Comedy Central, was the emcee for the evening and didn't deliver. He started off strong: "Welcome to Negro night here in Washington. Or as Fox will report, two thugs interrupt elegant dinner in D.C." But the rest of his jokes failed to land, and the crowd began groaning and eye-rolling. The energy was sucked out of the room by the end of the speech, which Wilmore punctuated with a racial slur. "So Mr. President . . . I'm gonna keep it one hundred. Yo Barry, you did it my n—a," Wilmore said to Obama to close it out. I wasn't going to lose sleep over it, but you could tell the mostly white room was uneasy about the n-word being dropped. Al Sharpton was telling people afterward it was in "poor taste." And the reverend knows a thing or two about taste, right? At least he knew what *not* to taste. Al looked skinnier than the Hollywood stick figures I'd just interviewed. As I wondered whether I was in better shape than Sharpton, we wandered upstairs to the bar to have a drink and recap the night. But it wasn't over yet.

Media companies usually throw after-parties the night of the WHCAD, but Fox doesn't waste money on that. So the Fox talent and producers were at the hotel bar figuring out what to do. We heard the MSNBC party was a good one and debated whether to go. Screw it, we said, Biz Markie was DJ'ing. So we hopped in an SUV and headed over to the venue, the US Institute of Peace, in Foggy Bottom. It didn't live up to its name.

After jawboning the PR and security staff, I and about six other Fox personalities made our way in. It was a well-appointed, gorgeous interior, and very crowded. Maybe we stuck out, but probably not, since everyone there was wasted.

Suddenly, some guy comes over to me and asks me to meet Amanda Terkel, the ThinkProgress blogger I confronted for targeting a rape victims charity. I was in a jolly mood, so I say, sure, bring her over. The guy says he wants me to "make up" with her. Why not? No hard feelings, let's see where this goes, so I say, "let's make up." The guy disappears for a second and comes back saying Terkel won't accept my apology unless I "grovel." I don't feel the need to apologize, let alone grovel, but it is a fun night, and it can't hurt to play along. So I agree to apologize, but this guy starts dropping the F-bomb, and I get the sense that he's there to instigate something. He says Terkel won't come over, so at this point I'm over it. Some short guy walks past me, clinks my cocktail, and says, "She's psychologically scarred." Now it feels like a setup. This guy wants to act macho for Amanda on his home turf. He's being obnoxious and wants to recap my ambush, but I'm off the clock. I wrapped up the red carpet shoot hours ago, and it was time to unwind. However, the guy is now in my circle of Fox people, and I notice he's recording everything with his iPhone.

I knew the game better than anyone, so I nicely told him "get out of here." He didn't, so I grabbed the iPhone out of his hand and flicked it down on the ground behind him. He should have gotten the hint at that point; the game was over. But he fetched his phone and reappeared with it rolling. The guy, who's my height, walked back right to me and put the camera near me again. I'd had enough at this point. This wasn't going to stop until I left, and I wasn't in the mood to leave, so I grabbed the iPhone out of his hand again.

This time I put it in my pocket. I told him, "not tonight," expecting him to take a lap and cool off. Once I saw he could behave himself, I'd give him the phone back. But he wouldn't stop talking to me about Amanda Terkel. He demanded his phone back while his colleagues watched on. It was at this point that I should have handed the phone back, but I didn't trust him, so I told him to "take it back." This clearly escalated the situation and put the guy in an awkward position, because if he tried to take it back it would get physical. If he did nothing, he'd lose face. The guy squirmed around for a minute, acting shifty, not knowing how to handle the situation. I told him I'd give him the phone back when I was ready, or I'd throw it out the window if I felt he wouldn't act civilized.

I asked him to identify himself, and he actually spelled his name out for me like a student. His name was Ryan Grim, who I later found out worked with Terkel at *Huffington Post*. Finally, he worked up the courage to take his phone back. I gave him one warning not to touch me. He paused. Thought about it, then reached toward my front pants pocket, which was a creepy move. He was too close. So I grabbed him by his tux lapels and shoved him back into a cocktail table and chairs. A few glasses smashed, a small commotion, but it wasn't much. He picked himself off the ground, wet and disheveled, and I yelled to security, "Get him out of here!" I'm not sure where Grim went, maybe to clean himself up, who knows, but I stuck around the party for a little longer. The same short colleague of Grim's came back around asking for the phone. I handed it back to his buddy and left the party.

The next day the story was everywhere. "Brawl breaks out at Nerd Prom" was on the Drudge Report. There were no punches thrown. It wasn't a brawl, I wouldn't even consider it a fight, but the media had some fun with it. Roger Ailes ran into me by the elevators at Fox and pulled me aside. "Hey, champ, don't go into the other team's locker room after the game and spike the football." To Ailes, team Fox shouldn't be going to MSNBC parties in the first place. He was right.

O'Reilly ran the red carpet package and asked me about the "dustup" on air afterward. I told him I regretted it, and he needled me about how much publicity I got out of it. The Grim guy got more publicity than he ever will in his life, so you're welcome. Send me the dry cleaning bill for the tux. As for Amanda, I offered to apologize and be the bigger person, even though I didn't have to; I'm just gallant. Holding a grudge isn't healthy, but it's water under the bridge. Personally, what happened at the after-party, I'm not proud of it. Grim could have landed in serious legal trouble. I'm not sure who his lawyer is, but mine is Justice Kennedy.

CHAPTER EIGHT

How I Saved Nude Beaches

One day in 2011, Bill called me into his office and said, "Watters. We're going to do a new segment where we see how much young people know about America." (It turns out they know very little.) The premise was for me to go out on the streets and ask people in their twenties about politics, civics, history, and their feelings regarding current events. Bill said he created the segment to "get me out of the building," so I would stop "bothering everyone."

In the business, these are called "man on the street" segments (MOS). Senior Producer Rob Monaco, our tape specialist, created the "packages" that you see on air. Bill told Monaco early on, "Watters isn't funny. Make him funny." I still struggle to admit that Monaco "made me funny." Because it's partially true, and because giving credit to your producers goes against everything TV hosts have been trained to do. I'll only say this: Monaco is a true artist, who understands comedy, timing, tape, sound, and nuance like no one else. I'm incredibly lucky to have worked with him, and I am grateful to have had a producer with such a perfect sense of humor for what we were trying to accomplish. He's a master craftsman who delivered high-quality product consistently for years. And if I give him any more compliments, I'm going to throw up.

Now back to me. The branding of the segment has become folklore. Bill was always the one to brand new segments, "The Kelly File" with

Megyn Kelly, "Miller Time" with Dennis Miller, etc. In the center of the pod stood a massive bulletin board, where the week's segments were thumbtacked up on index cards so everyone could see the shows' rundowns. While I was still brainstorming what to brand my segment, Senior Producer Ron Mitchell, as a joke, wrote "Watters' World" with a Sharpie onto an index card, taped it on a picture of Kevin Costner, and slapped it on the board. Bill noticed the card and thought *he'd* already come up with the name, and announced "Watters! We're going to call your segment 'Watters' World,' after Kevin Costner's *Waterworld*, the biggest box office bomb of all time!" Bill was laughing heartily at this. "This better be better than the movie . . . no pressure, Watters." Nineteen ninety-five's *Waterworld* cost nearly $200 million to make, the most expensive movie ever made at the time, but took home just $88 million at the US box office. Kevin Costner starred as a weathered renegade floating atop a postapocalyptic ocean. Despite the film's epic flop, Costner was paid $13 million. I would *kill* to flop for that much money. Maybe in a few years, if I keep at it, I will. Fingers crossed.

I headed out to Union Square in Manhattan for my first official *Watters' World* shoot. First Lady Michelle Obama had just declared that young people shouldn't be on Facebook—and that was my line of questioning, to see if people agreed. We wrapped things up, took it into the edit room, and aired it the next night. The package was halfway decent, but one interview really jumped off the screen: a white dude in his twenties with a crazy T-shirt, hat, and sunglasses. He said, "Twelve-year-olds shouldn't be on Facebook because they put that they're eighteen and they're really twelve! And I'm like whoa! She said she was eighteen!" Throwing both hands up in the air, professing his innocence, he started laughing, giving me pause. "Did you get in trouble for doing that?" I asked. "They tried," he replied. "Who's they?" I asked. He became really serious. "Um, well, the detective." Wow. The dude admitted on national television that law enforcement had investigated him for unwittingly flirting with underage girls online. He was ripping cigs without a care in the world, chuckling, big personality, no filter. Afterward, Bill instructed me, "More guys like *that* guy, Watters." I immediately knew exactly what we were going for. Characters. Dear God, did I find them.

When I heard there was a mushroom festival in Telluride, Colorado, I demanded to go. I'd stumbled upon 'Shroomfest while researching possible *Watters' World* shoot ideas, and immediately knew the streets of this legendary mountain town would be teeming with characters. It was an annual event that brought chemists, poets, chefs, and curious travelers to Telluride where mushrooms were explored as a food and a "medicine." Because it's quite obvious that mushrooms have therapeutic qualities.

Events like these require credentials, which can be a headache. I flew into Durango, Colorado, drove two hours through winding, majestic mountain passes, and arrived at a four-star resort in Telluride for a meeting with the 'Shroomfest marketing director. My credentials still hung in the balance because her boss was nervous about Fox cameras filming. I rode a gondola up to a mountaintop dining room, where I soothed her fears over wine and received official permission to shoot. But the real headache came the following morning when I awoke with a dome-splitting migraine. Slugging down bottles of wine at an elevation of nearly nine thousand feet does more damage than at sea level. As I shuffled in to pick up credentials, I looked as bedraggled as some of the burnouts.

The village was nestled at the base of snowcapped peaks and was crawling with characters: ski bums, Rastafarians, college students, hippies, hikers, writers, cooks, explorers, bohemian chicks, and straight-up chill people. It smelled like bud, the costumes were colorful, and the sound of drum circles filled the air. I marched in the parade, danced to the music, and schmoozed with some dudes who were 'shroomin'.

A gentleman with a blazer over a Gremlin T-shirt explained what it was like to trip. "You'll actually see sounds." I let that marinate for a second and then followed up, "Can you hear smells?" This question stopped him dead in his tracks and we both just stood there quietly reflecting. Mind. Blown.

Other younger dudes said it was more of a "spiritual quest" for them, where they'd go out into the woods and watch the trees melt through the hills like a swirling screensaver. Definitely. One guy who looked like a hitchhiker was tripping so hard he couldn't stand up. He just went on and on about "the dragons." I asked him if he was worried about anything, and he responded, "Besides my two ex-wives? No." This eligible bachelor may still be loitering around Telluride if any ladies are interested.

An older hombre rocking a camouflage cap and a silk shirt with parrots was a little unsteady on his feet when I approached.

WATTERS: What's the *best* thing about America?
HOMBRE: I live here.
WATTERS: What's the *worst* thing about America?
HOMBRE: I live here.

These are the kinds of exchanges that make a shoot. So I dug a little deeper.

WATTERS: What's your governing philosophy?
HOMBRE: I need to get some marijuana.

• Pure gold. I also would have accepted "Do unto others as you would have them do unto you."

Psilocybin, the psychedelic property in magic mushrooms, was, and still is, illegal in Colorado. Let's just say law enforcement had a light footprint in Telluride.

There was a legit element to 'Shroomfest: mycology, the scientific study of fungi. Tents showcased tables of nonmagical mushrooms, booksellers abounded, and experts recruited folks to participate in "mushroom hunts." I passed on the hunt and was close to wrapping up when an irate man on a bicycle began yelling at me. Perhaps he overheard my interviews or maybe my reputation proceeded, but he was bright red in the face. "You're a professional negative thinker!" he yelled. This wasn't helping with my splitting headache. To de-escalate the situation I asked him, "Can you help me find what I'm looking for?" He responded, "I don't really want to. At this point in your life, you made so many bad decisions that have led to where you work. You deserve what you have earned. It's called damnation. Go away." Apparently not a fan. You never want to get angry and argue with haters in the field. Fighting with strangers isn't a good look. Get to know someone first, then fight.

As I was leaving, I happened to run into Fox News religion correspondent Father Jonathan Morris, at the time a Catholic priest. He insisted he was there to perform a wedding ceremony. Whatever you say, Father. He was probably tripping balls. God works in mysterious ways. When we aired the package a few days later, Bill proclaimed that Father Jonathan had been "busted." Whenever I see him in the building, I like to ask if he can sell me an eighth. But he never has any on him. When Bill saw me dancing in the package, he asked if I'd eaten any mushrooms in Telluride. Not in Telluride, Bill, no.

A majority of the *Watters' World* segments were Bill's ideas. He was an idea factory, constantly churning out topics, events, and shoot locations. But around 25 percent of the time, the segments were my ideas. Colorado's budding cannabis business had attracted my attention for several years. Interviewing people getting high was hilarious and made for great TV, since it was still pretty taboo. Therefore, I never missed an opportunity to suggest a shoot in Denver. Bill had worked in local television in Denver during his career—and was worried about the detrimental effects marijuana had on his old community. Our interests aligned, and I found myself shooting the Cannabis

Cup, 4/20 celebrations, "pot tours," and other "investigations" into marijuana legalization in the Mile High City. Most of the shoots had a hard news peg, such as a scientific study on the harmful effects of marijuana, a rise in homelessness, a spike in DWIs . . . but by the end of the shoots I felt half-baked by the contact high, laughing along with the knuckleheads.

Cannabis tourism is alive and well in Colorado. Before I embarked on my "pot tour," I learned that full-blown legalization had been a big boon for the hospitality industry. As I was eating lunch in the hotel lobby before the shoot, a bartender told me people from all over the country fly into Denver for a weekend and load up on edibles, like "cannabis candies." Because it's illegal in their home state, they'll check out of their hotel rooms and leave behind chocolates and gummies. When the Central American hotel staff come to clean the rooms afterward, the bartender tells me they'll eat the leftover candy, unaware it's cannabis, and an hour later the ladies are playing air guitar with their vacuum cleaners.

The pot tour was two hundred dollars a head. A company called "City Sessions" picked me up and drove us around for four hours in a luxury bus billowing with smoke. The crew and I rode around with a handful of pot tourists, visiting dispensaries, grow houses, glassblowing factories, and of course, a donut shop. We purchased some gummy bears (for a prop, obviously) and ended the tour at Red Rocks, the legendary outdoor amphitheater chiseled into the Rocky Mountains. We could barely see through the smoke inside the bus on the ride home to the hotel. The conversation kept coming back to the topic of Munchkins. Are Munchkins made from the hole of the donut? Like are they punched out, thus leaving the donut hole? Or are they made separately from deep frying little spheres? The debate was finally settled when we arrived back at the hotel. A cleaning lady explained, in Spanish, that Munchkins were not punched out, they were fried alone. "Botija no perfoardo," she claimed, holding her Hoover like Hendrix.

The "stoned homeless" edition of *Watters' World* was more news-worthy. After Colorado legalized recreational marijuana, Denver saw a sharp uptick in homelessness. Sure enough, when I arrived, the out-of-state homeless population was clearly visible. These weren't older, hard-core junkies. Instead, they were younger, more down on their luck, eighteen- to thirty-year-olds who'd migrated to Denver from surrounding states searching for a more hospitable scene and easier access to quality cannabis. This was the quality of life trade-off that comes with legalization. Colorado didn't mind, and the kids seemed more colorful than harmful.

I was invited to visit a dispensary with a homeless Hispanic dude, who sparked up right afterward. The smoke went right into my face as I interviewed him, and we soon both started giggling about rolling enchiladas and chicken chimichangas. Then I met a homeless girl named "Giggles," who wasn't funny at all. She was pissed. Her "companion" at the moment called himself "Nip" and was stroking a pussycat named "Kush." Later that afternoon, I met a homeless guy in the park named "Kush." Synchronicity. "I just met a cat named Kush," I said, smiling. "You mean Giggles's cat?" he said. "No, Nip was holding him," I said. I saw him putting two and two together in his head, and he became angry.

"You saw Nip with Giggles? Around what time was that?" asked Kush, putting his thinking cap on. As we sat there on the grass piecing together this homeless-stoner love triangle, all I could think about was *who owned the cat*? Giggles, Nip, or human Kush. If Kush jointly owned the cat with Giggles, did the human Kush name the cat Kush after himself? Like a father names his son after himself? Or did Giggles name the cat Kush and then happen to start seeing a guy who shared the same name as her cat? Was Nip cat-sitting Kush while Giggles "worked"? Was Nip short for *catnip*? Was I as high as the homeless guy?

Searching for more homeless wasn't hard; they were everywhere.

Ones with multiple personality disorders, abusive parents, some quite educated, and others quite disturbed. Many of them came from dysfunctional families; their fathers were drug addicts or their mom incarcerated. Certain homeless can't function in society and need to be taken care of by government programs, shelters, and churches. Another breed of homeless *choose* not to participate in society. Instead, they smoke, hang out, beg, hustle, and swing by outreach programs for free food and socks. One homeless twentysomething told me he was a "Facebook-aholic." He woke up and smoked each morning, then dipped into the public library and went on his Facebook page. We're Facebook friends now. I asked another homeless twenty-year-old if he was offered $50,000 a year salary to work at a good company, would he take the job? His answer was no. He said, "If I'm in an office, I can't do it. I have to be outside interacting with people constantly."

"So you want to do what I do?" I asked him.

"Probably," he said; "it wouldn't be that hard, though." Burned by a homeless stoner. Ouch. It wasn't the first time and wouldn't be the last. I asked a homeless female if she had plans to "get back on her feet." She looked at me and said, "I'm standing now, ain't I?" Then she burped into my mic. It smelled like chicken chimichangas.

Cannabis enthusiasts "celebrate" the flower on April 20. One trip took me to Denver for a 4/20 festival. There I stunned some celebrants with the news that "Easter is tomorrow."

"That kinda sneaked up on me," uttered one dude. A slacker eating a gigantic turkey leg and wearing a shirt saying "Drugs Are My Life" didn't know what the meaning of Easter was, while a young female rambled on about "chocolate bunnies." Clearly, this crew was not devout. Spiritual, perhaps. When I asked a new crew what they did last weekend, one answered, "I don't remember, so it must have been pretty good." Another answered, "I slept all weekend." And another answered, "I won a booty-shaking contest." Honestly, all of their weekends sounded great, and I was jealous. But it was time to get serious. I informed one young woman that "they just did a study that said just a *little bit* of weed smoking can kind of hurt your brain." She gazed at me and said, "Wait, what? So, you have to smoke *a lot*. Is that it?" We both laughed. There was something very likable about this woman. Then she strapped a gas mask onto her head and lit a bowl into it. The guy who slept all last weekend told me, "I haven't read the study but the study is false." How was this guy not a TV pundit already? Throwing around baseless assertions like that. If he could yank himself out of bed he'd get hired instantly with that kind of anti-intellectual firepower. But guys like this were everywhere. The park was crawling with dropouts spitting gems.

UNIDENTIFIED MALE: The key to life is happiness.
WATTERS: When's the last time you were sad?
UNIDENTIFIED MALE: Every day.

You have to be really baked to reconcile the many layers of meaning folded into this exchange. So. Many. Layers. But the booty-shaking contest winner finished it off with this head-scratcher.

WATTERS: I'm Watters. And this is my world here *(making the sweeping hand motion).*
BOOTY-SHAKING CONTEST WINNER: Is that why you have a whale on your shirt?

These people were smarter than they looked. Why did I feel like I'd met my intellectual match at a stoner rally? I had to redeem myself somehow. I pitched shooting the Cannabis Cup in Denver and Bill green-lit it. It was a higher-end, ticketed event where an esteemed panel of connoisseurs crowned one high-quality strain the king. Sponsored by *High Times* magazine, the venue was packed with exhibits, cutting-edge gravity bongs, and merch. The objective was to discover how dialed in these people were.

A man dressed as Jesus described the crowd as "a gathering of five thousand friends that I haven't met yet." The messiah was definitely dialed in. He knew all about Easter also. But it was downhill from there. The sequester? Never heard of it. The ricin attacks? Never heard of it. Yet, extremely confident.

WATTERS: Are you worried about this ricin situation?
UNIDENTIFIED FEMALE 4: No.
WATTERS: But do you know what ricin is?
UNIDENTIFIED FEMALE 4: No.

I guess it's easy not to worry when you don't know what to worry about. Congresswoman Gabby Giffords had just been shot? No idea who she is. One young female didn't know who the Iranians were. "Uraniums?" she asked. Close, but no cigar. Foreign policy is an excellent topic for crowds like this, so I pushed a little further.

WATTERS: You're okay with the Iranians having nukes?
UNIDENTIFIED FEMALE 3: I mean, we have nukes, too, don't we?

Airtight logic. Let's let our enemies have nukes. Definitely would win a Democrat primary with that idea.

After feeling like the smartest person at Cannabis Cup, I got a little cocky and tried to rub it in. Boy, did that backfire big-time.

WATTERS: Do you ever feel like you might want to put the dope down and watch a little more TV?
UNIDENTIFIED MALE 5: I could probably *keep* smoking the dope and *still* watch TV.

Again, another rake to the face. Outwitted by a stoner with a pony-tail and marijuana-leaf-shaped sunglasses. *High Times* announced the winner of the Cannabis Cup afterward. In third place was Kosher Kush. The second-place finisher was Chem Tange. And the winner was Platinum Girl Scout Cookies! But let's face it. Everyone was a winner. Except me.

The potheads were well grounded compared to the people I met at the twenty-fifth annual UFO Conference in Scottsdale, Arizona. A few hundred true believers were milling around a hotel ballroom, peeking at exhibits, reading literature, and "networking," when I arrived. As a seven-year-old, I'd seen a UFO hovering close above me at dusk on my front porch in Philadelphia. It was a small orb, speckled with lights. As I reached to grab it, the unidentified flying object slowly slipped out of reach and disappeared into the sky. To this day, my mom still remembers me coming inside that night and telling her what I'd seen. There's a perfectly logical explanation for this. Aliens have sent me to earth to test human intelligence. Surely, after seeing the results, they're not at all threatened.

Several of the attendees said they'd seen UFOs, too. One woman with bleach-blond hair described a "fun" experience being in her bedroom "surrounded by lights . . . for about an hour." "I call it a pajama party," she said with a smile. She seemed to me to be recalling a photo shoot, but who I am to judge? A woman with purple hair said she saw "a classic E.T." that "scared the crap out of [her]." I bet the E.T. felt the same way. Other attendees claim they were abducted. One dude, quite famous in the UFO community, told me he was "hit by a blast of energy and was injured unintentionally. I think they took me aboard just to revive me. These three creatures were standing over me. And the minute I saw them, I just flipped out." A young female, who happened to be a huge fan of mine, blew my mind. "I've actually been abducted to the moon," she claimed. "The facility, everything was silvery, metallic, super bright." I asked her if she was married and she said, "No, not anymore." I wonder if the trip to the moon split them up? She continued: "When I was strapped down on there, one of the little grays came and straddled me. They were taking tissue samples down in that region." I nodded. "A mantis comes in and gets right in my face and just looks at me as he's writing down things on a file." Probably the same thing happened to Neil Armstrong when he was there, I thought to myself. One small step for man, one giant step for the mantis.

It was the spring of 2016, so naturally I asked about the election. Everyone who'd seen a UFO, met an alien, and been abducted or probed enthusiastically supported Donald Trump over Hillary Clinton. Every. Single. One. There was no way Trump's wall was going to keep *these* aliens out . . . so they were probably just pissed about Hillary's emails. That or Benghazi.

I myself felt like an alien occasionally, such as when Fox would send me to Martha's Vineyard. Probably one of the most liberal enclaves in the United States, behind Cambridge and Berkeley, the island just south of Massachusetts is where wealthy New England families relax, fish, golf, and sail. Those unfamiliar with the area may remember it was where Teddy Kennedy drunkenly drove off a bridge in Chappaquiddick, leaving his date to die in the water. It's also the home of Vineyard Vines, the preppy lifestyle brand that emerged from the Edgartown section of the Vineyard. Elite black Americans traditionally summer in the town of Oak Bluffs on the Vineyard: from Harry Belafonte and Martin Luther King Jr. back in the day to Henry Gates Jr., Spike Lee, and Vernon Jordan now. Barack Obama gravitated toward the island for some rest and relaxation nearly every summer during his two terms. It's very hard work destroying America, and the man needed to unwind. Luckily, I got to "cover" his vacation for Fox. What a junket. A roving Fox reporter behind enemy lines looking for lobster rolls, I mean, liberals to interview.

The Vineyard isn't 100 percent liberal, though. If you speak to the fishermen in Menemsha, the local farmers in West Tisbury, or a few of the WASPs in Edgartown, the forty-fourth president wasn't seen as the Messiah. Especially because this Messiah creates traffic on the island. Since Obama played golf every day of his vacation, he'd bring parts of the Vineyard to a standstill, since the Secret Service has to block roads for motorcades. But other than that, Obama was worshipped. So for most of his vacations, it was my job to gently challenge the conventional wisdom.

After eight years of Obama in the White House, his supporters were still blaming Bush. The Obama cultists on the Vineyard were blind to the economic realities of the rest of America. High gas prices, flat wages, manufacturing jobs lost to China . . . they didn't want to hear it. ISIS and illegal alien violence were just phobias hyped by Fox. Skyrocketing Obamacare premiums? Somehow the fault of Republicans. My go-to question for most of my summer shoots on the Vineyard was, "What's Obama's greatest accomplishment?" It was like asking for a moment of silence. Sometimes ten seconds would pass before the Obama supporter would utter something about "hope." But hey, at least that's an honest answer. When they said "green jobs," our producer would insert the buzzer sound effect. Here's a taste of some of my exchanges on the Vineyard . . .

WATTERS: Why have wages flattened under the president's policies?
OBAMA VOTER: It's Boehner's fault.

Obama voters could wiggle out of blame with the best of them. It was Bush's fault, Boehner's fault, Fox's fault, McConnell's fault, and ultimately the American people's fault for not truly appreciating how great Obama's policies were.

WATTERS: On the border, major invasion taking place right now. The president really hasn't stopped that.

OBAMA VOTER: Are we talking about in Israel?

Not the Golan Heights, dear; the Tucson sector in Arizona.

WATTERS: Would you be okay if the president shipped all the illegal immigrant kids to Martha's Vineyard?

OBAMA VOTER: No.

WATTERS: Then why is it okay if the president ships them to other parts of the country?

Most of the "help" on the Vineyard were white European teenagers on summer work visas anyway.

WATTERS: Do you love Obamacare?

OBAMA VOTER: Yes, but it is not Obamacare. It is Affordable Health Care.

WATTERS: But how come it isn't so affordable?

OBAMA VOTER: *(silence)*

The truth was that most Obama voters weren't on Obamacare. They received their health insurance from their jobs, or in other cases, Medicare or Medicaid. Obamacare only applied to a small slice of Americans, who were frustrated that they'd been dropped from their existing plans. They'd struggled signing on to a broken website, and then saw their premiums double and sometimes triple. If you didn't sign up, and weren't covered, Obama fined you.

WATTERS: Why did the president lie and said, "If you like your health care plan, you get to keep it?"

OBAMA VOTER: Maybe there's a misunderstanding.

If Trump lied to Americans about being able to keep their health-care plans, kicked them off, launched a broken website, and doubled their premiums, it would be the biggest scandal since Watergate. But Obama did that, and it was just one big "misunderstanding."

WATTERS: When Reagan was president, the Democrats held the House and the Senate, yet Reagan still got things done. Why can't Obama?
OBAMA VOTER: Because Obama is black.

A black Obama voter wearing a golf shirt shopping at Vineyard Vines during a posh vacation had just played the race card. I guess you play the race card when it's the only card left to play.

WATTERS: What's Obama's legacy?
OBAMA VOTER: I think he's probably going to go down as one of the great presidents that this country has ever had.
WATTERS: Are you on drugs?
OBAMA VOTER: I am not on drugs, but I am on Fox.

Outwitted once again.

WATTERS: What do you think the president's signature accomplishments have been?
OBAMA VOTER: He recently released, like, hundreds of people from jail.

I would have gone with killing Bin Laden.
One of my favorite all-time *Watters' World* answers came from a young Colombian immigrant on the dock in Oak Bluffs.

WATTERS: What has the president done well on the world stage, do you think?
OBAMA SUPPORTER: World peace.

Ignorance. Is. Bliss.

Alan Dershowitz debated me at the Chilmark general store, Spike Lee blew me off at a film premiere, and Obama's press secretary took umbrage at my question, "Why was POTUS so thin-skinned regarding Fox News?" These Vineyard shoots were learning experiences. I learned that it was nearly impossible to get footage of Obama golfing (even from the bushes), that Ted Kennedy probably could have saved Mary Jo Kopechne since the water under the bridge was so shallow, and most important, never book a hotel in Tisbury (it's a dry town). The logistics of staying in a dry part of the island forced me to share a hotel bed with one of my cameramen. When I woke up, we were spooning each other. I won't say who was the *big* spoon. I'll just say it was really cold, that's all.

It was also pretty cold at the nude beach. From what I gathered. On the southwest part of the island were federally recognized tribal lands, where anything goes apparently. The town of Aquinnah, once the home of the Wampanoag tribe, was a tourist destination for nudists. The Gay Head cliffs, comprised of red clay, fed down sharply to an isolated white sand beach, speckled with free-spirited sunbathers.

How had I stumbled upon it, you're wondering? John Belushi's grave site was in the area. The *Animal House* actor and *Saturday Night Live* comic had overdosed on a speedball at the Chateau Marmont in LA and had been buried in a family plot in Chilmark on the Vineyard. I was interviewing a fan who'd made a pilgrimage to smoke some cabbage by his gravestone when he mentioned the nude beach a few miles away. His directions were a little hazy, but after some hiking down a remote bluff, I discovered the beach, where people were in the buff.

Wrangling guests to interview on a nude beach takes a delicate touch, which I've been blessed with. A fully clothed reporter traipsing through the sand, with a fully clothed three-man TV crew holding cameras and a boom mic, is a little off-putting to nude sunbathers, who believe they've found an idyllic and isolated area to be at one with nature. Did I mention I was carrying a Fox News mic flag? Mindful that I was ruining a serene experience, I fell back on my manners. "Excuse me, would you mind if we did a quick interview?" I would say, waving and smiling as oiled-up couples scampered away, looking for towels to cover up with. The best approach was to act completely casual about it, pretend like everything was totally normal, and try not to stare. But there wasn't much to stare at. That's the thing with nude beaches. You expect a fantasy, but you're hit with a horror show. Overweight, hairy, and heavily male. Eventually, the awkwardness retreated, and I got some takers. After some small talk, I was able to sweet-talk a few middle-aged dudes and a woman into going on camera. Again, the key was not to stare. And whatever you do, don't look down.

WATTERS: Do you think Obama would ever come down here?
NUDE MALE: No, I don't think he can.
WATTERS: Bad protocol?
NUDE MALE: I don't know. Probably.
WATTERS: If you have any advice to give to the president, what would it be?
UNIDENTIFIED MALE: Just hang in there.

The perfect line for the perfect setting. These people had clearly lost their shirts (and bathing suits) in the Obama economy.

I visited the bluffs every time I was assigned to the Vineyard. It was a hard job, but someone had to do it. Some correspondents go to war zones, I went to nude beaches. One summer I interviewed a woman who was with her female friend, both in their birthday suits.

WATTERS: What do you think of Obama?
NUDE FEMALE: Not much. I'm a fan of Bush.

I'm sure she was.

Once I'd brought the raw footage back to Fox, it had to be edited. Heavily edited. Pixilating private parts was considered a perk or a punishment, depending on who the editor was. Our main editor, Scott, thought he'd seen it all after the Martha's Vineyard shoots. But that was not so. Some producer with a sense of humor, or a grudge against me, pitched that I go to a nudist colony. Bill accepted. He said he wanted to give me "more exposure." Soon thereafter, I was on a plane down to Pasco County, Florida, to go deep inside "Caliente," a "clothing-optional" resort and spa. I wore a pink shirt with khaki pants to blend in. My attire was "flesh colored." But no matter what I wore, I definitely stuck out.

When I arrived at the resort, the marketing director was running late, so I showed myself around. I wandered downstairs to the gym and laid eyes on a sixty-year-old female bodybuilder type, doing chest flies topless. She had implants or was definitely getting her pump on. Hard to tell. I decided to get my pump on, too, and banged out some curls, without looking at the topless woman from *American Gladiators* in the mirror. After a few sets, I walked back upstairs and was greeted by the marketing director. Who was also topless.

"Thanks so much for coming, Jesse," she said with a smile. I was picking up a swingers vibe suddenly. Later that night, I found out my instincts were on target.

The "nudist colony" was basically your typical resort and spa with restaurants, bars, pools, tennis, and private cabanas and condos spread around several lush Florida acres. But nobody was wearing clothing. In the main clubhouse and restaurant area, men wore bathing suits (Speedos) and women were topless with just bathing suit bottoms or skirts or wraps. But in the pool area, everyone was full-on naked. There's "good naked" and there's "bad naked." And most of this scene was "bad naked."

The marketing director showed me the ropes, and I got started. Bill thought it would be hilarious if I interviewed the guests about government spending, gun control, President Obama, and never acknowledged that they were nude. The guests at the resort were evenly divided between Republicans and Democrats, and the rest were clueless, an accurate reflection of the rest of the country.

I played tennis against a topless woman. She beat the pants off me. It was very hard to keep my eye on the ball, so I made a lot of unforced errors. I was very distracted. She probably would have beaten me with clothing, to be honest. Losing to a woman at anything is embarrassing, but losing to a topless woman provides the only acceptable excuse.

I hadn't lost my sense of humor, and littered the interviews with puns and innuendo. *Do you have a concealed-carry permit? How do you keep abreast of the news? What keeps you up at night? Should Obama be hammering the Republicans harder? Are you concerned about the mountains of debt we're racking up?* (Before the package aired, the producers got cold feet about my double entendres and edited them out.)

The shoot wound down, and then things got weird. Groups of nudists convened at the upstairs bar in the clubhouse where I was having a drink. I waited for my car to take me back to my "clothing required" hotel. These people obviously didn't need alcohol to loosen up, so cocktails took the scene to a whole new level. The guests got more flirtatious and handsy-er with me, even the dudes. I kept checking my watch wondering where my town car was, but I was a sitting duck. The conversations began developing into a definitive plan for the evening. After a few more drinks, about a dozen men and women were going to spend the night on their friend's yacht, where there were "plenty of beds." Everyone was welcome, singles, couples, and of course, me. It looked like this was a swinger situation, on top of the nudist deal, and apparently I was being propositioned to be the "guest of honor" for a "cocktail cruise." These were waters I wasn't going to swim in, so I politely declined. One rail-thin, topless fifty-year-old wife whispered in my ear that it would be "very discreet," and that "everyone was a fan." I was flattered, because these people clearly had great taste, but demurred, and escaped the bar unscathed. The "swing vote" was definitely up for grabs in Florida.

CHAPTER NINE

How I Saved Christmas

Like Rodney Dangerfield's character in *Back to School*, I found myself, as a senior citizen, causing trouble on a college campus. Maybe not a "senior citizen," but it feels like that when you're waltzing around the quad at forty. But in my late twenties, I was young enough to blend in. How was I deployed? To go undercover at a gay, Ivy League sex party.

The Queer Alliance at Brown University threw a legendary party called "Sex, Power, God." Great branding, I know. The point of the party was to celebrate your gender and sexual identity. And consume lots of drugs and alcohol. It was 2005, and gay marriage was illegal in America. However, the culture was changing quickly. Fox was covering the developments intensely. Brown University, by far the most liberal Ivy, was on the cutting edge of the culture war. Somehow Fox got wind of the "Sex, Power, God" party and sent me to the Rhode Island campus to file a report.

I arrived at Brown and met up with a student who was scalping tickets to the party. Eighty dollars cash. Pricey, but I didn't haggle, although I should have, because I don't remember being reimbursed. The party was thrown in one of the classic stone buildings deep in the heart of the main academic section of campus. When I walked in around 10 p.m., the party was in full swing. The grand ballroom was packed with stripped-down male students grinding to house music. It was dark and hazy. The strobe lights lit up the high ceilings, where oil portraits of past school presidents sat perched, staring down at the action. Girls were there, too, also pretty stripped down. Everyone was dancing, having a blast, and making out. Sick party, but I had work to do, so I went downstairs to fiddle with the small handheld camcorder that I'd smuggled in under my hoodie. I ducked into a bathroom stall to adjust the settings and heard a couple having sex in the stall next to me. Either that or a maintenance man was struggling to fix the plumbing. I went back upstairs and shot some debauchery. No alcohol was being served but the crowd was drunk before they arrived, probably rolling on ecstasy, too; it was that kind of vibe. I witnessed another couple having sex behind the DJ booth but didn't shoot it. I have standards. Eventually the lights went on, but everyone kept going until pretty late. A bunch of students collapsed and had to be escorted outside into ambulances. In fact, a record number of students—two dozen—received emergency medical attention that night. They couldn't handle their alcohol, among other things. Student fees had been used to fund the Queer Alliance party, which took place on campus, and celebrated a then-controversial and nontraditional situation. There were a small number of students who objected to this. But the most objectionable aspect of the party was the way the student newspaper described me the following week: an "older man," "wearing street clothes," "videotaping in the corner," according to the *Brown Daily Herald.* This was not the fun-loving Rodney Dangerfield character I was going for; it was more Woody Allen.

After my exploits aired, Brown University was forced to reevaluate its on-campus party policies. Years later, after more controversy, the Queer Alliance shut down the "Sex, Power, God" party for good. When a buddy of mine in LA saw this, he called and joked, "Hey, Watters, there's a great party at the Playboy Mansion this weekend . . . want to come out and ruin it for everybody?" I didn't deserve any flak, though. There was a culture war raging, and I was a war reporter covering the action. Perhaps a different kind of action, but action nonetheless. Sorry if I put anyone on blast. Fog of war.

I returned to Brown to cover "nudity week" and was kicked off campus by the administration. Perhaps they objected to me wearing clothes. After being kicked off, I was then chased around by a male student wearing a dress. Some would think it was *me* who'd harass a guy wearing a dress, but no, I was the one who was bullied. This cross-dresser launched a direct attack on press freedom. They screamed at me, interfered with my interviews, followed me, and disrupted the shoot. The people screaming about tolerance are usually the most intolerant ones, nowadays. I bravely finished the shoot and suffered only emotional scars.*

Cornell University also booted me off campus. The student newspaper, the *Sun*, reported that 96 percent of faculty members who contributed to political campaigns donated to Democrats. So I visited the campus in upstate New York to ask students about political bias and indoctrination. Several students revealed that they tailor their papers to their professors' political leanings. If they bring up conservative viewpoints, they admitted their grades suffer. The author of the *Sun* report actually said professors had told her that "Republicans aren't qualified to teach there."

A few of the liberal students "didn't see anything wrong" with the bias among faculty. Others were still grappling with the issue.

WATTERS: Do you support diversity?
CORNELL STUDENT: Yes.
WATTERS: But you don't support diversity of opinion?
CORNELL STUDENT: *(crickets)*

---

* Again, I am the victim.

The vacuous thinking extended to other issues as well.

WATTERS: Do you think the phrase "Islamic terror" is offensive?
CORNELL STUDENT: Yes.
WATTERS: Have a lot of the terrorists these days been Episcopalian?
CORNELL STUDENT: *(crickets)*

Just because you're in the Ivy League doesn't mean you're more up to speed, either.

WATTERS: What's the national debt right now?
CORNELL STUDENT: $200 million.
WATTERS: Actually $18 trillion.

I don't mean to pick on Cornell. A Harvard student made a similar comment years ago.

WATTERS: What do you think about the Fast and Furious scandal?
HARVARD STUDENT: You mean the movie?

Back at Cornell, while I was conducting interviews, I was ordered to leave campus by the director of media relations, John Carberry. The jolly, bearded fellow told me he was not granting me permission to interview students but couldn't articulate the reason *why* he was not granting me permission. He clearly didn't see the irony of Cornell kicking Fox News off campus for asking about political bias on campus. Even the student newspaper editorialized in support of my interviews, although they took a nasty shot at my skills:

There is no question that the Fox News segment clearly sought to embarrass Cornell through its cuts to cultural clips and witless questions. Yet the University's response to the piece was far more embarrassing than reporter Jesse Watters' shoddy journalism techniques. By disallowing reporters to ask students questions on campus, Cornell gave Watters the ammo he needed to ridicule the Hill in a greater capacity. Instead, Cornell should have embraced the autonomy of its students, allowing them to offer their consent in regards to media inquiries, rather than acting as the gatekeeper to the Hill.

—*Sun editorial*

"Witless questions"? "Shoddy journalism"? How dare they. Maybe they were referring to the moment in the package when I asked the students if professors "passed around doobies" and "told students to make love not war."

Ivy League students weren't the only ones being indoctrinated. A junior at the University of Akron told me his professor "tried to convert the entire class to Islam." I would have prayed to Allah for an A back when I was a student (anything to boost my GPA), but this particular student resisted and received a lower grade. This was a constant theme on campus: students being punished for not adhering to the professor's political philosophy. Many students, lacking a partisan antenna, don't even realize their minds are being molded into Marxists at the time, which would explain why the latest generation believes capitalism is evil and Columbus needs to be canceled. Other students gleefully glide through life unfazed by the past, present, or future. I got a glimpse of this during my famous quiz packages, where I came face-to-face with a universal truth: Ignorance is bliss.

"In the interest of news analysis," Bill explained, "we convinced Watters he *must* go to Panama City Beach, Florida, for spring break." When I checked into my hotel just for one night, wearing a blazer, all alone, the desk manager asked me, "You realize it's going to be loud here, right?" Believing I was a businessman in town for a sales meeting, he took pity on me and upgraded me to a suite on the top floor.

"It'll be quieter up there," he promised. I took the elevator up to my room and slid the key card into the door, opening it up to what looked like a honeymoon suite. There was a pink hot tub smack in the middle of the bedroom, pink shag carpeting, and mirrors on the ceiling. I opened the balcony door and gazed outside to the Gulf of Mexico. The pool downstairs was rocking, and I realized there was no way I was getting any sleep that night. I'd accidentally booked a room at the biggest spring break party hotel in the panhandle. It was raging. I tossed and turned and fell asleep to the sound of Lil Wayne.

The next day I shot a wet T-shirt contest, a booty-shaking contest, and then hit the beach for some interviews. It was SEC week in Panama City.

WATTERS: Are you worried about the rise in gas prices?
FEMALE STUDENT: Gas prices are irrelevant to me.
WATTERS: How'd you get down here?
FEMALE STUDENT: Uh, I drove.

It's all good, though. Someone else probably paid for gas.

WATTERS: What's the unemployment rate at right now?
FEMALE STUDENT: The unemployment rate is ninety-nine percent.

This was around the time of Occupy Wall Street, so that number may have been fresh in her mind.

WATTERS: How's it going in Afghanistan?
FEMALE STUDENT: Afghanistan is Af-GONE-istan.

Couldn't argue with that. Several of the students said, "My dad is going to be so embarrassed when he sees this." This is one of many reasons I won't be sending my daughters to spring break. You'd be surprised how many people absolutely bomb my *Watters' World* quizzes and immediately afterward ask, "So where and when can I see this?" It's as if it doesn't matter *why* you're on television, as long as you're *on* television.

Here's a list of some of the dumbest things ever said on a *Watters' World* quiz.

What year did we sign the Declaration of Independence? 1964
Who won the Civil War? France (runner-up answer is the West)
Who did America fight in World War II? The South
Who did America fight in the Vietnam War? South Korea
Who bombed Pearl Harbor? America (runner-up answer is Spain)
Name one state that borders Vermont? What's Vermont?
What do you think of Ebola? It's nice.
What president said "there's nothing to fear but fear itself"? Edgar Allan Poe
Name the body of water on the East Coast of the United States? The Red Sea
Where did Columbus land when he arrived? California
What was Columbus looking for when he sailed here? Women
What happened on Easter? Apparently Jesus was born
What happened on Good Friday? Nothing, I don't shop
Was Jesus Muslim? He might have been, I didn't know him personally
What country did the Pilgrims come from? Israel
What have you heard about the whistleblower? Isn't Trump the whistleblower?
Who is Trump's vice president? Joe Biden
What is your number one issue when you go to the polls? The lines

These answers are hilarious but also terrifying. There's a sizable chunk of society who're completely oblivious to our history, our country, and our politics. I wouldn't call them "dumb" (although some could make that argument); rather they're unaware and unconcerned with America's past, present, and future. It certainly makes me feel superior while interviewing these people, which helps soothe my intellectual insecurity, but it also makes me wonder how the hell are Americans so out of touch. Playing the blame game is simple, so let's start with that.

The public school system is shot. History teachers and social studies teachers have failed. Students often graduate without any knowledge about their country or system of government. This lack of knowledge translates into a lack of interest in current events, since there's no frame of reference to interpret what's going on in the news. Once in college (if college is an option), students can choose to pick their majors with little or no requirement to enroll in history or political science courses. Furthermore, the professors that do teach these courses are overwhelmingly liberal, and as I've discovered, students feel compelled to regurgitate the professors' bias to get a good grade. The body politic is being pumped full of uninformed or indoctrinated youth, clueless about what's made America great, or believing that America was never great.

Having an oblivious electorate is dangerous. Politicians, the media, and business interests prey on an uninformed populace. It's easy to get rich and powerful when people aren't paying attention. It's even easier not to pay a price when you screw up. You can lie, cheat, and steal and get away with it as long as voters aren't curious. Obamacare was a huge waste of time and money, and a majority of the country doesn't even know how it works (answer: it doesn't). The intelligence community botched the Iraq War and later got caught trying to take out Donald Trump, but nobody was held accountable. The mainstream media roots for the Democrats, hides facts that don't fit its agenda, and consistently gets the big stuff wrong (elections, pandemics, weather, economics), but viewers still tune in. Big-business CEOs won't respect freedom of speech in America if it's "offensive" to CNN, but will do billion-dollar deals with Chinese communist officials who force people into "re-education camps."

Powerful interests tax and spend, open our borders, police the world, spy on us, and lie to us while we remain in the dark. This is why we have big debts, dumb wars, and less freedom. A population paying attention would never let this happen. *Watters' World* is a wake-up call. Countless individuals would thank me after my street interviews: "Thanks so much, I actually learned something today," they'd say. "I feel like I'm back in high school," or "That was a good refresher," they'd tell me. So in a sense, *Watters' World* was an educational experience.

You're welcome, America.

People always ask me, "Jesse, are the people you interview really real?" Yes, they are. "Jesse, do you edit out the smart people?" No, I don't. Here's the truth to how it works. When I'm prowling around looking for people to interview, I'm looking for people who catch my eye. My two main criteria are: (1) a distinct "look" and (2) a big personality. The second I engage with a person, I can immediately tell if they have the type of energy that translates on TV. Sometimes a guest has a "great look" for TV, but their energy is low. Other times a guest's "look" is vanilla, but their answers are gold. Each *Watters' World* shoot is a search for two or three great guests with a strong look-to-personality combo, with additional guests sprinkled into this mix.

What do I mean by "a distinct look"? Meaning if I see a middle-aged man wearing khakis carrying a briefcase and walking next to a college-aged girl with a bright pink mohawk, I'm going to stop the chick with the mohawk. That doesn't mean I'm ruling out middle-aged men. Some middle-aged men have said some wacky stuff, but I'm going to approach mohawk girl *first*. And since I don't have all day, I need to be selective. I do my best to balance male and female, black and white, but it depends on what neighborhood I'm in and what the topic is. But the demographic mix isn't my main thought. I'm first focused on finding young, playful characters who jump off the screen.

Great hair, tattoos, or piercings will get you flagged. A distinct face always works. I'm talking about a model, a preppy guy, a stoner, an athlete, an alternative girl, whatever. Throw in a farmer, a banker wearing suspenders, a misfit, a sorority sister, a punk, a junkie, a yuppie, gay, straight, transgender—it's about casting. There's an exciting variety of styles in Manhattan (where I usually shoot), so these types are easier to find than in, perhaps, Iowa.

When you throw in a big personality, you're cooking with gas. A big personality always outweighs a great look, because as I know better than anyone, looks can get you only so far. The insane answer, or the hilarious exchange, or even a simple facial expression makes the moment. Sometimes a guest will unleash a burp during an interview. Other guests have broken into song. A ridiculous laugh, a snort, a flirtatious wink—all make the cut. Some people perform when the camera rolls, others don't. We made stars out of people whether they liked it or not.

If I had the resources, I'd film the conversation parents had with their children after watching them go blank on *Watters' World*. This is why I quiz my daughters during long car rides, just in case they run into the likes of me when they're older. So let this be a lesson: Pay attention, or you might disappoint your parents on *Watters' World*. You've disappointed them enough already. Don't do it on national television.

Young Americans are obsessed with political correctness. They're constantly being offended. Usually, they're not offended themselves; they're offended on behalf of other groups of people. Being that sensitive is tedious. But since there's no civil rights movement or no antiwar movement, the youth need something to struggle against, so their generation feels virtuous and worthy. The menace today isn't war; it's words. Very dangerous words. We used to spill blood to fight the English, but life is so comfortable now, we just fight the English language. Being offended is just a feeling, and today's culture war is really about young liberals' feelings being hurt because they've been conditioned to think everyone else should care. Once you take these people seriously, it gives them power. Instead, it's more fun to gently ridicule them. I don't go out of my way to be mean to people or offend people, but if they can't handle straight talk, that's their problem, not mine.

I visited various campuses to explore the reasons behind people's emotional overreactions to certain words and phrases. UNC Chapel Hill, Princeton, Georgetown all got the *Watters' World* experience. I'd politely describe it as a culture clash.

One student told me the phrase "Islamic terrorism" was offensive. It's not Presbyterians setting off bombs, so I never understand this complaint. The terrorists setting off bombs are Muslim, and they consider themselves warriors for Allah. If we can't accurately describe the enemy, how are we going to defeat it? Maybe that's why Obama never had a strategy. Most Muslims don't care that Americans call ISIS "radical Islamists." They care that the Americans bombed the hell out of ISIS. The politically correct school of thought says calling ISIS "radical Islamics" will anger peaceful Muslims so much, they'll join ISIS and kill Americans. This is how liberals blame Americans for terrorism. It's our fault they hate us. It has nothing to do with crazy Saudi Wahhabists pouring oil money into radicalizing the most dangerous young men in their kingdom and foisting them on the world so they never rise up at home. The Saudi royal family gave birth to ISIS and Al Qaeda. They import sex slaves, treat women like trash, and execute gays. But us saying "radical Islam" is offensive? The terrorists have bastardized Islam and murdered millions over the years. I'm more offended by the killing than what we call the killers. And if Muslim terrorists aren't true Muslims, that's fine, too. They won't get the seventy-two virgins when they're dead.

The phrase "illegal alien" is always described as offensive on campus. Here's an exchange I had with a student.

WATTERS: Is the phrase "illegal alien" offensive?

WOMAN: I prefer "undocumented" personally.

WATTERS: What would you call a person that came into the country illegally?

WOMAN: Stranger.

WATTERS: Do you believe in borders?

WOMAN: I wish the world didn't have any borders.

First of all, if you didn't have any borders, how would you have the Olympics? And second, who does the phrase "illegal alien" offend? The illegal alien? They're here illegally and aren't going to make a ruckus. Plus, they crossed the border; they know they're illegal. Mexican or Central American nationals who paid coyotes and risked their lives coming to America certainly don't care about cable news lingo. I really don't care what we call them; "undocumented immigrants" works for me, too. I'm sticking with "illegal" because it's easier to say and I'm used to it. Political correctness is a trivial pursuit for people who have it too good. Again, it's white college liberals being offended on behalf of someone else. I've interviewed illegals before and they don't care at all. I've always said that if I were a desperate, poor, ambitious Mexican national I'd likely come north and work my tail off in America. But since I have no skills besides TV hosting, working a regular job would be a challenge. Actually, maybe I'd just stay in Mexico and work at a resort.

There was a female student who told me the phrase "black crime" was offensive. When I asked her if she was robbed by a black guy, how would she describe him to police, she paused. "Would you tell police an Asian robbed you?" I asked. She admitted no, she would not. The conversation then turned to the topic of "white privilege."

"Isn't that how you got into Princeton? You're a woman and you're white." She nodded sheepishly, replying, "And I'm actually kind of upset about that." I was baiting her, but imagine feeling guilty about going to an Ivy League school because of your race and gender. If I'd gotten into an Ivy, I'd probably lord it over everyone, randomly squeezing it into conversations wherever I went. "When I was at Yale we used to . . . ," or "My roommate at Harvard has this boat . . ." Alas, I just wear a Dartmouth sweatshirt that I bought during a shoot a few years back. If I'm ever asked if I went there I just say, "My grandfather went to Dartmouth." That's actually true. And my sister also taught at Harvard. Shoehorning that into conversations is also deeply satisfying. She's a Democrat, so she must enjoy telling people her brother works at Fox News. Because Fox is basically the Ivy League of cable.

There's an unhealthy obsession with micro-aggressions on campus. I shot a package once on micro-aggressions, and I had to google what they were before jumping on the plane. Apparently, a micro-aggression is when someone unintentionally slights someone or some group of people, and is totally unaware of their own prejudice. Again, we're talking about victims of words. The difference here is that the victim can claim victimhood without the perpetrator of the "aggression" knowing what they did was wrong.

Here's a conversation I had with a student about micro-aggressions.

WATTERS: If you see someone and you say oh, *where are you from*?
UNIDENTIFIED FEMALE: That's just something that is really disproportionately targeting people and trying to pigeonhole them in a certain way. It might hurt someone's feelings and make them feel like they don't belong in the area. So it might be hurtful to them.

So if you think you're making friendly conversation, or you're generally curious about where someone grew up, be careful. You could be "targeting" someone and hurting their feelings. If you hear someone with a slight British accent, and you're wondering if they're from

Great Britain, South Africa, or Bermuda . . . tread lightly. The British are very sensitive about being pigeonholed.

Even social invitations are deemed "micro-aggressions."

WATTERS: Do you think it's offensive if I invite someone to play golf?

FEMALE STUDENT: It definitely could be singling out people who haven't had that experience with golf before . . . and maybe everyone doesn't like to go to the club.

WATTERS: Who doesn't like to go to the club? If I invited you to play golf—

FEMALE STUDENT: Uh-hm.

WATTERS: Would you be a little offended?

FEMALE STUDENT: I honestly, I mean . . .

If she doesn't want to play golf at my club, then I'll find someone else for the foursome. She's probably a terrible golfer who'll slow down the round. First, the Left is mad that men exclude women from golfing, then they're mad about being invited to play. Are the rules the same with tennis?

WATTERS: If a man says to a woman, "I love your shoes," do you find that offensive?

FEMALE STUDENT: Yes. I think that could really be taken as micro-aggression.

I thought women loved compliments? They're a very confusing group. I guess if a guy has a foot fetish, and he's staring at her feet like a creep, yes, that's crossing the line. But if a woman has nice pumps that look expensive, I don't see the problem. I appreciate getting compliments on my footwear. In fact, a woman once told me that women judge a man by his shoes. I also judge a man by his shoes. Does that make me a woman? Don't answer that.

"Labels" are a major focus these days.

WATTERS: Do you have a problem with "Christmas break"?
FEMALE STUDENT: "Winter break" is fine. Technically happening during winter.
WATTERS: What other holiday is around winter?
FEMALE STUDENT: Kwanzaa.
WATTERS: Should they call it Kwanzaa break?
FEMALE STUDENT: We should probably recognize a lot of holidays such as Ramadan.

Well. Ramadan is a month long so I actually would support Ramadan break. Who cares what they call a vacation, it's vacation! Call it whatever you want, as long as I'm off. If 75 percent of the country is off to celebrate Christmas, let's go with majority rules. Imagine Christians living in Iraq telling the Iraqi Muslims what to call their holidays? Go launch a War on Ramadan. Let me know how that works out.

I covered the War on Christmas from the front lines. Fierce battles would break out every year after Thanksgiving as forces of evil sprang into action. Much like the Cold War, there were worries about a "domino effect," so each assault on the holiday was met with stiff resistance, mostly by *The Factor*.

The town of Great Barrington, Massachusetts, attacked Christmas with a novel weapon: climate change. For many years, the charming New England town in the Berkshire Mountains generously draped red, green, and white Christmas lights all across Main Street. The festive display attracted tourists, helped local business, and warmed the hearts of all. But over the years, the town selectmen became more liberal and more anti-Christmas. In 2007, they voted to shut off the beautiful Christmas lights downtown. Their reasoning? Global warming. That's right. Those little Christmas lights were destroying the planet and needed to be turned off at 10 p.m. Surely there were more serious ways to conserve energy in a town of seven thousand. You could even use LED Christmas lights. Selectman Ronald Dlugosz stated: "I hate to be Scrooge here, but we're really doing a lot in this community to be fuel-efficient, to reduce our carbon footprint." I was immediately deployed to Great Barrington to confront the Scrooges. I walked into the town hall, waited until their weekly meeting had adjourned, and stepped into the room with cameras rolling.

WATTERS: You guys are attacking these Christmas lights here. And they're only up for a few weeks out of the year. And is this some sort of ruse to de-emphasize Christmas?

SELECTMAN: That's not an accurate statement.

WATTERS: What are your feelings regarding the Christmas lights?

SELECTMAN: They're my feelings. They're private, and they're none of your business.

SELECTMAN: First of all, I resent you coming in here and saying we're attacking Christmas or Christianity or anything. We're not doing that, okay? They're holiday lights. And we asked what we think are very reasonable questions in trying to save our environment. We don't think we should be just putting lights all over the place and impacting our environment.

Notice how the guy said "holiday lights." What holiday? Christmas, obviously. This was a two-pronged attack, on the name and the display. Weaponizing global warming was a cute tactic, but the rationale was too preposterous to succeed. The whole thing became a joke and backfired on them. Great Barrington learned its lesson after a flood of negative publicity. Last Christmas the lights shined as bright as ever.

The only thing sillier than calling Christmas lights holiday lights is calling a Christmas tree a "holiday tree." But that's what Rhode Island governor Lincoln Chafee did. He quickly came under fire as protesters turned out for the annual "holiday tree" lighting. His office was overrun with calls and emails. I caught an Amtrak to the Rhode Island capital and tracked the governor down outside his office.

WATTERS: Hey, Governor? Jesse Watters with Fox News; could we talk to you for one second?

GOV. LINCOLN CHAFEE, RHODE ISLAND: Sure.

WATTERS: We just wanted to know who exactly does a Christmas tree offend?

CHAFEE: I'm continuing the past practice that previous governors have instituted and calling this a holiday celebration. And that goes back to not only Governor Carcieri, Governor Almond, and maybe even before him. It's continuing a past practice.

WATTERS: Don't you think you calling it a holiday tree offends more people than a Christmas tree?

CHAFEE: Well, that's a debate that's been going on for many years. When I was in grade school we had to say the Lord's Prayer. That no longer has occurred in public schools. This is a continuing debate about the mixing of religion and government.

WATTERS: But Christmas is a federal holiday. You don't want to repeal that, do you?

CHAFEE: No, this is an ongoing debate about this subject, and as I just said the Lord's Prayer in schools, one of those. And, of course, the case has gone to the Supreme Court. And here in Rhode Island, the Pawtucket case, the creche that was on the town hall property. So it's an ongoing debate. And we're trying to uphold the values of Rhode Islandians and make sure that the purity of theology is kept separate from the pollution of government.

WATTERS: But don't you think a holiday tree, I mean, a holiday tree,
    what holiday is it? What holiday is it, Governor?
CHAFEE: *(Walks away)*

Maybe his heart was two sizes too small. Would he call a menorah
a "holiday candle"? Probably not. Chafee finally buckled under the
pressure of the people and *The Factor.* A year later, he flip-flopped
and officially pronounced it a Christmas tree. Once again, Watters
saved Christmas in New England.

I once rescued the baby Jesus from the clutches of Satan himself.
Boca Raton, Florida, traditionally erects religious displays in the town
square during the holiday season. Christmas trees, nativity scenes,
the menorah. However, in 2016, a satanic symbol was jammed next to
Jesus. An enormous black-and-red pentagram stood menacingly over
the manger. The inscriptions, "In Satan we trust" and "Hail Satan, not
gods," scratched into the occult structure left no doubt as to the purpose of the provocation. The city council stood by the display, arguing
that it was a religious symbol on the same level as the nativity scene,
thus constitutionally protected.

The Factor discovered that the satanic symbol was put up by a
Boca resident, Preston Smith. Preston was an avowed atheist who
happened to be a local middle school teacher. The symbol had nothing
to do with Christmas, and as an atheist, Preston wasn't displaying a
religious symbol, so the pentagram was unjustifiable. He may as well
have put up a swastika. I boarded a flight and staked out Preston at
his middle school. Little baby Jesus needed protection from the dark
forces of Satan. Like a crusading culture warrior, I confronted Preston
as he left school one afternoon.

WATTERS: Preston? We just wanted to know why you put up that
    satanic symbol on the public sphere there. Why are you try-

ing to attack Christmas? What do you have against Christmas, Preston?

Preston yanked his shirt over his face to hide his identity and scampered back inside the school like a coward. Days later, the satanic symbol was vandalized in the dead of night. A pickup truck drove over it, knocking it to the ground. The next Christmas, the public square was free from evil. Preston picked the wrong people to mess with. Just another victory in the War on Christmas. Chalk one up for the good guys.

A Chelmsford, Massachusetts, elementary school banned Santa Claus and candy canes, until I visited and kicked up dust. Bar Harbor, Maine, removed a Christmas tree honoring veterans because it was "tacky." But after I barged into a town council meeting and scolded them, they moved it to another town where it's properly celebrated. Plantation, Florida, sued a family over their massive Christmas light display. After $500,000 in litigation, and a feature on *Watters' World*, they lost in court, and the lights remain. Like the Battle of the Bulge and the Battle of Iwo Jima helped secure victory in World War II, these yuletide battles for religious freedom were critical in securing victory in the War on Christmas. The war has basically been won, although each year there are a few skirmishes that sprout up. But we can say "Merry Christmas" and call it a "Christmas tree" because Santa's little helpers didn't give an inch. That's the lesson here. Meet every attack, no matter how big or small, with the full force of the United States military. If that's not available, then the full force of the next best thing. In this case, me.

The War on Christmas is part of the Left's War on History. Erasing our connection to the past makes it easier to change the future. The future they want is radically different from what we cherish as Americans. Hating America is taught in school, and it takes only one viral video or one unapologetically patriotic president to unleash that hatred. In the summer of 2020, the hatred was unleashed, and our entire history was targeted for destruction. When liberal mayors didn't stop one statue from being toppled, it was open season on everything.

American history needs to be learned, not destroyed. Knowledge leads to growth and understanding; ignorance leads to hate and violence. The arc of American history has always been toward *more* freedom, justice, and equality. Our history is something we should be proud of. From the Revolutionary War to the Civil War to the world wars to the War on Terror, Americans of all stripes have shed blood for liberty and freedom. Peace was achieved, and our lives improved. We're still a young nation, nearly 250 years old. You don't judge 1820s America by 2020 standards. You judge the 1820s by which people helped build what became 2020 America. As individuals, we can acknowledge our sins, cleanse, repent, and grow. As a nation, we should do the same. America should retain our collective memory, to remind ourselves who we are, where we've been, and where we're going. A man without a memory is lost, and so is a nation. Our civilization is too valuable to be cloaked in darkness. We can't learn from the past if we erase it.

The leftists who already live here want to destroy it, even though they don't even know a thing about it. This war on history is an ignorant movement. Tearing down statues of Lincoln, Jefferson, Jackson, and Washington is flat-out stupid. Mobs even vandalized statues of Gandhi and famous abolitionists . . . and even desecrated a World War II memorial. This blind rage is motivated by hate and insecurity, not intellect. They're not advancing anything. They're just destroying everything. This is the behavior of invading armies, not our own citizens.

If a statue is the biggest obstacle in your life, then your life is pretty good. Don't tear down statues, build more statues, or do something so great that when you die, a statue is built of you. If a town wants to take down a Confederate statue, take a vote and take it down professionally. Dangerously tearing down public statues at midnight is a criminal act. Allowing this to occur without repercussions only gives vandals more license to act.

Cultural destruction won't stop at a few controversial historical figures. This mob has been indoctrinated to believe that *all* of American history is evil. They believe *all* of America is polluted by slavery and racism, so *all* of America's history and heritage and foundations deserve to be demolished. So they make no distinction between statues. They don't see distinctions between Grant and Jefferson and Columbus and Lee and Washington and Jackson. This isn't a mob of cultural historians deciding which monuments are unworthy—it's a wrecking crew. Statues commemorating cultural icons such as Arnold Schwarzenegger, the Texas Rangers, and Stevie Ray Vaughan were vandalized, as were places of worship, police stations, and CNN's Atlanta headquarters. The mob can tie everything in America to racism somehow to justify its destruction. The names of thousands of colleges (Duke University), the names of thousands of streets (Madison Avenue), the names of thousands of cities (Washington, DC), thousands of products (Apache helicopters), and the names of thousands of songs, books, and mascots. This is anti-intellectual cultural warfare that needs to be stopped in its tracks before it starts demolishing people instead of statues. Statues don't enslave us. They remind us why we're free.

I'm very proud to be an American citizen. Do these people have any clue about other countries and cultures? Read about what the Europeans did during the imperial era, what Japan did to China, or what China does today! The atrocities that Arab and African nations inflict upon each other make American history look like child's play. Perhaps the left-wing mob should brush up on what Stalin did to his own people, or what the Mayans and Aztecs were up to for centuries before

Europeans arrived. It wasn't pretty. To use the mob's logic, every single country in the world has to destroy every physical rendition of its history because its history is filled with sin, bias, and violence. The history of the human race is rough stuff, but anyone who knows history knows America is an exceptional nation. We should be building on this and celebrating it, not tearing it down.

CHAPTER TEN

How I Saved Hollywood

Sometimes you have to go behind enemy lines to get the goods, and that's exactly what I did at the Sundance Film Festival. Just outside of Park City, Utah, each January, independent films are showcased for fans and critics. The actors are flown in, and everyone mingles at premiere parties. Liberal icon Robert Redford hosts the entire event, and because lodging is so expensive, they keep the riffraff out. Celebrities can casually mill around town. Lots of drinking and eating and screenings in a freezing cold mountain town. Buzz is generated on many different levels, while films (and actresses) are picked up. So instead of asking actors about their films, I asked them whether they were disappointed in Barack Obama, who in 2014 was reeling from the Obamacare debacle and several scandals.

Things got off to a crazy start. I arrived in the morning, met the crew, and registered our credentials. As we were leaving the media check-in area, none other than the head honcho, Robert Redford himself, strolled right past us. He was the biggest "get" of Sundance, and a Watters-Redford exchange would surely get big play on Fox. I wheeled around and huddled the crew up, flipped the mic on, and told them we were going up to Redford immediately. The cameraman and audio tech nodded, powered up, and followed me back into the lobby.

"Mr. Redford, it's Jesse Watters with Fox News, may I have a minute?"

What happened next was unexpected.

"No interview! Not with Fox!" shouted Redford. The Sundance Kid whipped around and bolted through the lobby. But I was right on his tail. A huge commotion ensued as he scrambled and flailed around looking for an exit strategy. I zigzagged right next to him, asking him what he had against Fox News and what he thought of Barack Obama's sinking presidency. For a legend like Redford to act like a cornered animal at his own festival was quite bemusing. His unmistakably leathery face, jutted jaw, and sandy hair cut a jib in our frame that would play on *The Factor* to big fanfare. Dodging and weaving in an angry huff, even making contact with our camera, only added to the drama. I took mercy on him after a while and let him leave. What a lucky break, I thought. Couldn't have a hotter start to the shoot than that. I gathered the crew outside and asked to see the tape.

"I didn't shoot it," said the cameraman.

"What!? What the hell do you mean?" I said, my voice trembling with increasing rage.

"Mr. Redford said no interviews at the beginning, so I turned my camera off."

"You don't work for Redford! You work for me!" I screamed at him. People started to look at us from across the lobby. I never yell like this, but this was unacceptable.

"Yeah, well, this is a small town, man," the cameraman explained. "And you'll fly out of here tomorrow, but I still need to work here. I can't ruffle Redford's feathers like this, man." If he called me "man" one more time . . .

I absolutely unloaded on the guy. The guy told me nobody had ever spoken to him like that before. I don't recall what I said, but, eventually, I cooled down, and we all regrouped. I reiterated the plan: This was a run-and-gun, sights-and-sounds, on-the-fly, man-on-the-street package. These weren't prearranged, sit-down interviews. The crew said they understood, and we carried on, but I was still livid.

We hit up a red carpet for some premiere and ran into Jonah Hill. He'd starred in *Superbad* and *Get Him to the Greek* and was starting to take off in Hollywood.

"You're getting pretty famous now," I complimented him.

"No, not really," he demurred.

"You're getting there," I said, thinking he was being modest.

"No," he said. "I think you think I'm Jonah Hill and I'm not."

Damn. This wasn't Jonah Hill. It was an actor named Josh Gad, who was a dead ringer for Jonah Hill. Apparently, he'd played Olaf in *Frozen*. I'd heard his voice probably two dozen times since my daughters loved the movie, but I never knew what he looked like. My cameraman started chuckling. He was taking pleasure from me goofing things up. I swear to God he and I were going to come to blows later. But I gathered myself and powered through it.

WATTERS: What do you think the most important problem is in America right now?

GAD: The one that's most personal to me is global warming.

WATTERS: It's so cold I can't feel my toes right now.

Gad was frozen. Time to move on.

Richard Kind was also doing appearances. Famous for roles in *Mad About You*, *Spin City*, and *Curb Your Enthusiasm*, he had a nice little thing going.

WATTERS: What do you think the most important problem is in America right now?

RICHARD KIND, ACTOR: I think that the disparity between the rich and the poor.

WATTERS: So, instead of taking the really wealthy and then shrinking them down to the size of the poor, maybe we should lift the poor up instead.

Richard was kinda speechless after that. Sometimes when you live in a Hollywood bubble, you don't often hear ideas that contradict your own. You're welcome, Richard, and you didn't even have to watch Fox.

Throughout the day I ran into some other names, including the magnetic Brooke Burke, who was not concerned with Obama surveilling her emails and phone calls at all. *Playboy* playmate and Hugh Hefner girlfriend Kendra Wilkinson was a big fan of Fox. *SNL* star Bill Hader said he too was a fan (very sarcastically). Rose McGowan didn't want to talk about Obama at all; she was "ready for Hillary." She should've been ready for Trump. The silver-haired John Slattery humorously blew me off after taking a swipe at Fox, which I ignored since he killed on *Mad Men*. At the same tent, where the celebrities received grab bags full of free goodies, was Philip Seymour Hoffman. I encountered him respectfully in an atrium while he smoked a cigarette and asked for an interview. He quietly said no, which normally wouldn't have caused me to waver, but in this instance I did. There was something about him that made me feel like he really deserved to be left alone. A strange aura hung around him, a sad, dark aura. A month or so later he died from a heroin overdose. It all made sense when I saw the headline. What a tragic loss. A very talented artist who entertained us all with his special gift.

The night was winding down and I found myself at a party. The band Capital Cities was playing to a small crowd. There was a rumor that Elizabeth Banks was appearing later, so we staked out the room. After an hour or so, we spotted her. She was young and recognizable after her performance in *The 40-Year-Old Virgin*. I went in for a direct hit as she walked out of the event space. But as I asked her about President Obama—and we both walked briskly outside—I realized my cameraman wasn't following. What was the point of all this if it wasn't being filmed!? I stopped the interview and Banks continued to walk away. I turned around to see my cameraman just standing there.

"It didn't seem like she agreed to do the interview, since she didn't stop, so I didn't follow you."

It happened again.

"Are you kidding me!?" I was screaming again. "It's called a walk-and-talk! A walk-and-talk! You talk and you walk! What's so hard about this?!"

"I'm sorry," he said. But he didn't really mean it.

It was late. We ducked into a steakhouse to get dinner. I had the crew with me. As the correspondent, I usually expense dinner for the crew after a long day on our feet. I was not in a good mood. If it's a great shoot, I'll get a steak to reward myself. But I didn't deserve it. The Redford interview had been a major bust, and the Elizabeth Banks miss was like salt on the wound. I ordered the chicken instead. The next thing I know, the waitress was taking the order for the cameramen, and I almost spit out my Shirley Temple.

"I'll have the bone in rib eye," he announced casually, as if he had just closed a deal. My face started turning red. It was the most expensive entrée on the menu . . . and I'd ordered the chicken! I wasn't going to say anything. I thought to myself, I'm going to settle down and let it pass. Until he continued . . .

"And for sides, I'll have the—"

That's when I lost it.

"No sides!" I screamed. I pounded my fist on the table. Everyone's silverware rattled.

"No sides!" I emphasized again. "That's enough!"

The fact that this cameraman, who'd completely sabotaged an A-list celebrity shoot, actually had the gall to order a $75 steak and proceed to order $15 sides . . . not just one side . . . he'd said "sides" plural . . . was too much for me to handle. The entire table sat in silence for a few minutes until the bread came out, and the conversation slowly returned. I could barely look while the cameraman's steak came to the table sizzling hot. He even got a special steak knife. I chewed my chicken while he cut into his Delmonico, inspecting to see if it was cooked to his liking. He mumbled that it was too rare, but saw me staring daggers at him from across the table. He didn't have the nerve to send it back.

The next morning I got a problematic phone call. The cameraman had quit. The Fox crew desk told me the cameraman "wasn't comfortable with my style of reporting" and was refusing to show up. The fact is, I'd rather have a bad cameraman than no cameraman. I was completely screwed. There was a red carpet that morning, and the closest cameraman we could book was, at a minimum, two hours away. This was a catastrophe. I had Robert De Niro, Mark Ruffalo, and Marisa Tomei appearing that morning with no way to shoot it. I called our executive producer, David Tabacoff, and he relayed the message to Bill, who told me to conduct the interviews like an old-school print reporter, scribbling their answers down on a notepad. That he wasn't happy about the situation would be an understatement.

Luckily, I was able to wrangle a freelance producer who came in a clutch. She showed up to the event with her iPhone and shot my interview with Mark Ruffalo on her iPhone. It was 2014, so it was probably an iPhone 2.

WATTERS: With record unemployment—and the Benghazi scandal and the Obamacare debacle . . . are you disappointed in the president?

RUFFALO: Oh, Benghazi scandal, we kind of know that—I mean, you and I agree that that's BS now, right?

WATTERS: Why is that BS? An American ambassador was assassinated, and there was no protection for him, and he wasn't rescued.

RUFFALO: Well, what was the scandal, though?

WATTERS: Well, because there was no protection for him and was never rescued.

RUFFALO: But who cut the—who's cutting the protection, who's cutting the budget.

WATTERS: Who did?

RUFFALO: The Republicans.

WATTERS: I'd hoped you know, the Senate Intelligence Committee determined the cuts had nothing to do with the protection.

RUFFALO'S HANDLER: Sir, I'm so sorry, we have to move on.

And just as we were really getting into it, Ruffalo was cut off by his thirty-year-old female flack. Ruffalo is a die-hard progressive, but at least he seemed to be conversant in the subject matter. Marisa Tomei was appalled that I even dared ask her about politics.

WATTERS: Do you feel let down by the president?

TOMEI: I don't know why you're being provocative but—yuck.

"Yuck." At least she didn't say "ew." She acted like I was asking about her sex life. Perhaps she'd rather talk about that than the president of the United States. I guess I should have asked her about *My Cousin Vinnie* instead.

Last stop was Robert De Niro. He was at Sundance promoting a film he'd produced honoring his late father. He was known as a Democrat, but he hadn't bared his sharp political fangs like he has today. This was a kinder, gentler De Niro. But the way his event was run, you'd think the Dalai Lama himself was going to grace us with his presence. My newly hired freelance cameraman had finally arrived, so we entered the space together. Tightest security for someone besides the president I've ever witnessed. Extremely uptight PR women with headsets wrangling us, sitting us down, and nearly patting us down. When De Niro entered the small space, a quiet swept over the room. There was intense, almost submissive respect for the Academy

Award–winning actor. Everyone was whispering and basically bowing toward him. He was a short man, not charismatic, plainly dressed, and deadly serious. It was decided ahead of time by the Secret Service–like PR squad that I wasn't allowed to ask De Niro a question. But when has that ever stopped me? After he spoke, he began taking questions and when there was a lull, I spoke loudly . . .

"Bill O'Reilly has a question!"

The room grew silent. Then a small eruption ensued as a whirl of PR people descended on me. I was in the early process of being hushed and then physically removed, until De Niro responded.

"No, it's okay, I'll answer the question."

The PR team began backing off immediately.

"Are you disappointed in Barack Obama, Mr. De Niro?" I asked him respectfully.

He looked at me, paused, considered the question, and carefully responded.

"He's a guy who means to do the right thing. He has to pick his battles, but his heart is in the right place. He's not a schemer, and he's not devious."

"Bill O'Reilly says hello, by the way."

Everyone started laughing. It was contagious and De Niro started laughing along. He cracked a sly smile and said, "Oh? Tell him I said hello." And just one corner of his mouth slid upward, creating the classic chuckling mobster grimace that De Niro is known for. I wasn't sure if he was going to bury me in the desert later. But I did know I was having steak for dinner that night. And some sides.

Sundance was a challenge, but shooting the Academy Awards was like shooting fish in a barrel. I didn't have to chase anyone down. All I did was stand there, and they came to me. Well. They actually came to *Entertainment Tonight* host Nancy O'Dell. But I happened to be standing right next to her, so in order to get to her, they had to go through me first. Let's just say when they got to Nancy, some of them were a little bewildered.

Backing it up a bit, each year *The Factor* would take a trip to Los Angeles. This was branded "*The Factor* in LA Week." Bill would take meetings, interview celebrity guests in studio, visit the Reagan Ranch, whatever he planned. While the producers finished taping the show at 2 p.m. Pacific Time because of the time zone differential, they all went out exploring town, having dinner, and enjoying the atmosphere. Bill would send me all over Southern California on wild shoots. I was sent to Watts to interview Crips, to Koreatown to ask about "Lil Rocketman," to Venice Beach to quiz burn-out surfers, and to San Diego to shoot a belly dancing competition. One time I shot a Katy Perry concert at the Ford Theatre in LA. In order to get in, I had to pay five hundred dollars for a ticket because it was a Katy Perry concert/Obama fund-raiser. The next year, some liberal publication was scouring the Federal Election Commission reports and discovered that I had "donated" (ha) to the Obama presidential campaign. Rumors swirled that I was a big phony. Mocking Obama during my street interviews while secretly donating to his reelection campaign.

I'd like to apologize to Mitt Romney if my five hundred dollars put Obama over the top. What can I say? I'm a big Katy Perry fan.

But for Academy Awards week, I had to lather myself into an LA state of mind. I was assigned to cover the 1 percent in Beverly Hills. Where to find them? Shopping on Rodeo Drive, of course. After test-driving the newest Porsche 911, I ventured into the House of Bijan. You can't just wander into a store like this. You need an appointment, which I had. The House of Bijan is known as the finest boutique clothing store in the entire world. It was Michael Jackson's favorite store. Billionaires like Jeff Bezos and Saudi kings shop there. The proprietor informed me the House of Bijan dressed the last five presidents, with the exception of Jimmy Carter. I told him to consider that "a badge of honor." He laughed knowingly. After introductions, I was taken upstairs to the second-floor men's collection and was mesmerized by the obscene luxury. I was shown a crocodile jacket. "How much?" I asked. "A hundred ten thousand dollars," he said, showing me the price tag. What a load of croc. The store was crawling with hired models in extremely revealing cocktail dresses for some reason. To make the extravagant purchases a little easier to swallow, word was that they accompanied some of the shoppers home after the bill was rung up. One young lady showcased a diamond necklace for a cool half million. A risky move to put that much money on a pair of heels, but those are the risks the House of Bijan takes to attract the 1 percent. That night on the set with Bill I wore a $900 silk yellow tie the proprietor had "loaned" me. It came with a matching pocket handkerchief. Before the segment taped, while sitting across from me in the studio, Bill told me, "Take the pocket square out, Watters . . . who do you think you are, Brit Hume? You're a man of the people. If you wear one of those again, I'll burn it on the set." I wasn't that mad about it. I was terrified I'd spill coffee on it and owe the House of Bijan hundreds of dollars I didn't have.

Bill announced I'd be covering the red carpet of the Academy Awards that weekend, so the promotion was in place. Thankfully, none of the liberal Hollywood actors watched Fox, so they had no idea what was coming.

I'd been up late the night before at a pre-Oscar party, interviewing unsuspecting actors about politics. Every single one of them artfully dodged. "Is Obama doing a nice job?" I asked Stephen Dorff. "I don't know, man," he said smiling and walked away. Actress Tara Reid said, "Don't make me look stupid." She must have been a fan. On what shape the nation is in, actor Jason Segel said, "I don't have an opinion on that for now." Lame, but smart answer.

So when I arrived at the red carpet, I didn't know what to expect. After passing through TSA-level security, I arrived at my position. It felt like being crammed into a juice box. A New York City subway at rush hour was roomier. Well over a thousand reporters, producers, still photographers, and cameramen were squashed behind two football-field lengths of velvet rope. My cameraman was perched behind me on a tiny riser to save space. This came back to haunt me.

As we settled into our position, awaiting the celebrities to slither by, I noticed a disturbance in the force. Sasha Baron Cohen, playing a Muslim military dictator, had screwed with Ryan Seacrest. Flanked by two models in skintight fatigues and sporting an absurd amount of medals on his chest, Cohen "accidentally" spilled the "ashes" of his cremated friend, Kim Jong Il, all over Seacrest's tuxedo. He was whisked away by security while Ryan stood there perturbed, trying his best to play it off, feverishly wiping the ashes off his evening attire on live TV. It was nice to know I wasn't going to be the biggest wiseguy on the carpet.

All of the other entertainment reporters were asking the actors about their films, but I had no clue who was nominated and for what. It didn't matter at all because I was there to talk politics. It was February 2012, the country was limping out of the Great Recession, gas prices were over four dollars a gallon, and Occupy Wall Street was forming.

I'm not a movie buff, but I know the famous faces. "Is that Meryl Streep?" I asked my cameraman. "No, Glenn Close," he said. "What do you think of the state of the nation right now?" The actress, whom I later loved in *Fatal Attraction* and *Jagged Edge*, responded, "I think we're kind of pissed off right now in the country." Not as pissed off as Ryan Seacrest was, but yeah, pretty pissed.

Nick Nolte, whom even I knew from *48 Hours*, seemed either enlightened or intoxicated. "The country is in a wonderful position," he explained. "For the first time I think we're really on a cusp of looking in a true perspective." I wasn't sure what he was saying, but I liked the way he said it.

Heads suddenly began turning and the carpet started buzzing. Angelina Jolie had arrived. She was presenting that evening and there for Brad Pitt's *Moneyball* movie. Clearly the biggest star in Hollywood. After posing for the still photographers, her handlers skipped the interviews and rushed her past the legion of reporters. But as she raced by my position, I caught her attention with my commanding voice.

"Bill O'Reilly wants to know how you think the country is doing right now!"

She slowed down, gliding by me, her presence radiating casual glamour, smiling, uttering a thoughtful and sophisticated response, "That's a longer discussion than a red carpet." Technically, Fox was the only outlet she spoke to that evening, not even *Entertainment Tonight.* I was clearly destined for greatness and had a job as a Hollywood reporter if I ever get canned from Fox (which, statistically, isn't out of the realm of possibility).

Just when I started getting cocky, I got snubbed big-time. Cameron Diaz and I made eye contact. She approached me in good spirits. But then looked down to see my Fox News mic flag. A look of revulsion crossed her face. Turning to her publicist, she said, "Oh no, I don't do Fox News." I've never watched *There's Something About Mary* since.

Dissed by Diaz, but Michael Moore couldn't have been nicer. He recognized me, chatted for several minutes, declaring "I occupied Wall Street before there was Occupy Wall Street." Actually a gregarious guy. It's harder to demonize people when you meet them in person and have a friendly chat. But I'm a professional, so I dig deep and demonize with every fiber in my being.

Sandra Bullock had game. I asked her, "Is Bill O'Reilly fair and balanced?" She winked and retorted, "Mentally or physically?" P. Diddy, or whatever he was calling himself at the time, called me out. "Are you trying to be the next Bill O'Reilly, because that's not a good look for you, son."

"You don't think so?" I asked.

"Not a good look for you, son, trust me," Diddy said, patting me on the cheek like the Godfather. I was a fan, and still am, and took it in stride.

Things got a little more awkward with James Earl Jones, whom I asked about high gas prices. I don't believe he understood the question. "It's gasoline," he explained. "You got to pay. You got to run your car; it's gasoline." I doubt James Earl Jones fills up his own tank or knew the effect astronomical prices were having on working Americans. But his voice gave me a warm and fuzzy feeling. You could probably run your car on that.

The second-best-looking man on the carpet, besides me of course, was George Clooney. He was all class as he slung his arm around me. He and O'Reilly had publicly tangled over 9/11 a few years back, so George was familiar with *The Factor*.

GEORGE CLOONEY, ACTOR: Are you really going to ask me political questions right now?
WATTERS: Yes.
CLOONEY: Good.
WATTERS: Are you an Occupy Wall Street kind of guy?
CLOONEY: Well, I think they have an interesting message.

Deft dodge but he was game. I continued in a friendly manner.

WATTERS: Is Bill O'Reilly fair and balanced?
CLOONEY: Listen, I'm going to stay out of the fight with Bill.
WATTERS: All right.
CLOONEY: For once in my life, wish him nothing but the best.

Again, staying out of trouble. Everything was kosher so far. Until this . . .

WATTERS: Is Obama doing a good job?
CLOONEY: Yes, he is. He's the president of the United States.

The actor got hot under the collar. I'd set him off. He began to scold me.

CLOONEY: He's not Obama. He's the president of the United States.
WATTERS: Thank you.

Then he stared daggers at me, clearly taking umbrage with how I'd addressed the president. If looks could kill.

I usually use "President" when referring to a president, but sometimes it saves time when time is tight and every second counts, or sometimes it's a more casual setting. Once the carpet cleared I googled Clooney and the following popped up from a *GQ* interview he did.

"Let's face it: Bush is dim."—George Clooney

Thanks for the lecture, Clooney. We'll both work on our formalities.

The next day, I appeared on *The Factor* and watched the interviews play out. Sadly, something stuck out that could not go unnoticed. Because the cameraman had shot me from above *and* behind, I discovered . . . that my hair was thinning. Yes, my balding head was featured prominently in every single shot. This was something that I'd obsess about for a while. But at least I didn't get fake dictator ashes dumped on my tux.

CHAPTER ELEVEN

How I Saved America's Cities

Not only did I fight in the War on Christmas, but I also fought in the War on Women. On their side, of course. The War on Women began when Obama ran for reelection. Mitt Romney, of course, was responsible for waging the war, along with Fox News and every single Republican in America. Barack Obama was clever in creating wedge issues to ignite anger with groups he needed to turn out on election day. Single women were part of the successful Obama coalition, and they were cast as victims of Republican male oppression. Any pro-life legislation was deemed a "war on women." Any sharp criticism of a female politician, female celebrity, or female activist was an act of war. Any gender wage gap that existed was workplace discrimination. It didn't matter that Hillary Clinton herself paid men more than women in her office; that was swept under the rug (by a woman). The point was to inflame women into voting against Republicans. Mitt Romney, responding to an attack during a debate, declared he has "binders full of women" that he examined when making hiring decisions. The Democrats, with the help of the media, turned this into a sexist gaffe, and Romney was on the ropes for a week. Yawn. The scandals of 2012 seem so petty now.

Of course, there were legitimate issues surrounding women's rights and pay and criminal justice. I'm not ignoring that. But the "war on women" card was played overzealously to the point of frivolity. Not wanting your tax dollars to pay for free birth control was Armageddon. Congressman Paul Ryan joked, "Now it's a war on women; tomorrow it's going to be a war on left-handed Irishmen or something like that." That the party of Ted Kennedy, Bill Clinton, Bill Cosby, Jeffrey Epstein, and Harvey Weinstein was accusing Republicans of a War on Women was an irony ignored in the media.

Never one to lie back and let others do the fighting for me, I decided to enlist. In 2014, I flew out to the National Organization of Women's (NOW) conference at an Albuquerque Hyatt. It got off to a rocky start when I asked, "What are you gals trying to accomplish today?" The woman I was interviewing objected to the term *gal*. "I'm not a gal," she brusquely informed me, her voice deeper than mine. I hadn't gone through basic training so mistakes like this were bound to happen. Intelligence gathering seemed like a better approach.

"Have you ever burned your bra?" I asked her.

"Why bother," she replied. "I don't wear one." That was clear.

When I asked, "Where do I sign up to fight the War on Women," the gals told me to join a chapter. "If you need protection, I can protect you," I promised, making a muscle and inviting them to squeeze my bicep. Offering to protect them was "sexist," I was told, even though women do need protection. I was confused. I needed to enhance my situational awareness.

Patricia Ireland, the former NOW president, explained that "the whole structure is designed for men to be dominant." I had no idea Mrs. Ireland was into S&M. I had a lot to learn. My fact-finding mission continued. A nice young lady asserted, "There is actually an all-out war on women raging right now." Now we were getting somewhere. "Do I get a weapon?" I asked. Apparently not. In fact, nobody was armed. "Have you ever been wounded in the War on Women?" I inquired to a young blonde. "Kind of," she answered. "Shrapnel?" I wondered. She smiled. Hopefully there was a medic around if things got serious. "Men have been ruling the earth for so long," I explained, "what are we doing wrong?" The deep-voiced woman broke it down for me.

FEMALE: Men think literally.
WATTERS: Uh-hmm. How should I be thinking?
FEMALE: Circularly.
WATTERS: Like a womb?
FEMALE: *(disapproving smirk)*

But just as I was getting my first taste of action, the conference flack confronted me in the Hyatt lobby. "You don't have credentials, and I'm going to have to ask you to leave." I'd been seeking credentials for months, and had flown out with the expectation that I'd be credentialed upon arrival, assuming NOW was just disorganized. "We're not allowing you to cover the event," she informed me. And just like that, I was being dishonorably discharged. Moments later, two uniformed Albuquerque police officers marched into the lobby to escort me out. NOW had actually called in reinforcements.

"I'm just here to fight in the War on Women," I explained to the police. "There's a battle going on."

"The management doesn't want you on the property . . . so unfortunately, sir, we're going to have to ask you to leave." Were these military police?

"I feel like I'm being discriminated against," I told the officers. I was getting a big anti-male vibe. Maybe this is what the women go through. As the police escorted me out of the hotel, I walked by the flack again and pleaded my case. "I'm on *your* side!" I exclaimed. "I'm sure you are, Jesse," she said sarcastically. I thought liberals loved allies. I guess not. Outside, a third officer made me sign a document acknowledging that if I returned to the property I'd be arrested. It was my first sight of combat, and I'd almost become a POW. Would

I be bound and gagged? I wasn't going to take my chances. Patricia Ireland may be into that scene, but I wasn't.

I did several tours in the War on Women. The city of Philadelphia, in 2013, slapped a tax on lap dances, and I fought a bitter rearguard action against it. Many municipalities are broke and resort to taxing everything. Philly had tried to tax soda and cigarettes . . . and in the dark of night slipped in a tax on strippers. This stealth tax rubbed many women the wrong way. The city already imposed an "amusement tax," which is a percentage of the admission fee ($20 cover charge) paid to enter a club. But in a stroke of greed, the city decided the $20 a patron gives a stripper to perform a lap dance needed to be taxed, too. Many freedom-loving Americans argued this amounted to double taxation. This is not what the Founders wanted. Regardless, Democratic Philadelphia mayor Michael Nutter audited five years of lap dances and assessed clubs $800,000 in back taxes, plus interest and penalties.

I was deployed to Cheerleaders, one of the Philadelphia strip clubs under siege, and assumed my post defending women's rights. I interviewed a stripper who said, on a good night, she could go home with $500–$700 cash. What the hell was I doing in TV? I thought to myself. Nevertheless, I persisted. "When you've got moms with kids to feed at home, girls trying to get through school, and on top of this, the city wants their hard-earned money? That's absolutely ridiculous," explained a gentleman who'd clearly spent considerable time (and money) inside strip clubs. His economic argument was airtight. Another woman explained it this way: "You're just trying to make a guy a little bit happier and have him go home in a slightly better mood than he was before." She was the Betsy Ross of strippers. America may be an imperfect union, but it is a union nonetheless.

Next stop, City Hall. After I stormed Mayor Nutter's office demanding answers for this grave injustice, his press secretary made himself available to me. "Doesn't the mayor think there might be a better way to go about raising revenue?" I asked. Nutter's flack squabbled with me. "There actually is no such thing as a lap dance tax. There's an amusement tax. Everyone needs to pay their fair share." But it was an "unfair share," since a double assessment was slapped on. Curiously, it was Democrats who were fighting the War on Women and *Watters' World* was on the side of the angels. Literally. One stripper I met was named Angel.

A year later, the city's Tax Review Board said the lap dance tax was not proper. But Nutter kept waging war. Finally, Judge Ellen Ceisler struck down Philly's lap dance tax. My fight for women's rights was won. I consider myself a feminist.

I consider myself somewhat of a cultural anthropologist, too, exploring remote lands, sometimes hostile territory, engaging with the natives, and returning with a greater understanding of different social customs. I was able to release my findings to the public and interpret these strange behaviors to a larger audience. *The Factor* didn't have the budget to send me to investigate the long-lost tribes in the Amazon rain forest. Instead, I flew to San Francisco several times to explore what was becoming close to a separatist movement within the continental United States.

Having shot pieces in North Philly, South Central LA, East St. Louis, Detroit, and the South Side of Chicago, I was always tuned into my surroundings. In Englewood, on Chicago's South Side, I was looking for trigger pullers to come on camera. I turned to my guide, a local, and asked, "Am I safe here?" He turned to me laughing and explained, "We don't shoot white people. Y'all our best customers!" In Detroit, I was taken around by investigative reporter Charlie LeDuff, who knew everyone and could've been mayor if he decided to run. In North Philly we hired armed security. Which was good, since I didn't have to rough anyone up myself. Gotta keep my hands healthy, so I can hold the mic. But San Francisco was a different animal. No producers or security were necessary. It wasn't that dangerous; it was just like stepping into a foreign country, where pretty much anything goes.

The Bay Area holds an annual "Naked Bike Ride," where thousands pedal through the streets in the flesh. There was a ballot initiative banning circumcision spearheaded by a group of "intactivists," who'd gathered enough signatures to hold a vote on making it a misdemeanor punishable by up to a year in prison for "mutilating" the foreskin. San Francisco has an Antique Vibrator Museum, which got a lot of buzz when it opened. The homeless population was out of control, as permissive politicians allowed encampments all over city property. Many neighborhoods allow for public urination and defecation. There's even a "poop app" to let pedestrians know which blocks to avoid. City-sanctioned public drug injection sites, coupled with lax drug law enforcement, make the city by the bay a den of open drug use. In fact, right next door in Oakland, peyote is decriminalized (I may have to visit next time I'm out there). Prostitution is barely prosecuted, either, so when the sun goes down, it's game on. San Francisco is a notorious sanctuary city, too. Local law enforcement does not cooperate with federal immigration agents, so when criminal illegals get busted, the locals let them go before ICE can detain and deport them. During the battle of gay marriage, flamboyant male activists cross-dressed as nuns invaded Catholic churches and disrupted communion. The fight for gay marriage was just, but that tactic was disgraceful. San Francisco is a beautiful town overall, don't get me wrong, but let's just say I enjoyed "visiting." It's not a place I'd hang my hat.

"This city is a land of opportunity, but it's also a city of freaks," one San Francisco resident explained to me. Each trip I made to the city by the bay got progressively worse. City Hall is surrounded by swaths of junkies and homeless, which politicians ignore as they march up the steps to their offices. Mothers roll their strollers over hypodermic needles, drug deals go down in open daylight, aggressive packs of burnout runaways with half-ass face tattoos and dreadlocks drag their dogs around and drunkenly fight and stumble around looking for spare change and smokes. These street kids can be volatile, sometimes agreeing to interviews, but other times, dropping their pants and mooning my cameras. The Haight-Ashbury neighborhood, home of the original hippie movement and sixties rock music scene, has lost its vitality and fresh spirituality. The authentic counterculture is gone. It's now just a commercialized throwback running on fumes from fifty years ago. What's left is a strident anti-cop culture, a dirty drug culture, and the unmistakable smell of urine. A drunk Spanish guy told us how outraged he was after getting ticketed for peeing on the sidewalk. "The cops usually let me go wherever I want!"

Some neighborhoods look like "no-go zones" for police officers. The Tenderloin area appeared to be one of those. Situated in the middle of some of San Francisco's nicest downtown shopping and tourism destinations are a few blocks of absolute sickening degradation. It's sad that American cities feature areas like the Tenderloin. I shot a little after dark there, and it's truly heartbreaking. Dozens of men and women in tattered rags strewn about the sidewalks in stupors, half-naked addicts marching aimlessly down the streets menacing anyone on their path, begging zombies, drunks, and crackheads. All had descended into this decaying district to dance with the devil and flirt with death. Filthy hotels rent by the hour where people check in to shoot up or turn tricks or both. Crack vials covered the pavement like ice cream sprinkles, lazy fights were breaking out around every corner, and men cruised around in their cars with the windows open looking for a fix or a cheap deviant sexual score. I'd found "rock bottom," where people would trade their bottom for a rock.

The citizens of San Francisco are tolerant of what they witness on the street, but also fearful. I spoke to several people who described their fears for their children whose schools are exposed to dangerous vagrants. But the political correctness that runs rampant in the area prevents them from articulating their concerns too boldly. Being offended is worse than being physically harmed to some degree. Nearly every single neighborhood has a dark underbelly that seeps into normal society in ways that most cities don't experience. Sometimes this can produce deadly results.

In 2015, a beautiful thirty-two-year-old named Kate Steinle was strolling down a San Francisco pier with her father. In an instant, she was dead. She was shot by an illegal immigrant from Mexico. Jose Ines Garcia Zarate had seven felony convictions and had been deported five times. He had a dozen aliases and was involved with heroin manufacturing. Democrats constantly claim the border is secure, yet Zarate kept sneaking across over and over and over again. The most maddening part of the tragedy is that it could have been avoided. Zarate was in custody in San Francisco on a drug warrant when ICE slapped a detainer on him, asking the police to notify them before releasing him so he could be transferred and deported. But San Francisco is a sanctuary city and ignored the feds' request. The jail released Zarate and months later he killed Kate in broad daylight.

Zarate had a history of inhaling toxic fumes and shooting dope. After his arrest, he told investigators he'd been aiming at seals in the bay. The gun he used was stolen from the car of a US marshal. Zarate claims he "found it" and fired it accidentally, hitting Kate Steinle in the chest. He dumped the gun in the bay and fled on foot. The Board of Supervisors and Democratic mayor Ed Lee had instituted the sanctuary city policy that allowed Zarate to roam that fateful day. In fact, the Mexican national admitted it was the city's sanctuary policy that attracted him to the area in the first place. Even liberal California senator Dianne Feinstein blasted the mayor's dumb policy: "The tragic death of Ms. Steinle could have been avoided if the Sheriff's Department had notified ICE prior to the release of Mr. Sanchez [Zarate], which would have allowed ICE to remove him from the country." But the city's political leadership refused to own up to their mistakes; instead they pointed fingers at Republicans and Fox News. So I pointed the finger right back at them.

I sat quietly in a row of seats in the back of a room in City Hall as the San Francisco Board of Supervisors gaveled the hearing to order. It was your typical hearing . . . arrogant local politicians going through the motions of government, completely unfazed by the real concerns of real constituents. Eleven know-it-alls making $140,000 a year sat around an old oak horseshoe table, where they overrode citizens' grievances and cast votes on items they were unqualified to decide on. My cameraman had set up his tripod in the corner of the room, and the hearing was captured in a wide-streaming shot online. Fox had sent me to confront the supervisors on the fatal consequences of their sanctuary city policy, and ask if they'd learned from their mistakes. I waited for a while, as locals registered their complaints about unfair zoning, homelessness, handicapped access, and bizarre ordinances. Mostly, the supervisors feigned interest and whispered to each other, basking in their relevance and enjoying their perch as the arbiters of city life. They nonchalantly ruled on beefs from average Americans until it was my turn. But I was not your average American. I'm slightly *below* average, which makes me able to do things others won't do.

When it was my turn to make a public comment, I stepped up to the lectern and addressed the supervisors.

WATTERS: Good afternoon, Supervisors. My name is Jesse Watters with *The O'Reilly Factor* at Fox News Channel. I would like to address your dangerous sanctuary city policies. I would like to show you a picture here. It's Kate Steinle. She was murdered by an illegal alien who had been deported five times and over six felony convictions. But for some reason the city of San Francisco let this guy out.

The supervisors just sat there in silence. Many of them wouldn't even look up. They just bowed their heads and refused to acknowledge the crime that was committed in their city. I continued.

WATTERS: You guys aren't even looking. Look at the picture. Are you afraid? You guys don't have anything to say?

It was a shameful display of cowardice. As I spoke about Kate, I got more and more angry. I explained how their policies had let the killer out, and how this wasn't the first time illegal alien felons had been allowed to prey on American citizens in the streets of San Francisco. After repeatedly asking the supervisors if they would reverse the sanctuary city policy, I asked if they had anything to say to Steinle's family, perhaps an apology. I was met with stone cold silence. The only time they spoke was when they dismissed me when my allotted time was up.

SUPERVISOR: Thank you very much. Next speaker, please.

You could hear the room rustle with discomfort at what we'd just witnessed. The people were aghast at how callously their leaders had treated a dead woman. Refusing to look at her picture and acknowledge her family's suffering. I walked out of the room and headed straight for Mayor Lee's office. His spokeswoman, Christine Falvey, refused to let me into his office to speak with him.

WATTERS: I just have a few questions. Please tell him *Watters' World* is looking for him. All right? Thank you. I came all the way from New York just to get a few answers, you know, about the sanctuary city policy.

FALVEY: He did send out a statement about this issue. It's a very serious issue.

WATTERS: Is taking it seriously just sending out a little piece of paper when someone is murdered because of a policy you support? That doesn't sound that serious to me.

FALVEY: I don't think that is characterized correctly.

WATTERS: How is that mischaracterizing?

FALVEY: We have taken it very seriously.

WATTERS: How did I mischaracterize, though?

FALVEY: It's deeply sad for the family. And the mayor is going to continue to work on this issue. It never should have happened, and he wants to make sure it doesn't happen again.

WATTERS: How is he making sure it doesn't happen again, specifically?

FALVEY: On a number—he is working on a number of issues.

WATTERS: Like what?

FALVEY: He will be—he is working.

WATTERS: Because this is several times this has happened in your city. How many dead people does it take?

FALVEY: I really thank you for coming by.

The mayor wasn't working on anything. Falvey was lying and squirming. Months later, the city would reaffirm its sanctuary city policy. This was a personal flashpoint for me. Heartless and disconnected politicians were favoring criminal illegal aliens over their own citizens. San Francisco specifically seemed like a separatist region, flaunting public safety. For what? To win the Hispanic vote? (President Trump, a border hawk, won 35 percent of the Hispanic vote, outpacing McCain and Romney.) To keep illegals working cheaply under the table in exchange for donations from industry? It was a betrayal of Americans and American values. No amount of public shaming would open their hearts and minds. San Francisco and cities like it exist in a liberal utopia where local media doesn't challenge politicians, colossal public policy failures are excused as the cost of compassion, and concerns of average citizens are ignored in favor of special interests.

It makes perfect sense that the leader of the Democrat Party hails from the San Francisco congressional district. These San Francisco values have polluted her party and have made it nearly impossible to make deals for Americans. Pelosi shut down the government to prevent our border from being secured, held up stimulus checks for Americans because President Trump wouldn't send checks to illegal immigrants, and distracted the country from coronavirus with a six-month-long partisan impeachment charade. Even while the Speaker screamed about the dangers of in-person voting, she was caught on camera casually strolling inside a locked-down salon without a mask. But who am I to judge. Great hair, don't care.

In many ways, I consider what I did in San Francisco City Hall to be a failure. The *Washington Post* called my actions "good journalism and outstanding television." I refuse to accept the compliment. Not because the *Washington Post* later called me "officially out of control," and "Fox News' next big headache." I refuse to accept the compliment because it was a waste of time. Did we get justice for Kate Steinle? Not really. The San Francisco prosecutors overcharged Zarate and botched the trial. A jury acquitted the illegal immigrant of murder charges, agreeing with defense counsel that it was just an accident. The only charge that stuck was a felon in possession of a gun, which was later overturned because on appeal, a liberal judge concluded that Zarate didn't "possess" the weapon long enough to legally "possess" it. The Steinle family sued the government for negligence and lost thanks to the Ninth Circuit Court of Appeals. And "Kate's Law," which *The Factor* spearheaded, requiring a mandatory minimum five years for illegal felon reentry, was bottled up and blocked by Dick Durbin in the Senate. Where is Zarate now? He was incarcerated by the Federal Bureau of Prisons until July 2020. We don't know his status as of this time. It's possible he was released due to coronavirus concerns, released on his own recognizance, or deported. We don't know. But if he was deported, he certainly knows how to sneak back in. He's done it five times. And yes, he'd be welcomed back into San Francisco. But Zarate, just don't perform an illegal circumcision! That can get you into really big trouble there.

Bill de Blasio is doing his best to turn New York City into San Francisco. He took over a clean, safe city from Mayors Bloomberg and Giuliani and mismanaged it like a drunk Soviet. Traffic, open drug use, and homicides are up, while the quality of life goes down. De Blasio failed to stand up to the rioting looters, and Black Lives Matter mobs took over chunks of the city, erecting encampments on city blocks where "protesters" polluted and assaulted police officers. Buildings deemed "architectural masterpieces" are defaced with graffiti, the rats are back, and the combination of coronavirus and crime destroyed property values and forced many to flee. Rents are falling and businesses are closing left and right.

The signs of New York's demise were clear early in de Blasio's tenure when the homeless population exploded and became emboldened. I was commuting daily into Penn Station, the midtown belowground hub for trains, subways, and, increasingly, vagabonds. I have a special connection with the homeless. There really isn't much separating me from a homeless guy. I could get fired at any time and have no skills to fall back on to make a living. Math is challenging, science is beyond me, and business bores me. Surviving in the wilderness is, as you know, out of the question, so when I see a homeless guy begging for change, I see myself six months after saying the wrong thing on the air. This is why I give homeless people money when I see them on the subway. That, and because I want liberals seeing Jesse Watters give homeless people money on the subway. It throws them off. It also embarrasses them, since they aren't giving a dime.

Most of the homeless are substance abusers or have mental health problems or both. So we need to help them get back on their feet. The Big Apple doubled its spending on homeless to more than $3 billion a year, but its homeless population hit an all-time high. More money doesn't always fix the problem, does it? What the mayor doesn't understand is that you have to get the homeless off the street, get them clean, and get them treatment. Open some institutions if you have to.

The city's budget is nearly $100 billion a year. Where's the money going? Nobody knows. The mayor's wife lost $850 million earmarked for mental health and nobody blinked an eye. If that happened in the private sector, she'd be in prison. Except bail reform would have her sprung and still skipping around.

As I strutted around Penn Station, with the cameras this time, it was a sad state of affairs. A child told me she was "scared." A woman said a homeless man "attacked" her and grabbed her face. A business owner explained, "Every morning we have to mop the floor from human waste." Commuters, children, and merchants felt constantly threatened, bothered, and harassed. In Penn Station, you're not allowed to loiter, sleep on the floor, or panhandle. These violations should either get you kicked out, fined, or thrown in jail. But de Blasio directs the NYPD not to enforce it. Several homeless men and women told me the police let them sleep unbothered for "up to eight hours." Many of them were addicted to crack or had drinking problems. One woman explained she makes money from prostitution to feed her habit. Others collect bottles and cans to recycle and make about twenty dollars a day. All had some stipend from the federal government, as well as Medicaid.

I caught heat from the liberal media for airing this package. They said I was "dehumanizing" the homeless. It was actually the opposite. I gave them a voice, shook their hands, and exposed the failure of liberal policies. When have you seen the mainstream media interact with the homeless and do in-depth features on them? Almost never. The liberal media ignores the homeless, until conservatives draw attention to them, at which point we're called cruel for pointing out a problem.

Rudy Giuliani's homeless policy was compassionate. You were not allowed to sleep on the street. Police and social workers would escort you to a shelter or to a facility for a health evaluation. This dictum was applied consistently for years, until people stopped living on the street, moved elsewhere, or sought help. Letting people live on the street for long periods of time makes their mental health deteriorate and exacerbates their addictions. If you live on the streets for too long, you'll hurt yourself or someone else. If your brother or sister descended into homelessness, you'd try your best to rescue them. Because you love them. Any mayor who doesn't try to rescue the homeless doesn't love them. And any mayor who lets people urinate all over the city doesn't love the city. You don't let someone pee on something you love. I believe it was Shakespeare who said that.

Things got so bad in New York that families of NYPD officers killed in the line of duty were refusing to let Mayor de Blasio come to the funerals. The streets were filthy and unsafe. Al Sharpton was calling the shots on crime prevention, not the mayor. *The Factor* had invited the mayor on the show numerous times, only to be rudely blown off. It wasn't due to a tight work schedule. Reports were that de Blasio woke up late, rolled to the gym, and didn't arrive at City Hall until 11 a.m.

I ventured uptown to the Bronx, where Comrade Bill was holding an event for affordable housing. Sitting nicely in the audience, I waited my turn, and politely took the microphone when I was called upon.

WATTERS: Bill O'Reilly has a question for you.
DE BLASIO: Okay. Are you his emissary?
WATTERS: Yes, I am. You don't know *Watters' World*?
DE BLASIO: Again, please?
WATTERS: I'm Watters, and this is my world right here. *(Crowd laughs)*
DE BLASIO: Okay. Continue *(smiling)*.

(Once I'd hit him with my tagline, he was on the ropes. The tagline establishes dominance and can have a bewildering effect on a subject.)
WATTERS: We've been trying to book you on the show for weeks.
     And your staff hasn't been very respectful toward us.
DE BLASIO: I'm sure they're very respectful.

WATTERS: Actually not.

DE BLASIO: I'm sure they are.

WATTERS: We're just trying to get to know you better. What's the problem?

DE BLASIO: Oh, I appreciate the invitation and my staff will follow up with you.

(He attempts to end the conversation and unsuccessfully call on another reporter.)

WATTERS: But they haven't been following up, and that's why I'm here.

DE BLASIO: I'm glad you're here.

(He's squirming. Sweat is glistening on his forehead.)

WATTERS: We're fascinated by the de Blasio mystique.

DE BLASIO: Okay. Let's take some serious questions. Go ahead, Henry.

(The mayor tries to call on a friendly reporter named Henry.)

WATTERS: Can you help us out, Mayor?

DE BLASIO: I've talked to you, my friend. Henry?

WATTERS: You haven't responded. Will you do the show?

DE BLASIO: Henry, just start talking, Henry.

HENRY (A FRIENDLY REPORTER): I'm not going to rescue you.

WATTERS: You need rescuing. Thank you very much.

DE BLASIO: I never need rescuing.

WATTERS: Thank you very much.

DE BLASIO: I just want a real question. Go ahead, Henry.

As the mayor was grasping for a lifeline, one of his armed security guards walked up to me, grabbed me by the arm, and physically escorted me out of the event. This was not an attack on the First Amendment. The mayor was not waging war on an independent media. My press freedoms were not at risk. We were not approaching a constitutional crisis. I was just being persistent and sarcastic to a cowardly mayor who couldn't take the heat. I should have peed onstage instead. Then he would have let me stay.

Years later, de Blasio used his enforcers on me again. I was cohosting Fox's New Year's Eve show in Times Square. The temperatures hit record lows, and during a commercial break, I left the set to warm up in a heated tent. But as I approached the tent, a security agent put his arm to my chest, stopping me in my tracks.

"What's the problem, Officer?" I asked.

"He doesn't want you in here," said the security agent.

"Who doesn't want me in here?" I asked. "Anderson Cooper?" I wondered, thinking I'd accidentally entered the CNN tent.

"No. The mayor doesn't want you in here," explained the security agent. I immediately recognized the agent. He was the same one who'd booted me out of the Bronx press conference.

"But it's twenty below," I said.

"Sorry," said the security agent.

"Tell him it's Henry."

We both laughed. We both knew his boss was a joke. When de Blasio ran for president a few years later, the rest of the country got to know, too.

CHAPTER TWELVE

How I Saved the Environment

Armed security is a big asset. Without it, you're totally exposed. In more ways than one. There was a top editor at a major media outlet who tangled with *The Factor* and didn't come out on top. Perhaps he did, literally, but I wasn't there for that. Although I was pretty close.

I'm not naming this man, because I'm a good person and don't want to ruin his life. I doubt he'd do the same for me. But that's the difference between us. I'm a nobleman, and he's a ruthless scoundrel. The view is quite beautiful up here on my high horse.

This man had run an extremely unfair piece about Fox and our contributors. It twisted words, took things out of context, and smeared with innuendo. Your typical nasty attack job. *The Factor* didn't turn the other cheek. Hiding behind the masthead and ducking accountability wasn't allowed. You had to answer for it. Especially if the attack was personal in nature, which it was. Calling someone a racist and an accessory to murder was fightin' words. This was media combat, and we were in the trenches. The pen is mightier than the sword, but the camera works even better.

Before we broke out the camera, we invited the man on the show, seeking comment. We were ignored. But before we uncorked the ambush, I poked around his office building in midtown Manhattan to catch a glimpse of him and ascertain his schedule. He kept an interesting schedule, indeed. Almost immediately after I arrived I saw him leave the building. It was a chilly winter day. He was bundled up in a parka, walking briskly in a light snow. I kept a safe distance and watched him closely. This was good, I thought to myself. He leaves around lunch at this time and goes to his favorite deli or coffee shop. Tomorrow, I'll be back out here with my camera crew and nail him.

He continued to walk crosstown until he hit Sixth Avenue where he turned and headed north. He was actually nearing Fox News. There were plenty of lunch places closer to his office. He looked like a man on a mission. I kept up the shadow. He continued to walk north until he ducked into a bank. I stood outside and watched him withdraw money from the ATM and leave. Everything seemed normal, just getting some cash out at lunchtime. Then he turned onto Forty-Fifth Street. About fifty yards later, the man quickly stepped off the sidewalk into what looked like a low-end pizzeria. Okay, I think to myself, he's grabbing a slice for lunch and should be out in a minute. He likes the slices here, although he passed a few other pizza places, and this spot seems random and, quite honestly, a little dingy. As I waited outside across the street in the cold, the minutes passed by. Ten minutes, twenty minutes, thirty minutes. What was he doing in there that whole time? It wasn't the kind of place you had a lunch meeting. I called back to the office to deliver a situation report and was told to maintain the shadow.

I decided to look inside the pizzeria. This was risky since I'd gained some notoriety and was recognizable to an alert *media guy*. But as I walked inside, I saw he wasn't in there. I even checked the bathroom. Empty. Had I lost him? I rushed outside and looked at my watch. Exactly an hour had passed since the man had gone inside. Suddenly he emerged from a tiny entrance right next to the pizzeria. I snapped a picture quickly as he left. Where had he been, I wondered, as he walked west on Forty-Fifth. I tailed him through the snow until he made it back to his office.

Confused, I hustled back to West Forty-Fifth Street to see where he'd vanished for an hour. Right next to the pizza joint was a small step up to an entryway. The door was closed. Apartment numbers corresponded with access buzzers on the wall outside. I picked a random one and pressed. The door clicked, so I opened it. The space was tight. A staircase fed up one flight lined by unpainted walls. As I walked up the stairs, it didn't strike me as the kind of place a man of his stature would go. This was basically a crummy walk-up apartment unit sandwiched between a pizza place and a locksmith on a midtown cross street. There were places like this all over Manhattan. You stroll by never noticing them, and even if you do, you don't think much of them.

I reached the landing on the second floor and came to a door. 2A was the apartment number. There were only three apartments in the building: 2A, 3A, and 4A. My game plan was to check them all to see where the man had been this whole time. Not knowing what to expect, I winged it, and knocked on 2A. The door opened, but not all the way. But it was enough to see what was going on.

A very attractive blonde, maybe thirty years old, was standing in the doorway. She was wearing a tight white T-shirt with jeans and was barefoot. She looked a little like Elizabeth Shue, but with longer hair. I could see into the apartment behind her, an unmade bed. There was no furniture, just the bed sitting in the middle of the apartment, with rumpled white sheets hanging off. I immediately figured out what was going on and went into character.

"Hi, I'd like to book a massage," I said, smiling.

"You're supposed to call ahead first," she explained nervously. "How did you get this address?"

"My friend was just here earlier. He told me about it. How much?"

She peeked her head out of the doorway a little and looked to see if I was alone.

"What's your name?" she asked.

"Mike."

"Okay, Mike, call this number." She took out a piece of paper and wrote it down. "Ask for Vanessa. They'll handle it, but you can't just show up here." She handed me the piece of paper.

"Got it. Will call. See you later this afternoon, Vanessa. Sorry for showing up out of the blue like this."

"Just call the number. Okay? Bye." She smiled knowingly but hurriedly and closed the door.

It all made sense now. The ATM withdrawal, then the full hour upstairs. I walked up the next two flights of stairs, knocked on both apartments, but nobody answered. Vanessa was the only one in the building when our *editor* was here.

Back in the office I explained the situation. We all had a good laugh. The next step was to call the number. We gathered in an office, called the number, and hit "record" on a recording device.

A woman answered. "Hello?"

"Hi, this is Mike, I'd like to book a massage."

It wasn't really a massage, we both knew that. The woman took down my phone number and got into the particulars.

"What kind of masseuse would you like? This afternoon we have available a black, an Asian . . ."

"My friend says Vanessa is great. How much for Vanessa?"

"Massage is two hundred dollars an hour plus tip," the woman on the phone explained.

"You pay girl cash," she added.

"Is she good? Will I be happy at the end?"

"Yes, you will be very happy."

I don't remember if we officially booked the massage on that call. If I did, I'm sorry to have stood you up, Vanessa. How were we going to handle what we had here? The decision was made. It was time to ambush the guy.

He lived outside the city with his wife. About a week later, I staked out his house on a Saturday.

After a little wait, his car pulls out of the driveway, and we start a tail. It isn't long until he pulls into a 7-Eleven. After he goes inside, we follow him in with a cameraman.

We find him in the back by the fridges pulling out a Snapple.

"Hello, I'm Jesse Watters with Fox News, how are you?"

He looks at me, sees the microphone flag, and notices the camera in tow.

"Fine. What are you doing here?"

"We wanted to talk to you about a column." I reviewed for him what had been written and asked what justified such slander. We went back and forth about a minute; he dismissed me, argued, and stood his ground, while making his way to the checkout counter. After refusing several times to apologize, it was time to change the subject.

"By the way, on February thirteenth, you went to an ATM and then visited an unlicensed massage parlor on Forty-Fifth Street."

He froze.

I continued sarcastically. "Was there an editorial meeting in there or something?"

He stopped looking at me. "Unlicensed massage parlor" was me beating around the bush. The ATM reference was included to remind him there was electronic evidence and surveillance footage. This wasn't the crime of the century, but we wanted him to know he'd left a footprint.

He gathered himself finally after an extremely long, awkward pause. The only thing he could muster was, "No."

I continued to share details of his rendezvous while he rang up his Snapple. Customers were excited by all the fuss. We followed him outside to his car. While he had been chatty earlier, after I mentioned the massage, he went stone-cold silent. After he left I went back inside and got myself a Snapple. Peach-flavored iced tea.

Did we ever air the footage? Nope. Why hurt a man's marriage and embarrass him professionally like that? I have standards. We did notice a change of tone from his outlet for several years afterward. Perhaps, thinking that a shoe could drop at any time, they kept their powder dry. Whenever I pass the pizza place on Forty-Fifth I always think of my guy who went in for "a slice."

There were other times when I wish I hadn't opened the door. Al Gore comes to mind. The former VP was scheduled to deliver a speech at Duke University. He'd been dodging *The Factor* for a decade. Gore had gotten rich pushing global warming and had even received a Nobel Peace Prize for his work. But personally, Gore's mansion and round-the-world travel were huge carbon emitters, and he rarely had to answer for that. Additionally, he was campaigning globally for government spending on green technologies that he was heavily invested in, like software that measures emissions under a "cap and trade" system. Most of his "science" was never challenged by the mainstream media. Around this time, a hack had uncovered some damning emails from within the man-made global warming scientific community. Released data and emails showed climate researchers manipulating temperature reading charts to highlight only increases in global warming. The scandal was nicknamed "Climategate." One scientist writes, "Where the heck is the global warming? The fact is that we can't account for the lack of warming at the moment and it is a travesty that we can't." Another scientist admits how to use a statistical "trick" to "hide the decline" in global temperatures, maintaining the famous "hockey stick graph." Widespread evidence of cherry-picking data and stonewalling skeptics raised questions as to the true motivations of these so-called scientists, many of whom are recipients of millions of dollars in government grants. If the warming slows, so does the gravy train. Being the "greenest guy at Fox," I flew to North Carolina to have a friendly chat with Gore about all of the above.

Confronting Gore at Duke was challenging. It was a private university with vice-presidential–level security. But I took a shot in the dark and got lucky. Gore would probably stay at the nicest hotel in town, so I headed there the morning of his speech. Since I used to be a bellhop, I knew what to do.

"Did Al Gore check in here?" I asked the bellhop, as I slipped him twenty dollars.

He glanced around before confirming, "Yup, last night."

"Thanks. Have you seen him this morning?" I asked.

"I think he's in one of the conference rooms meeting with people . . . but it's a private event," he said. I told him I was with Fox. "Big fan," he said.

"Appreciate it," I said, nodding my head. Bellhops live by a code: Money talks. At that stage of my career at Fox, this bellhop may have been making more than I was, so I had to expense that tip.

I sauntered into the hotel lobby, found the bar/grill room, and plunked down in a soft wingback. The hotel was a four-diamond so I ordered some delicious bisque while I waited. Plus a Shirley Temple. After lunch, I poked around the hotel's first level. Plush carpeting, rich mahogany, oil paintings . . . a lot different than the La Quinta Inn that I was staying at. Around the corner was a sign saying PRIVATE LUNCH and a velvet rope cutting across the hallway leading to the ballroom. Bingo. All I had to do was wait . . . and order another Shirley Temple. Soon enough, Gore emerged and walked quickly through the bar area, where I intercepted.

WATTERS: Mr. Vice President, Jesse Watters, Fox News. How are you?
GORE: How are you? Fine.
WATTERS: Hey, why won't you come on *The O'Reilly Factor*, Mr. Vice President?
GORE: I don't like him. *(fair point . . . but I was undeterred)*

WATTERS: You know Bill is not a big anti-global-warming guy. Mr. Vice President . . .
GORE: I don't like ambush journalism.

Nobody "likes" ambush journalism, except the person doing the ambush.

WATTERS: Yes, but why won't you come on the show? Come on, it will be fun. There's two sides to this story.
GORE: Well, I'll consider it.
WATTERS: You will consider it?
GORE: Sure.

At this point, I was breathing down Gore's neck with a microphone and he was frantically jutting around the lobby looking for somewhere to go.

WATTERS: All right. Great. So, while we have you here . . .
GORE: You don't have me here. *(cute response)* I'm not doing an interview right now. *(You kind of are, actually.)*
WATTERS: What's your reaction to the fact that the arctic ice is actually increasing? *(This was a phenomenon that global warming scientists were having trouble explaining.)*
GORE: I'm not doing an interview right now.
WATTERS: One last question for you.
GORE: I'm not doing an interview.

He'd left the luncheon to go to the men's room. This is where things got a bit awkward. Gore had finally located the men's room near the hotel lobby and escaped inside, followed by yours truly. Because I'm so tenacious, I followed the former vice president into the men's room with my cameraman filming. As I stood in the doorway by the sinks, Gore sidled up next to the urinal, cocked his head, and said, "Are you really interviewing me while I'm going to the bathroom?" The answer was yes. Had I no shame? Realizing Gore had asserted the moral high ground over me, I tucked tail and left the bathroom. But when he came out I pounced right back on him.

WATTERS: Are you embarrassed at all by Climategate, sir?
GORE: I'm not doing an interview right now. I'm having lunch.
WATTERS: Do you stand to make any money from cap-and-trade?

Finally, Gore returned to his private lunch. I walked back down the hallway and went to the bathroom. After all those Shirley Temples, I really had to go. As I walked in, I saw Gore had left in such a haste, he'd left the water running in one of the sinks. I quickly shut it off before any more water was wasted. And just like that, I'd regained the moral high ground.

There's a lot of misinformation out there about global warming and I take zero responsibility for it. In fact, it was my job to correct the record. During Earth Days, or record blizzards, I ventured outside to ask regular folks about the climate. Here are a sample of their answers:

WATTERS: Which country, do you think, is the biggest polluter?
FEMALE: I would pick South America.

South America is not a country. The correct answer is China. By a mile.

WATTERS: How much, do you think, has the earth warmed over the last fifteen years?
FEMALE: A hundred degrees.

We'd all cook to death if that were true. The correct answer is .11 degrees, if you believe the scientists, who have a troubled track record. I've always wondered what the baseline was. How do we know what the world's temperature was in 1830? You're saying man, who couldn't even figure out indoor plumbing at the time, was able to get an accurate reading of the entire earth's temperature? How exactly?

WATTERS: What is global warming?
MALE: I don't really know what it is, but I just believe in it.

It's like believing in God, I suppose.

WATTERS: Is there a climate change when there's a lot of snow?
WOMAN: Yes.
WATTERS: Would it also be climate change if there was no snow?
WOMAN: Yes.
WATTERS: So, it's climate change either way?
WOMAN: Yes. There's change.

When someone flips a coin and says, "Heads I win, tails you lose," you're being scammed. But when liberals do this to you, they call it science. When you ask a question, they call you a "science denier." Most liberal arguments aren't arguments at all; they're juvenile rhetorical traps to *prevent* an argument. But the more facts and information you acquire, the less sense liberalism makes. Therefore, loads of resources are directed at preventing the public from seeing both sides of an argument and accessing raw data. But with the explosion of the internet, Twitter, talk radio, podcasts, and Fox News, the American public can hear alternative opinions, see court filings online, research statistics, and make their own determinations about public policy debates. For far too long, the mainstream media has been gatekeepers of relevant information, only communicating cherry-picked information to support their liberal narrative. This monopoly is ending. When the curtain is peeled back, Americans can see live congressional hearings streamed to their phone, read through inspector general reports, review video clips of politicians saying the opposite of what they said a month ago, examine corporate political donations, watch raw footage of riots, or see the internal partisan samples that media companies use to weight their polls. This is eye-opening, especially when you put it up against what the mainstream media is reporting. Critical information is left out of their reports, video is suppressed or edited deceptively, and numbers don't add up. Americans are rightfully frustrated about being lied to and manipulated by a propagandistic press as they continue to dig deeper on their own for the truth.

This righteous anger has given rise to a new populist groundswell in this country. Many on the right are exasperated at the media, big tech, big business, big labor, higher education, federal law enforcement, and the political class in Washington. They believe that powerful interests are misleading them and dividing them for profit. Whenever their corruption is exposed, they usually get away with it, or worse, there are two standards of justice depending on your profession, political party, or bank account. This anger is growing and is on a collision course with the ruling class. The more the ruling class tries to tame it, the more boisterous and unpredictable it becomes. Those who try to tame it will be engulfed in its currents, but those who can ride it will be carried to shore in victory.

There are many on the left, real Americans, not just in the political class, who are joining forces with the corporate media, big tech, and powerful interests to suppress information. Monopolistic control of information, while regressive, does further the political aims of the left. It allows them to control the narrative, to wield power over Republicans on campus or on Capitol Hill, and censor speech and opinion they disagree with.

Hillary using "BleachBit" software on her server, FBI director Robert Mueller's team destroying their iPhones, Obama's IRS "losing" thousands of incriminating emails—these are assaults on transparency that liberals are comfortable with as long as their political objectives are secured. Merely asking questions about the origins of Covid-19 will get you labeled a conspiracy theorist. Questioning the science surrounding lockdowns or global warming will get you tarred and feathered in some circles. The search for truth, for answers, or innocent questions about conventional wisdom are deemed "dangerous." The media is uninterested in a former president flying around in the jet of an international underage sex trafficker, allegedly partying on Jeffrey Epstein's island with minors. Flight logs, photographs, and eyewitness testimony put Bill Clinton in highly questionable circumstances, but the media won't pursue it. In fact, ABC killed a bombshell exposé from an alleged Epstein victim because it jeopardized the network's comfy access to the royal family. Never mind the royal family member was photographed with an alleged sex trafficking victim. The MeToo movement didn't blink.

After a three-year investigation into Trump-Russia collusion, at the end of which investigators determined there was no collusion, there is zero interest in determining how the whole charade began. A presidential campaign had never in the history of American politics been spied upon by the incumbent administration of the opposing party. Foreign spies, undercover FBI agents, wiretaps, doctored evidence, and national security leaks were deployed against an American campaign and a presidential transition and administration. The media was complicit, as were Democrats, the CIA, and the FBI. This was a historic abuse of power and a violation of American citizens' constitutional rights. Documents that shed light on these political crimes have been hidden for years. Documents and congressional testimony that have been made public substantiate these unlawful actions, but the Left will not acknowledge them, even after smoking-gun evidence proved Hillary Clinton concocted collusion to distract from her email scandal. They ignore them, smear you as a wing nut, or justify the intrusive actions on grounds that continue to crumble under their feet.

The game is simple. The ruling class hides the truth and lies about those who seek it, and the Left sides with the hiders and liars. Joe Biden was credibly accused of sexual assault. He denied it. But when the accuser said Biden's Senate records might hold evidence to bolster her claim, Biden refused to release them. The media yawned and said, "Okay." The Democrat primary voters blew it off, too. Why? Because Biden had the best shot at beating Trump, and he wouldn't survive a scandal like this. It was all about power.

Ex-cons with felony warrants for sexual assault can resist arrest, go for a knife, reach for a gun, spit coronavirus at an officer, and days after the officer-involved shooting be hailed as heroes in the media. The details of the arrest will be buried or scrapped from the news reports. Sometimes exculpatory evidence for the officer will be held for days before being released. Video evidence will be edited, and headlines will be skewed to paint the suspect as a martyr and the officer a cold-blooded killer. By the time all the information comes out, if it ever does, the damage is already done.

Whether it's a corrupt judge, a crooked politician, or a shady executive, they'll go into lockdown mode after a scandal, and the media and their liberal allies will circle the wagons. If you have the right connections, the right party, or enough money, you can cover up your bad behavior and make your political opponents look like the guilty party. All in a day's work.

Bias isn't what's in the news. Many times bias is what's *not* in the news. Republican achievements in the Mideast are largely ignored. The Mideast peace deal, the obliteration of the ISIS caliphate, the removal of major ground forces from Iraq and Syria are largely unknown to the general public because they've been largely exiled from broadcast, cable, and internet news rundowns. Conservatives generally have to work harder than liberals to consume fair and balanced news and information. Any liberal can passively let the mainstream media news wash over them. The search engines, social media platforms, and internet news sites are managed by liberals; the three broadcast networks, ABC, CBS, NBC, plus CNN and MSNBC, are left, as are all of the major metropolitan newspapers. If an independent thinker wants to read about racial riots, the Russia investigation, or the impeachment trial, they're better off watching raw footage online, reading unredacted documents, or perusing witness testimony. Following conservative journalists on Twitter is like being a part of the counterculture. Every single second there is an army of citizen journalists fact-checking and exposing liberal media lies and the politicians who echo them.

Censorship and suppression are now the allies of the Left. Conservatives have now become the renegades and crusaders for truth. We're the ones asking the questions that powerful people don't want asked. We're the ones filing the Freedom of Information Act requests, ambushing the politicians, and demanding accountability for dirty scoundrels. We want to see how the math adds up, where the money went, and what the real agenda is. Why can't we know how Biden's family members got rich? If coronavirus came from a lab or a wet market? Or who the whistleblower is? Eventually we found those answers out, but we went through hell doing it. It shouldn't be this hard. It shouldn't be so wicked to be curious about our own country.

The more information is democratized, the thirstier we get for truth. There's a rabid hunt for answers in America that's causing everyone to go at each other's throats. Conservatives and independent thinkers are on the warpath for facts while powerful interests feed the country empty calories. We get spoon-fed small morsels of spin and half-baked nothing burgers that insult our intelligence. Momentum is building against the gatekeepers, their credibility diminishes daily, and the fact that the Left is okay with it makes conservatives into the underdogs for the first time in a while. We fight harder as underdogs. We're the underdogs of the internet era. And just like the colonists, we'll throw off the king's shackles and usher in an independent era, free from tyranny, where everyone is free to live and learn and prosper. Knowledge is power, and we're coming for the crown.

CHAPTER THIRTEEN

How I Saved My Mom's Texts

When I joined *The Five*, we were moved to 9 p.m. This meant that my liberal mother had already had her vodka when the show aired. After a drink, she can become quite passionate about politics. During the show, my iPhone would beep with text messages from my mom. This drove my co-host Dana Perino crazy until I figured out how to put my phone on silent. The texts were scathing critiques of my commentary. I read a few aloud during the commercial break and everyone laughed. We decided to feature them on air as my "One More Thing" at the end of the show branding it "Mom Texts." It was like reading hate mail, but from your own mother. The audience enjoyed it. Responding to the mom texts was a bad idea. It would take me down a dark liberal rabbit hole. Therefore, I'd like to respond to my mom's texts here, because she's unable to text back.

1. "I cannot and will not identify myself as the mother of Trump's wing man. Change it up."

    You can and you will.

2. "You are on 'Fantasy Island'! And don't make statements about what I as a Democrat want. Illegal immigration?"

    Prove to me that you don't want illegal immigration. I'm waiting . . .

3. "Brutal and mean and not American and ludicrous and where is your voice, Jesse? Sad. Words matter."

   I'm sensing deep disappointment here.

4. "WHAT R U TALKING ABOUT!!!???"

   All caps. Wow. I must have said something really accurate.

5. "What makes you think it's appropriate to viciously disparage, insult and dismiss a member of Congress? How does that behavior contribute to any sort of civil discourse? Humility helps; character counts. Think about that, Jesse."

   I've thought about it and will continue to disparage.

6. "Oh, my goodness! And you actually believe Trump is not divisive!!! You've been swallowed by semantic quicksand!!!"

   "Swallowed by semantic quicksand." I'm going to steal this line.

7. "Please pronounce your 'ing's. The word is 'putting' not 'puttin.' Peekin'? Restockin'??"

   I'm having flashbacks to middle school.

8. "I am honestly concerned that your colleagues have begun to roll their eyes at your diatribes."

   I've noticed it, too. I expect it from Juan but not from Dana.

9. "I cannot watch today or tomorrow, so bring back the kind Jesse."

   He never left.

10. "You are screaming at Juan and so disrespectfully. Tone it down!"

    I'm sorry I can't help it.

11. "Remember to respect your elders and I mean Geraldo!"

    #respectthemustache

12. "Do not throw your hat in with Rasputin."

    I'm assuming you mean Putin here.

13. "Eyebrow problems? Did you dye your eyebrows black?"
    Mom, no! I have YOUR eyebrows!

14. "Commitment to the world's environment is both lofty and critical. Are you proud to go public with the fact that you do not recycle!!!? Sad."
    Not proud. Recycling can be difficult.

15. "We need to be worried about the stability of the Republic!"
    Please read something else besides the New York Times.

16. "When you are good, you are so very, very good, and when there is a performance like last night's, I become so distraught that you have moved ever closer to that imaginary line that cannot be crossed."
    I think it's safe to say we disagree on where that line is.

17. "I have delighted in your more measured and thoughtful language and approach to issues these last months, and I've said that to you. So then I began to wonder, is this Mean Mondays? Because this only happens on Mondays."
    Nobody is in a good mood on Mondays, Mom.

18. "I am tired of the 'FOX and Friends' fellow."
    Sorry, Kilmeade. Mom's not a fan.

19. "Enough. Think about how to make the world a better place."
    That's exactly what I'm doing.

20. "All I can say is thank God for Juan Williams. Really, Jesse?"
    #prayforjuan

21. "Jesse, really good show. But how about trying to come up with more meaningful and impactful 'One More Things.' Your score on that front is not soaring."
    You didn't like my monkey fight video?

22. "On Chapter 5 of 'Fire and Fury.' An absolute must-read."
    This is where she gets her information from.

23. "Daddy does not like Greg's heavy metal transition music."

    Daddy is not alone.

24. "Jesse, we're all excited about the Philadelphia Eagles, but this does not merit your losing of all your 'ing's . . . 'gettin,' 'goin' . . . 'winnin' . . . Or is this 'Bro Talk'?"

    "Bro talk." LMAO

25. "How can I get Trump fired?"

    Haha. Get a job "counting" votes.

26. "Life is bigger than Hillary. Stop behaving like a one-trick pony."

    I'd stop talking about her, but she won't go away!

27. "WRONG!!! Trump is NOT at 50 percent approval ratings. Like Juan, I worry about your sources! Where do you get your information???"

    Rasmussen

28. "I am worried, Jesse, and I am very worried about that unusual jacket you are wearing!"

    Must have looked pretty dapper that day.

29. "Remember, confidence is silent and insecurity is loud."

    Deep thoughts by Mom Texts.

30. "If Trump fires Rod Rosenstein, we will have people marching in the streets. Trust me on that. And I will not be alone."

    Viva La Revolution!

31. "Jesse, you have not come a long way until you stop featuring yourself in your 'One More Thing' sections. Humility is something to consider."

    I've considered it.

32. "How insulting, Jesse, the former head of the FBI is a good actor. And who might you be?"

    A bad actor?

33. "Is Stormy beating Trump at his own media game?"

  I'm going to leave this one alone.

34. "The dark jacket is a vast improvement over the Ferris wheel operator getup you wore yesterday and need to lose—not to denigrate Ferris wheel operators."

  We wouldn't want to do that, now would we?

35. "You look very handsome, and I do not want that text feeding your ego going public."

  Too late!

36. "Be so careful, Jesse. Trump will be impeached if he fires Mueller. We live in a country of LAWS."

  Well, you were right about the Trump being impeached part.

37. "Obviously, Dana has balanced sources, Jesse. Your interpretation of the nothing burger is not only pitiful but inaccurate and woven from tattered cloth."

  It's clear Dana is your favorite.

38. "Jesse, you used to read veraciously. What happened? An occasional novel would be in your very best interest."

  You misspelled voraciously.

39. "Stop it right now! You are being obnoxious to your co-hosts! Who are you!!"

  I'm Watters, and this is my world.

40. "I'm going to ask that you pick up the Comey book, 'A Higher Loyalty.' Please do this for your mother."

  I'm going to ask that you pick up "Art of the Deal." Please do this for your son.

41. "Stay away from speaking for Trump. Don't be an ass."

  Hahaha. Have another.

42. "What happened to the rule of law? Stop this, Jesse. You sound like an immoral crook."

    Crooked Jesse.

43. "Where is your moral compass?"

    I lost it in the woods on a leadership hike.

44. "Those colleagues of yours are breathtaking at multiple levels, and I am not referencing Diamond and Silk."

    How dare you?

45. "STOP TALKING ABOUT YOUR HAIR!"

    My hair has become part of the show, Mom. Accept it.

46. "Jesse, any political arena is fraught with name-calling, as well as wretched accusations by all sorts of players but not by the president of the United States. To normalize this behavior, calling a woman horse face, demeans you and makes you appear crass and awful and also misogynistic, as well as off the mark. Catch yourself before you fall over the edge of what's right, Jesse."

    Trump has gotten you to defend a porn star.

47. "How do we all seek a more civil discourse if you continue to fan the flames?"

    Civil discourse? This is cable news.

48. "You need to be better informed regarding issues of sensible gun control measures."

    Okay, Beto.

49. "Stop making sweeping and generalized and inaccurate statements about what Democrats are seeking. Note those who won the election on this issue, just as reported by Dana."

    Stop. Citing. Dana.

50. "The caravan is real, Jesse. The point others were making was that Trump only stoked caravan fear for election purposes! He hasn't mentioned it since!"

    He has mentioned it since, although they've splintered away into smaller groups to avoid detection at our border. Many more Central American migrants have been contained by Mexico as a result of favorable court rulings on Trump's new asylum policy, a deal struck between the US and Mexico, and stronger enforcement on Mexico's southern border. Don't mess with me, Mom.

51. "Manafort is a criminal."

    Short and sweet.

52. "You do not have the expertise or knowledge to question the special counsel's investigation until you know what they know. Hush, Jesse."

    I knew that they knew there was no collusion. YOU hush.

53. "We are a nation of laws. Please tone down the strident attack on our court system. You end up presenting as lacking a moral compass, honey. We all know you are a Trumpet—you need not scream it."

    When you slip in a "honey," the criticism stings less.

54. "Please bring just a tad more measured caution to your heretofore overly excited support of this president. What you are presenting is really out there, Jesse. And above all, please stay in your wheelhouse. You can have an opinion, but let's acknowledge that you have no legal expertise."

    Acknowledged. Nor financial or scientific expertise.

55. "Do not accept an offer to be chief of staff."

    I couldn't afford the pay cut.

56. "Do not minimize Stone's actions. He used your form and please remember you do not have a law degree."

    I'm detecting some academic snobbery, Mom.

57. "Stop sparring and yelling at Juan, you are making Dana cringe."

    Why must I constantly cater to Dana? What is going on here?

58. "Do your research about border security, you don't sound like you have any facts and you look tired after a vacation."

    Ouch.

59. "Good recovery on the gay march comment."

    Phew. That was a close call.

60. "I'm offended by a great many of your comments."

    Snowflake.

61. "Jesse, you eat too much meat, when we all need to be eating more of a plant-based diet."

    You cook steak literally every time I come home.

62. "You are so misrepresenting these women when you lump, clump and generalize and label them. How does that foster conversation, Jesse?"

    Lumping, clumping, generalizing, and labeling is how I put food on the table.

63. "Please bring back Dana; you have lost the balance."

    I can't anymore.

64. "Stop yelling at Juan."

    If I had a nickel . . .

65. "And you must stop being a Trump mouthpiece. Do not name call and parrot Trump's insults. That is beneath you."

    Is it though?

66. "One positive, your tie knot looks better and you are buttoning your top button."

    I'll take it.

67. "Stop, stop, stop, you're screaming. This President is devious and
dishonest and dishonorable. Of course, he needs to be investigated."
You investigate crimes, not people. Also, nice alliteration.

68. "You are actually throwing out accusations of illegal activity to the Obama
administration. You're in a position to do that? Who are you, CIA?"
No comment.

69. "Jesse, please remember that you have spent months defaming and
delegitimizing and trashing the efficacy and integrity of the Mueller
investigation. So, does it not strike you as just a tad disingenuous and
unethical to now embrace its conclusions with glee? (and smirks!!!)"
It wasn't an investigation, it was a cover-up (smirking).

70. "Dana corrected you about your Michelle Obama statement. You
said, she quote called in a favor. That's slander. And when you make
incorrect statements like that, you are liable."
*Are you an expert in libel law? Did you pass the bar? Do you have a
law degree?*

71. "Nunes was an unethical threat."
A threat to the deep state.

72. "Honey, speak with the English majors in your family. Your analogies
are wretched, and they missed the boat."
*Honey, what's a good analogy for non-published English majors
criticizing published History majors who communicate for a living?*

73. "You do oppose white nationalism hate crime—right?"
Oh my God, Mom.

74. "You are making such sweeping and generalized statements about
The Left. Every show for the last 2 weeks you've railed against The Left
making all sorts of inaccurate and offensive pronouncements. And I
know this to be true because I am certainly Left of You, yet I fiercely

take issue with and disagree with your inaccurate portrait. You are not speaking for me. End It. Please."

The Left is always demanding apologies.

75. "You never had education debt Jesse—you cannot make light—it's paralyzing—it was an incredible gift we were able to provide you."

I wasn't making light, and thank you.

76. "Thank you Dana—she's solving the issue with ideas!"

Well, what the hell am I doing???!!!

77. "Please don't air the altered Pelosi video today or on your show. Don't play Jesse, please."

It's called a meme, Mom.

78. "Stop rewriting history Jesse."

History is always written by the winners.

79. "And you are an expert on big-city government?? Thinking of running for office? Hmmm? San Francisco has a large homeless population in part b/c a person can survive on those streets and not freeze to death in January."

I agree. But stop fetishizing "experts." An "expert" is just some liberal with a degree who provides a quote to a journalist that backs up the predetermined agenda of the story. Notice how the "experts" quoted by journalists never support the conservative side of the argument.

80. "Please respect (and do not trash) Mueller."

You mean the highly conflicted Mueller and his crew of 13 angry Democrat hit men?

81. "What are you angry about? Perhaps you have work burnout?"

Covering Trump can be exhausting.

82. "Could you please seek something redeeming for your 1 more thing—just occasionally?? Your choices are terrifyingly questionable!"

"Something redeeming" is not on-brand.

83. "Talk about using your power! You've single-handedly tanked the economy of the Dominican Republic!"

    I think if was the half dozen mysterious tourist deaths that did that.

84. "Kelly Anne C behaves unethically but will Trump acknowledge that? Betcha nope. That's why I continually find myself aghast—why does he not heed the rules? He is supposed to model ethical behavior and he lies daily. You call it humor and exaggeration? He lies. We taught you never to lie. And when you did, you confessed (b/c you were afraid Santa wouldn't come!)."

    True story. The fear of no Christmas gifts acted as a truth serum.

85. "Honey, let the Dominican Republic alone. You are not helping."

    I smell foul play . . . but would agree to an all-expenses-paid fact-finding junket to help clear the air.

86. "I hope with all of my heart that, as frustrating as you may find your differences, you continue to respect and honor that person to your right—and hear Juan's Voice!!!!!"

    I hear Juan, I just have a hard time listening to him.

87. "I hope your Squad criticism can be just a tad more measured today; how disparagingly you spoke about them yesterday . . . perhaps try not to communicate such disdain for diversity—When you laugh at their perspectives—which are real for them—just as your point of view is real for you, please don't sound like an old white guy who lacks any understanding of otherness. Love you so."

    Love you too.

88. "Words matter—remember? And so do your words, Jesse. Please stop with the blanket and uncritical support of this man. Where is your measured sense of weighing the nuance, the implications, the effects on others? Your stance as a Trumpian warrior at all costs creates such a one-dimensional picture of your thinking. You sound like Flat Stanley."

    Who's Flat Stanley?

89. "I hope you have some time to speak with Dana about the drift that has occurred b/c of her absence; I suggest that you stop the one-upsman business with Juan and that everyone listen with greater care and stop disparaging the other party in such black-and-white rhetoric. I want to listen but I am desperate for some thoughtful balance please. I am not a wretched human because I am a Democrat!"

    Is Dana paying you for each pro-Dana text?

90. "I think you just said something terribly inappropriate but I missed it! Good show!"

    Just the usual inappropriate stuff, nothing to worry about, thanks!

91. "Jesse—stop making sweeping statements about individuals you don't know; YOU are sounding like Joe McCarthy—an individual you clearly need to undertake some research about! Weren't you a history major . . . ??"

    I'm getting the feeling you think I have no idea what I'm talking about.

92. "FOX just sanctioned a private gun seller to advertise on The 5??? It was at 5:45—would you learn about that please / it was creepy and weird."

    Your Connecticut upbringing is glaring.

93. "Jesse, stop pointing."

    Can't stop, won't stop.

94. "Your commentary of late—such as the ease and expediency of making decisions when they are just about you—and the remark you made recently implying the worthlessness of community service . . . signals SURELY a moment for a more value-laden One More Thing—perhaps something that supports a cause that might benefit OTHER PEOPLE vs. your eating cookies . . . a notion to be considered, don't you think?"

    Don't OTHER PEOPLE like eating cookies?

95. "Stop yelling!"

    YOU stop yelling!

96. "I don't think you have any idea how strident and screaming you are!
You are struggling honeybun!"
"Honeybun" makes any Mom text go from average to savage.

97. "Bring it down a notch J; you are translating as wild and too emotional/
whew—please."
Men can't show emotion?

98. "Your colleagues can share perspectives and not scream—listen to
them."
Stop comparing me to Dana. I know that's who you're referring to.

99. "And it is obnoxious and insulting when you say Juan 'go back to
school.' I hope you can find an ounce of grace and apologize to him."
If I apologized to Juan, it would set a very bad precedent.

100. "Sweetheart, I know that what is taking place politically is unsettling—
we get that, even in Peru. But we have actually heard from dearly loved
and deeply respected people in the States that you are behaving as if
'unhinged.' I mom-texted you before leaving to please tone it down and
to stop screaming—that was last week!! please honey, be careful and rein
in your tone and language. If others are communicating the 'unhinged'
message to us when we are out of the country, 'tis something for you to
weigh and think about. Don't make me worry abroad—please."
*I want to know who called me "unhinged." Was it my sister? Because
if it was, that doesn't count.*

101. "You are already smirking—just please don't scream and be sarcastic-
'tis Congress' right and role to investigate."
'Tis? Is this a Christmas bedtime story?

102. "Good show—you weren't 'unhinged!'"
Why do you keep using that word?

103. "Will you be fired for saying 'God damn'?"
No. But sorry.

104. "Devastated by Shepherd Smith's departure! Such sadness and such a loss."

    "Devastated?" The only shows you watch on Fox are The Five *and* Watters' World.

105. "Schiff is not totally corrupt honey—that is a partisan comment and inaccurate."

    I can't believe you're defending Pencil Neck.

106. "The Republicans cannot defend their demon except to argue process."

    "If you quit on the process, you're quitting on the result."—someone

107. "You are screaming, honey? Why?"

    I think you just have the volume turned up too high.

108. "You were hilarious."

    Positive reinforcement!

109. "The Ukrainians DID know $ was being withheld."

    You mean when Biden withheld it?

110. "This is an impeachment investigation. And this is a legitimate process—albeit frustrating for you-"

    That would explain THE SCREAMING!

111. "Pay attention to your sources—QAnon??????"

    Mom, are you Q?

112. "You cannot be a white supremacist—you were born and raised in Philadelphia!"

    The city of BROTHERLY love!

113. "Sweetheart—don't disparage Ukraine and its people. People are people all over the world and to say we don't care about them sounds like what your president said about African countries."

    America First!

114. "Name calling has been a hallmark of our current leader—how about NOT joining the verbal tirade, Jesse. Shifty? Sleepy? Please; you do not need to be a Copycat."

    Mom texts is a verbal tirade.

115. "And Jesse, no one watching television wants to see you pantomime peeing—really I do mean this and I suspect your producers are in sync with me. Once again, you've caused Dana to cringe."

    The show mustn't hinge on Dana's cringe.

116. "The reason that Juan and Dana are part of the larger conversation is because they speak specifically and thoughtfully—what's with your ranting? And what's with a constant disparagement of an investigation!"

    Stop siding with the hard news division!

117. "Honeybun—let Greg be the hysterical ranter—do not join him—speak to content."

    Yes. Please bash Greg. Takes the heat off me. Can I give you his cell?

118. "You are screaming."

    It's your TV volume again

119. "OMG don't watch this process?? You are insulting me and Americans and denigrating a process that is part of our constitutional obligation. This may not be an impeachable offense and any subsequent trial may indeed acquit him but that has no bearing upon our responsibility to understand what has occurred! Whew—cannot keep this tuned in to be ridiculed by Gutfeld or that judge. And your vocabulary has become stuck on that word 'sham.'"

    First, "that judge" is the amazing Judge Jeanine Pirro. Second, I can tell you're beginning to doubt what Adam Schiff is selling. Third, "sham" is a great word.

120. "And for all of the shouting please be assured that despite your WRETCHED political orientation I love you forever!"

    Love you too!

121. "Sweetheart, Greg is being awful to Emily—laughing at ridiculing-mean."

    He can be such a jerk sometimes. Let's talk about him instead.

122. "I want Nunes and Giuliani phone records . . ."

    You've been radicalized.

123. "That grammar usage was really cringe-worthy! 'Her' and Beto?????
    Oh my goodness' Jesse."

    My bad.

124. "Now wouldn't it be important for you to re-enter your commentary
    role with just a 'tad' of measured reflection vs ALL IN FOR TRUMP NO
    MATTER WHAT!!!!! Tucker has a different opinion/ might you?"

    I'm going to be more like Tucker. Is that really what you want, Mom?

125. "Did you behave with a modicum of respect? We were at the film
    1917. . . ."

    Yes. With a modicum. Did you get popcorn?

126. "One more thing . . . don't diminish yourself by referring to Adam
    Schiff with Trump's moniker."

    Shifty or Pencil Neck?

127. "OMG let me pray for you—and I know Nancy Pelosi is already."

    Nancy is definitely NOT praying for Jesse Watters.

128. "Jesse you can not appear on the 5 and not have followed all
    testimony up until 4:59 pm—irresponsible and uninformed—your
    business is the news."

    Can you have Dad text me instead?

129. "Truth and Right Matter."

    Okay, Joe Biden.

130. "Do NOT say that you don't recycle!!!! You MUST and you DO."

    Do I? and do you and Dad even recycle?

131. "Bloomberg/Klobuchar"
     You are bad at this.

132. "FYI—your microphone is too loud and all of your lectures (which Dana has to keep cutting short) were louder than all the other voices noticeably so honeybun = adjust."
     I'm too loud, you mentioned Dana, and called me honeybun. Only thing missing is that I'm not an expert.

133. "And for heaven's sake please stop the media bashing???? You are the media."
     Not the fake news media, though.

134. "No name-calling / labeling—don't pretend to be such a Trumpet that your ethics and kindness are compromised / your mother."
     Are you signing off now?

135. "I do hope you can convey some level of measured thoughtfulness (and humor) about your President's rants and behaviors—he's one scary and powerful loon and I believe we had all better pray!!"
     He's YOUR President too. #powerfulloon

136. "The tearing of Donna's materials is inexcusable, obnoxious and beyond wretched as well as utterly disrespectful behavior. Apologize."
     I'll apologize to Donna for ripping her notes when Pelosi apologizes to Trump for ripping his speech.

137. "Lesbian Muslims aren't a population you need to feature in your commentary."
     Let's agree to disagree.

138. "You were hilarious except for the condom metaphor. . . . I love Geraldo."
     A lot to unpack here.

139. "Please stop with the insults!"
     Crazy Bernie is his name, Mom.

140. "The television just went poof and there was an explosion on the
street! And now you are not on air (and you do look handsome tonight!)
CORONA is a comin'!!!!!!!"
Now who who sounds "unhinged" . . . ?

141. "Stop screaming at Juan!!!!"
NEVER!!!!

142. "Your hair looks great LONGER."
Careful. My ego may grow, too.

143. Your sideburns do appear uneven. . . ."
Aaaaand you've brought me back down.

144. "I count down every show hoping you make it through!!"
Me too!!

145. "At the beginning of this disaster your words were measured and
reasoned and so responsible—now—as you know—this is a situation
where there are different strokes for different folks regarding reopening
through the country ///NY is utterly unique in that half the nation's
deaths are from our state and we MUST follow science and Cuomo in
this region. PLEASE PLEASE don't use your voice to undermine what
must happen in this area for us to resume safely. And, Jesse, NYC will
not be the same city (ever)."
*Did science tell Cuomo to force coronavirus patients into nursing
homes?*

146. "You're not listening—all of your 5 compatriots told you loudly
not to put poop in another's garbage can. Was that your nod to Earth
Day?"
Hahaha!

147. "Please Jesse don't be 'Trump Drunk' - it doesn't suit you."
Better than being "Biden High."

148. "I like your messy room metaphor except that it's TRUMP running from room to room making a mess everywhere he goes. . . ."

One day I'll use a metaphor that you'll like. One day . . .

149. "Thinking that your attack on the Director of the CDC had to do with his appearance—your not liking his 'look' or how he sounded / not with his expertise. Just like your mockery of the newsman who appeared to be sleeping // maybe judgment needs to be suspended here and based instead on a person's competency vs their 'look'?? Thoughts??"

How did my hair look today?

150. "Jesse—are you kidding me??"

Now what?

151. "Trump is utterly consumed by everything Obama and has never stopped accusing, insulting, and fabricating information about the former presidency. Whew!"

What are your thoughts on Obama's birth certificate?

152. "And, darling, you know the drill—Obamagate is T's transparent effort to throw mud and change the subject. . . ."

Is this Mom or Juan texting?

153. "Jesse—'Putin, goin', doin'—Please! Find the 'ing' to your verbs - you sound as if you were raised by wolves."

Greg will be threatened if I sound too smart.

154. "Susan Rice's emails do not raise any new questions—they confirm what we all have known for 3 years—that the intelligence community had rational questions re: Flynn's communications with Kislyak."

Wrong. Newly released documents revealed it was an illegal sting op from the jump.

155. "You are beyond blessed to have a job—keep behaving."

I'm trying.

156. "Random hope . . . Just try to be a tiny tiny bit less obsequious in your Trumpian applause today. Remember you're not on the White House payroll. And you cannot see Dana's eyes. . . ."

    I'm going to have to talk to Dana about this.

157. "Greg has lost weight."

    It's the Peloton.

158. "Jesus. I just ordered a bathing suit from Lands End and I've been on the phone with Laura from Chicago who LOVES YOU. I mean really-ordering a bathing suit!"

    I'm kind of a big deal.

159. "PLEASE Do not go toward attacking others—Tis about pulling together—STAY THERE Jesse/ please—you can do this."

    Sometimes I feel like you don't know me at all.

160. "Your comments about voting by mail are inaccurate and entirely irresponsible—you are giving credence to Trump's undermining of a process and behaving like his pawn."

    While you were quarantining in Maine I filled out your absentee ballot in New York. MAGA Mom!

161. "Listened to the entire Biden speech and Kamala's speech and then listened to you // you were accurate, thoughtful clear and forthright with editorializing—summary so impressive, thought you were David Muir. Then I thought you monitored your team effectively without being obnoxiously dismissive or disrespectful. Wow. Take a bow."

    People compare me to David Muir all the time.

162. "I am getting excited about Kamala Harris. Please teach Tucker how to pronounce her name."

    You're the only one getting excited about Kamala Harris.

163. "You'd better put your tie back on and trim the mullet!"

    Done and done!

164. "Greg does look exactly like a middle school math teacher!"

    He missed his calling.

165. "Thank you, Dana! Wear a mask! And Jesse this virus is rogue—it's
    not something we know about—we are dancing in the dark!! It is a new
    phenomenon—protocols have changed just as you stated but to not
    support mask wearing is characterized by our narcissistic President."

    *Mom. I wear a mask. And just sent you and Dad a bunch from
    Rhoback!*

166. "Jesse—do not denigrate experts—you sound like Trump. And let's
    please remember you are not an expert regarding this virus. Listen and
    hush."

    I will hush if you call it the China virus. Deal?

My mom's texts don't define our relationship, though. I avoid talking
politics with her as much as possible in person. She's a great woman,
wife, mom, grandma, and professional. As she reads this she's probably laughing, learning, and scrutinizing my grammar. Dad, I hope
you're not jealous that you didn't get your own chapter. I got my sense
of humor from you, so this entire book basically is a testament to Stephen Watters. And so everyone knows, I pop my collar because my
dad does. You have him to blame. The provocative pop distinguishes
the protagonist's swagger on camera.* I got my fashion sense from
him as well. And his competitive streak. Oh, my goodness, am I just
like my father?

---

* When comedian Dennis Miller saw me wearing a pink polo shirt with a popped
collar, he said I looked like "gay Dracula." Don't worry, Dennis, I don't bite . . . hard.

CHAPTER FOURTEEN

How I Saved the Primaries

The first time I met Donald Trump was in New Hampshire. The real estate tycoon and *Apprentice* star had, for months, been questioning whether President Barack Obama had been born in America. The "birther" conspiracy was engulfing the far-right sector of the internet, and Trump was leading the charge, demanding that Obama release his long-form birth certificate. He claimed to have dispatched investigators to Hawaii to dig around. Trump had become active on Twitter as well, weighing in on politics or pop culture in his typically provocative style. It was April 2011, and the buzz was that Trump was toying with running for president. In fact, polls showed him ahead in a Republican primary. Personally, I was a fan of *The Apprentice* and saw the birth certificate gossip as an ugly joke for drama. The birther stuff was already out there before Trump lit it on fire. Hillary Clinton's people in Iowa and longtime confidant Sidney Blumenthal began circulating emails about it in 2008. Her pollster Mark Penn even drew up a memo floating a line of attack against Obama's so-called foreign roots. Birtherism was below the belt and crazy. It was a tactic designed to attract controversy, therefore attention, and galvanize anti-Obama sentiment. Politics is a dirty and tough business . . . and people go to great lengths for power. The scurrilous allegations made in nineteenth-century American politics make questioning an opponent's birthplace seem G-rated.

I'd set out to shoot a *Watters' World* on Trump's visit. He was to arrive to a Portsmouth airfield by helicopter, hold a press conference demanding Obama release his birth certificate, visit a diner, and deliver a private speech to a New Hampshire Republican organization. Visiting New Hampshire, an early primary state, showed Trump knew how to play the game. Trump shaking hands at a diner made people think he may actually be taking the game seriously, because the Donald doesn't do diners.

Dozens of reporters were staged in an airplane hangar awaiting Trump's chopper. While we waited, our BlackBerrys began buzzing with breaking news. President Barack Obama, after years of speculation, finally had released his birth certificate. There's no doubt Obama purposely released the document immediately before Trump was to deliver his highly anticipated birther press conference in the Granite State. It was a perfectly timed political masterstroke that would certainly ruin Trump's big moment in New Hampshire when he landed. But that's not what happened at all. When Donald Trump's helicopter landed, he emerged in his dark suit and red tie, strolled up to the microphone, and declared victory.

I just accomplished something that no one else has been able to accomplish. I was just informed while on the helicopter that our president has finally released a birth certificate. I want to look at it, but I hope it's true. That way we can get on to much more important matters. So the press can stop asking me questions. He should have done this a long time ago. Why he did not do it when the Clintons asked for it, and why did he not do it when everybody else was asking for it, I do not know. But I am really honored, frankly, to have played such a big role in hopefully—hopefully getting rid of this issue. We have to look at it. We have to see if it is real. Is it proper? What is on it. I hope it checks out beautifully. I am really proud, I am really honored.

Now we can talk about oil. We can talk about gasoline prices. We can talk about China ripping off this country. We can talk about OPEC doing numbers on us like nobody has ever done before. We can get on to issues and hopefully when I sit down with interviews, people do not start talking about birth certificates like they have been doing.

A smile curled across my face. What I was witnessing was a master class in public relations, taking a sure loss and flipping it on a dime into a win for himself and for the country, while making Obama and the media responsible for "this issue." It was an "issue" that he himself had magnified, but he was "honored" to have proven that Barack Hussein Obama was a constitutionally legitimate president. As if he were a forensics expert, Trump would still have to "look at it," of course, and "hopefully" it was "proper." Of course. It was definitely devious, but I marveled at the theatrics of it, since Trump had mere minutes in the helicopter to reboot the narrative back to his advantage. It was like holing out of the bunker for birdie.

What impressed me next was the way he dominated the throng of reporters. Used to watching Republican politicians cower in fear of reporters and tiptoe around tough issues, Donald Trump commanded the hangar of media like someone who was in charge of them, not the other way around. He dismissed silly questions with, "Are you an intelligent person?"

He cut them off, holding his hand out like a stop sign, effectively quieting questioners. One reporter asked a question and was met with a sharp attack. "You're an Obama fan," declared Trump.

Taken aback, the reporter said, "Why do you say that?"

Without missing a beat Trump said, "Because of the questions you're asking me." It all happened so quickly and naturally that reporters were having a hard time keeping up. Here was this big celebrity presence, speaking concisely and powerfully in a way that Obama never did. Obama spoke for an hour without making headlines, taking forever to spit out a sentence, and pausing in between words with "ahs" and "ums," boring me to tears. But Trump was the polar opposite of Obama. He created a palpable energy that was undeniable.

With the press pushed back on its heels, Trump pivoted from the birth certificate to what he saw as signs of American weakness that needed fast fixing. This was 2011, and the very same themes he touched on that spring day were the ones he won with in 2016.

"I would come down really hard on OPEC," declared Trump. At the time, high gas prices were killing Americans. Five-dollars-a-gallon gasoline in several states was destroying the middle class, and President Obama said he had no control over it. Trump was flabbergasted by this, announcing he'd get on the phone with these OPEC countries and drop the hammer until they increased production. "Look at Saudi Arabia, we protect them . . . look at Kuwait, we handed Kuwait back to the people," Trump explained, referencing our military umbrella protecting the House of Saud and the First Gulf War, where we kicked Saddam out of Kuwait. Barack Obama was unable or unwilling to use American leverage to keep oil prices down, while Trump saw the levers of power just sitting there ready to be pulled. Sure enough, gas prices under President Trump years later averaged just down around $2.50 a gallon. (Domestic oil production is up nearly 40 percent over Obama's last year in office.)

On foreign policy, Trump showcased his reticence toward foreign military adventurism. "Nobody knows what's going on in Libya; it's a total disaster," stated Trump. Obama and Hillary had been convinced by the Europeans and several Arab nations that America needed to intervene in a civil war, on the side of mysterious "rebels," and overthrow Muammar Gaddafi. "The rebels are controlled by Al Qaeda and Iran . . . you could end up with WORSE than Gaddafi." Trump was right. After America "led from behind" and backed a European-led assault on Libya, we lost our ambassador Christopher Stevens and three military contractors to an Al Qaeda attack. Years later, Libya has descended into a failed state, a hotbed of terrorist activity and black market oil and arms trafficking. "We come back and we have nothing," Trump continued, while "wealthy" Arab nations don't pay jack. We should be charging them to do their dirty work, or at least "keep the oil."

"China is ripping us off . . . taking advantage of the United States . . . and manipulating their currency," roared Trump, who was way ahead of the curve when it came to confronting China. "How can we ever be strong if we have other countries making our products?" This was the economic nationalism that won the American rust belt back from the Democrats. Returning the American manufacturing base was always very important to me, ever since Pat Buchanan championed it during the late nineties. Trump said he would place tariffs on Chinese imports to correct their behavior and buy time to build American factories. It was a strategy he used once in office, forcing China to the table and negotiating a new trade deal. "Remember, we have all the cards, and they don't," announced Trump. The current leaders of the country didn't utilize the full power of the American toolbox to strengthen our position in the world. Trump was aghast at this gross incompetence. As I listened, it all sounded so obvious. He bemoaned that a Maytag plant had pulled out of Iowa and left for Mexico. This was someone who truly cared about American jobs.

"The world changes," Trump said. "The world will always change. You cannot just have an idea . . . and say let's go through a wall for it. Sometimes you have to be able to go under the wall, over the wall. I always said, have a goal, work hard, but you have to have a certain flexibility." Trump, in that New Hampshire airport hangar in 2011, was describing his life philosophy. He spoke about the need to sit down and talk to people, people you don't like, and negotiate a deal for America.

I listened intently. It was an inspiring performance. Donald Trump was putting America First. As a patriot, the message resonated with me.

There was a common sense that was woven into his approach to military intervention. There was a knack for leveraging power to achieve results for the workingman. And there was an open-mindedness to negotiation that aimed for action, and wasn't so ideologically intractable.

He finished the event with a rhetorical flourish that would become familiar years later. "I want to make this country *rich* again. I want to make this country *powerful* again. And I want to make this country *respected* again." And with that, he turned and walked into his black stretch limo. When it arrived at the diner, I was there to greet him.

One of the reasons I was in New Hampshire was to ask Trump about his feud with Charles Krauthammer. Trump's statements about "taking the oil" from countries "we liberated" like Iraq, Libya, and Kuwait caused Krauthammer to call Trump "nutty."

"That kind of talk is the stuff you expect from a guy at a bar at closing time with slurred speech," Krauthammer told *The Factor*.

I was waiting when Trump's limo pulled up to a diner in Manchester, New Hampshire. He emerged and immediately was swarmed by a gaggle of reporters. Since I had the size on most of the guys, I got right in there next to Trump and asked him to respond to Krauthammer.

"Charles doesn't like the idea of us taking the oil. . . . We won a war. . . . We spent $1.5 trillion on this war. We lost thousands of soldiers, great military people, and thousands and tens of thousands are wounded. And I say take the oil. Because what's going to happen is Iran is going to take the oil the day we leave." Trump ended up being partially correct. Once Obama pulled out of Iraq, the Iranians began to dominate Iraq's economy, forcing their neighbor into pipeline deals, receiving trucks of oil daily, and even seizing tankers. "Iran's not taking the oil, not if I'm president," declared Trump. "And Charles said 'that's impractical.' So honestly, Charles is a fool."

After I told Trump that Krauthammer had basically called him a "drunk" the other night on *The Factor*, Trump hit back. "They want to get some publicity off my back. . . . I'm leading all the polls. And he's just a sad fool." I felt conflicted because I admired Krauthammer, but also admired Trump. Now these two men who I greatly respected were shredding each other. I felt loyalty to Krauthammer since he was my colleague, but Trump was entitled to hit back. Reconciling these feelings was easy for me. I came to a place that would guide me going forward, when Trump and Fox people sparred. These were grown men. I didn't have to choose a side. Politics and media are a rough business. Trump jawboned Fox analysts to work the refs and get better coverage, and folks on Fox analyzed and reported on Trump because that's their job. I stayed out of the personal drama. I had enough drama of my own making.

Trump strolled into the greasy spoon with his dark cashmere topcoat followed by a pack of photographers. Stunned diners looked up from their plates of bacon while Trump worked the tight space like a pro. Trump wasn't a politician to these people, he was a celebrity. Republicans, Democrats, and those who'd never voted were in awe. He charmed every table in the joint, and moments later was gone, leaving people laughing and gossiping. I immediately realized the celebrity factor would supercharge his campaign if he decided to run. Interviewing diners afterward, I asked a woman what it was like to meet Trump. "I accidentally spilled syrup on his nice coat," confessed a gray-haired woman with her husband. "He looked at me, wiped it off, smiled, and said, 'You're fired!'"

She was still giddy from the interaction, blushing actually. "I told him I'm sorry. He was so nice about it." Her husband leaned over to me and said under his breath, "I've been married to her for fifty years and that's the first time I've ever heard her admit she was wrong. If he runs, that man *definitely* has my vote."

In summer 2015, Hillary Clinton and Jeb Bush were considered the two front-runners for their parties' nominations. The two most boring politicians in America. Until Trump came down the escalator. At his side was Melania, who was hard to miss. People thought he was using the announcement as leverage for *Celebrity Apprentice* salary renegotiations, and I myself was suspicious. I felt burned when he decided not to run in 2012. I didn't want to get burned again. But that moment at Trump Tower ignited something real. Nobody knew exactly what it was at the time, but the people responded to it. The media missed it completely, chasing each politically incorrect yet honest phrase around and around until news cycles were filled with punch-drunk pundits filling the airwaves with only one name: Donald Trump. Under the radar, Trump was forming a bond with the American people that would never be broken. That bond with his base grew stronger after each attack. It became unbreakable. It's this connection that's given Trump the blessing and confidence to fight some of the most challenging forces in American political history. Power comes from the people, and Trump recognized that.

I first noticed the Trump effect at the Iowa State Fair that summer. The fair is a staple of presidential politics. Politicians visit, act like real people, press the flesh, and eat fried butter on a stick without gagging. It's good old Americana. Candidates from both parties wear jeans, look casual, and try to generate excitement while walking around aimlessly past food booths and carnival games. Some draw small crowds, and others fail to get noticed. Donald Trump did it a little differently. He landed his helicopter smack dab in the middle of the state fair, walked out wearing a five-thousand-dollar suit, and took a huge bite of pork chop on a stick. Next thing you know, he starts giving little kids rides in his helicopter, buzzing above the grounds, the crowd in disbelief. And just like that, Trump wins the fair. They're still talking about it in Iowa.

Soon after, Trump was in the exact opposite environment of the Iowa State Fair: the US Open in New York. I happened to be at the tennis tournament, too, shooting a package for *Watters' World*, now an hour-long weekend show. A friend had a suite next to Trump's so I knocked on the door. A big tall security guy opened it and looked at me. "It's Jesse Watters with Fox News, can you tell Mr. Trump I just wanted to introduce myself." The security guy, Keith Schiller, looked me up and down, said nothing, and closed the door. I had no idea if he was letting Trump know I was outside or I'd been blown off. I waited a second and the door swung open.

"Jesse!" thundered Trump. "The superstar! Get in here! You're great. I want you to meet Melania."

He was a big presence, but he made me feel relaxed and right at home in his suite. Melania was on the couch. She stood graciously and gave her hand to me to shake. They both shared how much their son Barron enjoyed *Watters' World*.

"He waits up for the end of *The Factor* just to watch your segments," said Trump. I looked around and noticed a tray of sliders and pigs in a blanket. It appeared the pork-chop-on-a-stick routine wasn't a show . . . the billionaire actually liked fair food.

"Let's take a picture, get over here." He led me to the suite's seats looking onto the court at Arthur Ashe Stadium and waved to the crowd. He got a nice reception, and we took some pictures together.

"Let's take a look," he said, asking to see my phone. "No good. Bad lighting. Let's go back inside." He was right. The lighting *was* bad.

We took another picture inside and he inspected it again. "Much better. We want to look good, right, Jesse?" We chatted for a few moments more, and he thanked me for dropping by. "If there's anything I can do for you, let me know," he offered. I thanked him and left the suite. In the car home I looked at the picture. Trump looked good, but I looked terrible. Never stand next to a guy who's wearing a five-thousand-dollar suit. Especially when you're wearing shorts and a polo shirt. Advantage Trump.

Trump immediately put himself in the center of the ring when he ran in the GOP primary. In fact, before the first primary debate, he was already positioning himself at the presidential level. After the San Bernardino, California, terrorist attack, President Obama refused to blame radical Islam, wouldn't even say that phrase, and blamed guns instead. Trump came out and called for a Muslim ban and said if more citizens were armed, bullets would have been going the *other* direction, putting the terrorists down much sooner. The Second Amendment argument was common sense. The Muslim ban was a little dicey, and later transformed into a travel ban for a handful of Muslim countries with terrorism problems. But the sentiment hit home for most people. America had a problem with radical Islamic terrorists, and wasn't screening travelers strictly enough from hot-spot countries. The San Bernardino terrorists were allowed to pass through customs, when a cursory look at their social media showed jihadist rhetoric that should have been flagged.

Trump's bold, patriotic proposals were in direct contrast with Obama's, and catapulted Trump over his Republican rivals into a direct face-off with the incumbent Democrat president. Grabbing command of the national conversation early and aggressively, Trump was staking out powerful populist positions and causing everyone else (the media, Republicans, and Democrats) to react to *him*. It galvanized a lot of regular Americans, inspired conservatives, and drove the Left crazy. It also attracted so-called working-class Reagan Democrats. This strategy worked to his advantage brilliantly in 2016.

I sat down for my first interview with Donald Trump in January 2016. He squeezed me in before a rally in Iowa. Heading into the venue, I noticed scores of supporters lined up outside in below freezing temps. It's not easy to draw big crowds in Iowa, but he'd done it. We set up the cameras in an office down the hall from the main stage and waited. When Trump arrived he buttered me up. "Jesse, you'd be great on *Celebrity Apprentice*. You're quick. That's what it takes. Quickness. You have to be quick on your feet," he explained, snapping his fingers. I agreed, and spouted out something that made little sense, immediately casting doubt on how quick I was.

The way we'd arranged the chairs and camera angles was not to

Trump's liking. I had set up the shot to capture "my good side," which is my right. Trump had "a good side," too, apparently, also his right. But the camera was shooting him from the left. He let his staff know, but it was too late to reconfigure the shot. Advantage Watters.

My goal for the interview was to shed light on Trump as a person, not as an aspiring politician.

WATTERS: How did you meet Melania? Was it love at first sight?
TRUMP: I was at a party and I saw this very beautiful woman and I said boy would I like to get that phone number. It wasn't easy, took me about five weeks.

Melania really played hard to get. It's all about the thrill of the chase, isn't it?

WATTERS: Did you get on one knee when you proposed?
TRUMP: No, but it was a hard phone number to get.

Trump still seemed to be stewing over how long it took to land Melania. Also, I've always wondered about Trump saying he didn't get down on one knee. Would admitting it make him appear weak? Or does one not get down on one knee for one's third proposal? Was Trump still perturbed Melania played so hard to get that he didn't kneel? Was it a power move? I wisely decided not to follow up.

WATTERS: If you're fortunate enough to win, you will be moving into the White House. That's downsizing for you. Have you given that any thought, moving into the White House?
TRUMP: Well, you know, it's a special place. I mean, look what it represents. It is quite a bit smaller but these are minor details.

Not just "smaller," but "*quite a bit* smaller."

WATTERS: President Obama returned the Churchill bust when he came into office. Are you going to get that back from Great Britain?

TRUMP: I would love to have Churchill's bust back in the White House. He was a great, great man.

Busts need to be respected again.

WATTERS: Also symbolic, if you're fortunate enough to be in the White House . . . The first state dinner. Who are you going to invite?

TRUMP: You and Bill [O'Reilly] and the gang, right? We have to have the gang, have to get front row, center, probably not the Chinese to the first dinner.

WATTERS: Mexico maybe?

TRUMP: Probably not. We won't invite too many of the countries that are ripping us off, of which there are many, but you'll certainly be there.

Never received my state dinner invitation.

WATTERS: [What do you] eat for breakfast?

TRUMP: My big thing is dinner. Breakfast, Jesse, if I can avoid them, I'm very happy to do that.

WATTERS: You don't like bacon?

TRUMP: I like bacon and eggs. I do, if I have it, I like bacon, eggs, cereals, different cereals.

WATTERS: What kind of cereals?

TRUMP: Made in the USA. Has to be made in the USA, the cornflake-type stuff. Raisin bran, right out of the fields of Iowa.

It dawned on me that Trump was a savvier politician than he was making himself out to be. Turned a question about breakfast into a shout-out to Iowa farmers.

WATTERS: You getting exercise on the campaign trail?

TRUMP: It's a lot when you go from here to there and it's walking and it's fast walking and making speeches in front of—you know, tens of thousands of people.

"Going from here to there" and "making speeches" is the new CrossFit.

WATTERS: You played golf with President Clinton. What was that like?

TRUMP: I enjoyed it. I mean we had probably a couple of rounds over the years.

WATTERS: Does he have a good swing?

TRUMP: It's fine. It's really fine. He gets criticized. He actually plays very nicely.

"He gets criticized" but "actually plays pretty nicely," aka "I'm much better than he is."

WATTERS: You seem like a great guy to watch the game with but you don't drink.

TRUMP: I'm not a drinker.

WATTERS: Why is that?

TRUMP: I never really wanted to drink. I never acquired the taste, never liked the taste. I've seen instances, even within my own family, where people drink too much and it's not a good thing, and I don't like it. So I've stayed away from it. I don't really judge and you know, people like to do it but you have to do it in moderation. For me it's good, not drinking, I don't have to worry about moderation.

I'm glad Trump doesn't drink. More for me.

WATTERS: Have you ever smoked weed?

TRUMP: I have not. I would tell you one hundred percent because everyone else seems to admit it. Almost like, it's almost like hey it's a sign. No, I have never smoked a cigarette, either.

Complete opposite of Obama.

WATTERS: Do you have time to watch TV anymore? Are you binge-watching anything?

TRUMP: I watch *Watters' World*.

This guy was good. After a few more questions, we said good-bye, and Trump walked backstage. The venue was in the middle-of-nowhere, Iowa, but it was packed to the rafters. He hit his marks on China, trade, immigration, and ISIS. Unhappy with the event's sound technician, he announced he was refusing to pay. The crowd ate it up. When I flew back to Fox and screened the interview, I noticed something. Trump's shot was so tight that the Trump sign behind him was cut off. The word "RUMP" appeared behind him in the entire interview. Perhaps that's why I never got that state dinner invite.

CHAPTER FIFTEEN

How I Saved 2016

Trump blitzkrieged through the primary debates with hard-core economic nationalism and a potent dose of gut-busting middle school ridicule. It left seasoned politicians shaking their heads in disbelief. This wasn't supposed to happen. The pugnaciousness astounded political analysts. Trump was freestyling and shattering decorum, dunking on moderators, the Republican National Committee, the media, his opponents—anyone who got in his path. He tapped into a powerful vein in America. People were sick of Washington politicians boring them with cheap talk and platitudes and never taking real action on issues that affected their lives. Trump looked hungry. He was sharp, competitive, and had a clear, bold vision for where he wanted to take the country on trade, taxes, immigration, and foreign policy. It was time to put America first. More specifically, the people of America first. The people responded to Trump's message and especially his attitude. Attitude is everything in politics. Trump was audacious, and Americans responded emotionally, on both sides. He positioned himself as an avenger for the forgotten men and women of this country, who dismissed his transgressions and embellishments because he put them first, unlike the selfish, insincere ruling class whose greedy, globalist policies had laid waste to the once-proud working-class heartland.

The world has changed a lot since America bounded into Iraq, looking for WMDs and seeking to overthrow Saddam. I understood the rationale for the war post-9/11. The intelligence was wrong, though. Perhaps we got duped by sources, didn't have it nailed down, or were going in regardless. We'll never fully know. After the swift military victory, we didn't win the peace, Iran stepped in, and chaos reigned for years. Not until General David Petraeus's troop surge strategy finally took hold did Iraq start to settle down. Right as that happened, though, Obama won office and failed to cut a deal with the Iraqi leadership. We pulled out rashly and left a vacuum for ISIS to form, creating another bloody chapter of terror. But looking back, since most of the 9/11 hijackers were Saudi, knocking off Saddam and placing 150,000 soldiers in the heart of the Mideast was a blunt message to the Saudi royal family: Watch it, or you could be next.

America's relationship with Saudi Arabia makes sense when you zoom out. Why does America protect the Saudi royal family? Geopolitical analyst Peter Zeihan has explained eloquently why America has policed the world since World War II and why our role is now changing. After we fought simultaneously on two fronts, soundly defeating Germany and Japan, America could have taken the spoils and carved up the world however we wanted. European colonies could have been ours. Imperial Japan's Pacific playground could have been ours. We could have added states and territories on every continent. America would have controlled every single supply chain worldwide and there was nothing these broke and defeated powers could have done about it. But because of our geography, we didn't.

America, situated perfectly between two oceans, and facing no real threat of invasion from our neighbors, is in a unique position. Instead of a large standing army, we project power through our navy. Our complete dominance on the water allows America to stage attacks at the time and place of our choosing all over the world. Our carrier groups can move marines and aircraft to an enemy's shores, not to mention short-range missiles, and end a dispute with precision, speed, and overwhelming power. America doesn't fight wars on our shores;

we fight them on our enemies'. But if we had annexed large swaths of imperial holdings after World War II, fielding standing armies to administer resource production and maintain order among hostile locals would have been a massive undertaking. The money and manpower would have soaked America dry, not to mention the inevitable uprisings that would ensue. So instead, America arranged a world order based on naval supremacy, and free trade, in exchange for an alliance system to defeat the other new superpower, the Soviet Union.

In order for the exhausted European and Pacific powers to recover economically, America gave them free access to the biggest consumer market in the world: the United States. All nations, who were aligned with the Americans against the Soviet Union, were granted access to sell their goods to American consumers without tariffs. America would also guarantee the free flow of goods around the world with our dominant navy. This was called free trade. America would protect the sea-lanes for oil tankers to go from Saudi Arabia to Europe, and from Saudi Arabia to Japan. The free flow of oil on the world market, and the free flow of tariff-free imports into the American market, in exchange for military alliances against the communists, was how America ran the world during the Cold War. We used basing in Europe and NATO to thwart Soviet aggression in the West, and basing in Japan and later South Korea to contain Soviet aggression in the East. Proxy wars were fought to maintain the order, and America policed the world while the world got rich. Finally, Reagan's robust defense spending and confrontational approach to communism triggered the Soviet Union's collapse, and America won the Cold War. But what about the order we had created? Was it still useful once the Cold War was over? Not as much.

As America became energy independent and Russia posed less of a mortal threat, America felt less inclined to station troops in Europe, the Mideast, and Asia. America also didn't like allowing other nations to dump cheap duty-free goods into our market while they threw up pricy tariffs on our exports—while we floated a navy that guaranteed everyone's security and trade. That deal only made sense in exchange for their alliance against Soviet communism. With that threat gone, and these nations enriched from years of free trade and free protection from the American security blanket, what sense did it make for us to keep letting them keep a trade advantage? Does that phrase sound familiar? Enter Donald Trump. The businessman wasn't ideologically wedded to the old ways of Washington, and he instinctively saw the old order as a business deal that needed to be redone.

What are we getting for this? he asked.

NATO countries weren't paying their fair share of security costs but were slapping massive tariffs on our exports. We were paying a fortune to protect wealthy Saudi Arabia, a country with no real military, but the royal family was asking us to do their dirty work in Iraq and Syria while we were footing the bill. The rise of China had been made entirely possible through America's free trade order, but the middle kingdom was stealing our intellectual property, devaluing their currency, dumping cheap products, stealing our factories, and slipping fentanyl into our heartland, addicting our workers.

Trump set out to rebalance the world order in America's favor post–Cold War. It's been a wild ride. Republicans and Democrats will both zigzag toward this new order, which Peter Zeihan explains could actually be *disorder*. As America remains energy independent from the shale revolution, and our primary trade envelope continues to be in North and South America, other countries will fight to secure their own energy and natural resource supply chains, with America no longer securing the free flow of oil and goods throughout the world. The pandemic has accelerated this de-globalization. America will become more isolationist and remain wealthy, self-sufficient, and militarily superior. While the world returns to regional competitions, America will sit back and enjoy life between two oceans. The United States still has a global military but it no longer has global commitments. So don't mess with us. Without fear of fallout, when attacked, America can strike back in wildly unpredictable and powerful ways.

After seizing the nomination, Trump entered the summer of 2016 with some challenges. The RNC didn't really know what to do with him, donors were bewildered, and Trump's campaign was bare-bones. A small but feisty never-Trump movement within the GOP was irritating the nominee and wouldn't go away. But Hillary had her own problems. She had some difficulty putting down Bernie Sanders, even with behind-the-scenes help from the Democratic National Committee. The party was trying to paper over their ideological divide by ignoring it. Since Hillary was expected to win, a lackadaisical attitude took hold. They figured they could patch things up after November. The email scandal was also dragging on. Hillary and her lawyers had sat down with a team of FBI investigators during a Saturday in June, and her husband was caught chatting up the attorney general on a tarmac. Loretta Lynch was overseeing the investigation, so that didn't look good.

When FBI director James Comey announced a press conference on July 5, 2016, the political world held its breath. Most people expected Hillary to become the first female president. Would the FBI indict her and destroy her chance of making history? That answer we soon found out was no. Comey announced that Clinton was "reckless" and broke the law for setting up a secret server in her basement and mishandling classified information. But he gave her a pass, saying he would have to prove that she "intentionally" broke the law, and no prosecutor would take that on. Not only was that a misinterpretation of the statute, but many prosecutors had put people behind bars for doing exactly what Clinton had done on a much smaller scale. Democrats were ecstatic. Republicans fumed. This turned into an inflection point in the campaign that, in a strange way, helped Trump. The nominee began running against "a rigged system." With two sets of rules, for insiders and outsiders, Trump the outsider was representing millions of Americans who felt "outside" the system. The system where financial, social, and political connections determined your fate had left many people feeling forgotten, especially in the rust belt. Americans had lost control of their lives; while powerful forces on the coasts had reshaped the economy, those in the middle felt left out and left behind. The political establishment, the Clintons and Bushes and Bidens, had overseen the loss of factories, the importation of cheap labor, and the infusion of political correctness that strangled their true voices. The sweetheart deal given to Clinton was rubbing it in their eye. The Clintons got away with everything while the country suffered. Trump seized on this sentiment and used it as a rallying cry. "Lock her up!" folks chanted at rallies. It was a rowdy slogan, half in jest, perhaps not, that created a new dynamic in the race. Trump and his voters weren't just running against Hillary, they were running against everyone: the crooked FBI, the biased RNC, open borders, Wall Street, censor-happy big tech, the trigger-happy foreign policy establishment, the China-loving power brokers, the United Nations. . . . It was Trump against the world, and people love an underdog.

Trump started August down in the polls. So, Trump did what Trump does best: fired people and got to work. Paul Manafort got canned, and Trump hired some assassins. Steve Bannon, Dave Bossie, and Kellyanne Conway were brought on board, and Trump started working from a teleprompter. Republicans used to mock Obama for reading from a prompter, but Trump on a teleprompter was a beautiful thing. He began to hone his message and pound slogans like "America First," "Build the Wall," and "Make America Great Again." There was still the signature riffing, but the speeches were more tightly focused. He outworked Hillary all August, while she basically took the month off, doing sparse, low-key events every now and then in between Hamptons fund-raisers.

On September 11, 2016, Hillary was leaving a Ground Zero ceremony when she fainted. You'd faint, too, if you were married to Bill, I suppose, but it was caught on camera. Agents stuffing a limp, wobbly-kneed Clinton into a van was not a good look, especially for a candidate whose nasty, unexplained cough had been nagging her for weeks. Trump had been hammering Hillary for lacking the "strength and stamina" to be commander in chief, and here she was proving his point. It was early September and Trump's numbers had rebounded.

He and Clinton were basically tied going into the first debate.

Trump had a decent first debate, acted "presidential," but the media story line afterward was that he called a Latina beauty pageant contestant fat. It's true that when you're running a beauty pageant, and a contestant shows up overweight, that's a problem. But most presidential candidates don't have a history of hosting beauty pageants, so issues like this don't ever arise. I spoke to Trump after the debate in the "spin room," and he complained that his microphone wasn't working properly. It actually *wasn't* working properly, and the debate commission admitted the audio was "faulty." It was not the last time Trump would be stung by the debate commission.

Days before the second debate, the *Access Hollywood* tape dropped. Not good. Trump was on a hot mic with Billy Bush talking dirty about women. The campaign would later refer to it as "locker room talk." Trump issued a rare apology, while the RNC headed for the hills, and the media began writing his political obituary. But Trump doubled down. He invited every single one of Bill Clinton's alleged sexual assault victims to the next debate. He lined them up at a table (it was a pretty long table) and held a press conference. Yeah, he'd said something about women, but Bill Clinton had actually *done* some things, and got away with it. It was a total spectacle. Then Trump tried to bring the women into the debate hall and sit them across from Bill Clinton himself. The debate commission put a firm stop to that. The second debate performance was Trump's best. He methodically took Hillary apart and delivered the line of the night: If I were president "you'd be in jail." It was a drop-the-mic moment that couldn't have been scripted better. But something strange happened. Trump's great performance didn't show up in the polls. Hillary was up double digits in most polls, and it didn't make sense at all.

While Trump outhustled Hillary on the campaign trail, a series of events converged in late October to shift the race. James O'Keefe's hidden camera videos exposed Democrats bragging about conducting voter fraud. Obamacare premiums skyrocketed in several states. WikiLeaks dropped DNC emails showing Hillary took a "public" and "private" position on issues. Lastly, Clinton's State Department emails were found on convicted sex offender Anthony Weiner's laptop. I feel sorry for the FBI agent who had to inspect that device.* At the final debate in Las Vegas, moderator Chris Wallace asked both candidates if they'd accept the results of the election. Always one to be litigious, Trump said he'd wait and see how everything shook out. Hillary proclaimed not accepting the results of the election was tantamount to a "constitutional crisis."

On election night, Fox expected the race to be called early and for Clinton to be the winner. Exit polls predicted a good night for Democrats. Hillary, as she wrote in her book *What Happened*, actually took a nap that evening to rest up. She awoke to a nightmare. She'd slept through Trump winning Florida, North Carolina, and Ohio. I was watching the returns at Del Frisco's Steakhouse, across from Fox, with some friends. It was a rowdy group, cheering every time Trump won a state. When Trump broke through the "blue wall," I let out a holler. Out of nowhere, a young woman threw a drink right in my face. She bolted from the bar, and a member of my party confronted her on the street while she ducked into a taxi. She was a Clinton supporter who couldn't take "what happened." It was a sign of things to come. Things were about to get nasty in America.

Although Hillary called Trump to concede the next day, few Democrats accepted the results. Hillary accused Trump of colluding with

---

* Hopefully he wore gloves.

the Russians to interfere in the election, and the rest of the media followed suit. These false accusations dominated the news cycle. Several
Democrats claimed the election was hijacked and challenged the elec-
tors. Others labeled Trump an "illegitimate" president and boycotted
his inauguration. In their blind rage, liberals firebombed a limo at the
inauguration, which was later found to be owned by a Muslim immigrant. Oops. Celebrities expressed interest in "bombing" the White
House and "the Resistance" sprouted up into a hard-core anti-Trump
movement. I'd covered the rallies, and the only thing they were resisting was soap.

Trump was fresh off inauguration, so why not nab an interview? I
text Hope Hicks, his gatekeeper. After some back-and-forth, we nail
down the details. The president will be holding an afternoon rally
at the Bridgestone Arena in Nashville, Tennessee. The plan is for a
ten- to twenty-minute sit-down interview with POTUS in a backstage
holding room before his speech.

I let the bosses know immediately, because at this point, I'm shooting two packages a week for *The Factor* and at least one a week for my
Watters' World weekend show, so we have to coordinate scheduling. A
few years prior, before my weekend show, I was only doing one package a week until an executive called me up and said, "Watters, we're
going to put you on the air *twice* a week now. The audience likes you.
I can't figure out why, but they do." Years later, and we're still trying
to figure that out.

The key to balancing my weekend show with *The Factor* was this:
The Factor was number one. My weekend show was not. So when
I told Bill O'Reilly I was interviewing President Trump, instead of
congratulating me, he piggybacked my shoot. "Watters, before you
sit down with him, interview everyone lined up outside the arena, and
we'll turn around a package."

Whereas most hosts, before the first presidential interview of their
career, would be sitting inside calmly preparing, I ran myself ragged

through throngs of "proud deplorables" waiting outside, asking questions and taking selfies. One key to my success was doing what I was told.*

After an hour, Secret Service let me into the arena, and I found my way back to the interview site. Standing outside were Steve Bannon and Reince Priebus. I shook hands and started chatting with Bannon, whom I'd been friendly with for years. Brilliant guy, but he didn't have any time for the likes of me anymore. He was focused on defeating China's naval expansion. I was focused on fixing my makeup.

The room was ready. Flags were positioned perfectly in the background, the presidential water glass was prepared, two chairs faced each other, and the lighting was set. Secret Service swept the space. We got the two-minute warning. Then suddenly, the president of the United States thundered into the room.

"Jesse! How're we doing?!" His voice was booming, huge frame, larger than life.

He shook my hand hard as hell, patted me on the shoulder, and said, "You see how many people are outside? Maybe thirty, forty, fifty thousand wrapped around the block!" (Realistically, there were probably fifteen thousand people lined up outside. I'd just been out there. But who cares? I went with it.) "At least!" I responded, laughing.

Next thing I know, someone hands him a canister, and he beelines for a mirror. "Whooooooosh!" The president whips his arm in a circular motion around his head, creating an aerosol halo of hair spray above the infamous blond dome. Everyone just stood and watched. He looked very focused.

Son-in-law Jared Kushner followed him into the room. I'd never met him before. He's tall, skinny tie, patricianly, in control. He shook my hand and said gently, "I just want to thank you for everything you've done for my family." A month earlier, a nasty liberal professor

---

* Most of the time.

had accosted Ivanka on a commercial flight in front of her children. I'd ambushed the professor outside his apartment building the next week. Like a coward, he wouldn't apologize. Instead he put a hood over his head and scrambled back inside like a celebrity felon leaving a courthouse. "No problem, Jared," I said.

I sat down across from the president, and he started boasting about his numbers. "You see my approval rating, Jesse? Fantastic. Through the roof!" He was a month into his first term, and the Real Clear Politics average had him around 48 percent.

We knocked out the interview and took some pictures afterward. "Want to hitch a ride on Air Force One with us back to DC?" the president asked. Um, let me think about that for a second. "YEAH!" So after his rally we raced onto a press van and motorcaded to the airport.

Climbing onto the jumbo jet was like a lucid dream. I had sticky fingers because everything on board had the Air Force One logo emblazoned on it. Very hard to resist. Our Fox News crew was seated in a spacious middle section with six plush seats while the rest of the traveling press corps was stuck in the back in what appeared to be coach. The only other mainstream media guy seated in the special section with me was Mark Halperin, then of NBC News. He was quiet and probably didn't remember this, but I'd interviewed with him when he was at ABC News before I'd joined Fox. During the interview, he'd sniffed out that I was a conservative. As the interview ended (without an offer) he declared with authority, "It's our job to hold the powerful accountable." Halperin later gained a reputation for holding other things.

Once again, Hope Hicks delivered. After wheels up, she summoned us quickly to the executive suite on Air Force One, where POTUS was watching Fox News and holding court around a freshly lacquered boardroom table. DHS secretary General John Kelly was frowning, while Tennessee congresswoman Marsha Blackburn was enjoying herself. My crew flipped the camera on, and Trump welcomed me and showed off the room for a few moments. I went in for a joke: "Now that *you're* president, they'll have to rename it 'Hair Force One.'" The president didn't find it that funny. He shook my hand, slapped my back, and shoved me out toward the door where I came from.

Later in the flight, POTUS walked back to my section. The cameras were turned off. He dominated the room and made everyone laugh. At one point I teasingly asked, "Mr. President, why were you playing N-SYNC at your rally?" It seemed a little off-brand, so I was curious. "I love N-SYNC, Jesse. Lance Bass is *the man*." Lance Bass? I thought for a minute. Is he thinking of the same Lance Bass I'm thinking of? The president continued. "I was at an event in Manhattan a little while ago. There was this woman. A model. She was with some guy from the Jets. Football player. Like an Adonis. All of sudden, Lance Bass walks by and this girl leaves the NFL player and starts chasing after Lance Bass! I gotta tell you. Lance Bass gets tail!" Not the kind of tail he's thinking of. Hope and I looked at each other, and I spoke up. "Uh, Mr. President, Lance Bass is gay."

Silence for a second. The president looked at me. "He is?!" Genuinely surprised. Everyone started laughing. "All right, Jesse. I'm going to go back and talk to the failing *New York Times*. I'll see you later."

I began at *The Five* in April 2017. Greg Gutfeld says he hated me at first because he'd watched my *Watters' World* segments. Can you blame him? But I won him over with my charm and quick wit. I wasn't too witty, though. Can't have Gutfeld thinking I'm a threat to his brand. He's very territorial, and I respect my elders. The best part of working with Gutfeld isn't listening to his sharp takes on air; it's listening to his provocative ramblings in the commercial breaks. Here is just a small random sample of direct quotes uttered by Gutfeld between segments.

Charity sucks. It's the best thing you'll ever do, and they get all the money—GG

The cheapest form of phone sex is to call Victoria's Secret and ask
   them to go through the catalog with you—GG
If you're going to kill your spouse, take them hiking—GG
When you buy drugs on a Friday you can't do them all that night. You
   have to save some for Sunday brunch—GG
I fucking hate the ocean—GG

    Dana Perino was harder to win over than Greg. It took me a while
to figure her out. But I finally did. Dana has a secret life. She's a de-
generate gambler. I stumbled into a high-stakes card game in Hell's
Kitchen after midnight and there was Dana. Wired, eyes bloodshot,
cigarette dangling from her lip, blouse unbuttoned, chips stacked up,
surrounded by a table of tattooed, sweaty outcasts. We locked gazes
across the smoke-filled room and had an immediate and unspoken understanding. Dana wasn't the innocent farm girl from Wyoming supporting sensible solutions to complicated policy problems. That was
just what she wanted you to see. The real Dana plays for keeps. She
needs her fix. She doesn't care who you are or where you're from . . .
she's there to take everything you have. I backed away from the table
and as I left the room she did something that I'll never forget. She took
her cigarette and put it out on the arm of the man bringing her scotch.
As the man's flesh burned, his eyes watered, but he didn't flinch. He
accepted it. Dana owned this guy. She owned the room. She owned
the table. It was all about respect. This was a power move that sent
chills down my spine. Dana is cold as ice. This is a warning to everyone. Never cross her.
    We had our DNA tested on *The Five* and Juan and I have more
in common than you think. It turns out I'm 99.9 percent European
(mostly the British Isles) and .1 percent sub-Saharan African. I'm
actually more black than Liz Warren is Native American. Does this
make me a black Trump supporter? Doubt it. But besides our shared
racial background, Juan and I share another similarity: a love for

tequila. Sometimes I think Republicans and Democrats would get along better if they drank together, like the good ol' days. Or it could lead to a duel. Either way, if Juan and I can get together, then Ted Cruz and AOC should be able to get together. Maybe.

Co-host Kimberly Guilfoyle and I had a great run before she left to join the Trump team. I miss her kicking me under the table. When KG tells you to shut up, you listen. Kimberly whispers a lot. It all sounds very important, but I can never hear what she's saying. I nod in agreement, though. It definitely sounds like something I would agree with. I think. I'll never forget her advice to me when I joined *The Five*: "Don't screw this up, Watters."

Soon after joining *The Five* I was invited with a small group to have dinner at the White House. Upon our arrival, the president took us up to show us the Lincoln Bedroom. It wasn't the nineties anymore, so we didn't have to donate anything. Standing over the Gettysburg Address, the president said, "Some people say my Twitter account is the modern-day equivalent of the Gettysburg Address." I laughed. "Some people" was definitely him.

President Trump was a gracious host and gave us a short tour, expounding on the history of the White House. Walking down the stairs lined with official portraits of past presidents, President Trump said, "I'm going to have these moved around. Bush has too prominent a placement." He claimed the Clintons smuggled the White House china back to Chappaqua and joked that the Monet given to the White House by the Kennedys must be worth at least $20 million by now. "That may find its way to Mar-a-Lago when my term is up." Everyone howled.

We all sat down for dinner and talked for hours. Actually, I listened. Trump was on a roll, regaling us with campaign stories, gossip, and policy talk. The dinner was off the record, but I'll just share this. During dinner Melania graced us with her presence. She entered the room, and we all stood. The president lit up and made a big deal of the first lady's arrival. I was seated next to the president, so when I stood, Melania was right there. How do you say hello to the first lady? I wondered. She wasn't royalty, so I wasn't supposed to bow or kiss her hand. My mind was racing. There must be some sort of protocol? So I panicked and went in for a kiss. Yes. I approached Melania and put my hands on her side and leaned in to kiss her cheek. She accepted but then, in a moment of confusion, I went in for a kiss on the opposite cheek. It was a European greeting and wasn't Melania from Slovenia? But as I shifted back and dipped in again for the other cheek, she pulled away. Denied. This was awkward. I sheepishly stepped back as the president insisted she join us for dinner. "No, thank you," she demurred, smiling as she elegantly left the room. We all sat back down and I had to quickly change the subject to take attention away from what had happened. "What do you think Hillary's up to right now, Mr. President?" I asked.

"Crooked? What's she doing now? She's not being president." Everyone laughed.

Later that week, news broke that I had dinner with the president. CNN's Jake Tapper tweeted, "So you're the president of the United States of America. You can dine with literally anyone you want to. Titans of industry. Geniuses of the arts. Tech wizards changing everything. World leaders and humanitarian saints." He had a point. But if I were president, I'd want to dine with me, too. I make a great dinner guest, although the first lady may disagree.

CHAPTER SIXTEEN

How I Saved the Election

Joe Biden was on the clear path to securing the Democrat nomination by mid-spring. It was not an inspiring performance. Joe put on mediocre showings on the campaign trail, on the fund-raising circuit, and during the debates. Joe closed his first major speech in Iowa with his back to a listless crowd, uttering, "Look me over, if you don't like what you see, vote for the other guy." There was no fire in the belly, not even a spark. Many wondered if Joe was suffering from cognitive decline.

He announced he was running for Senate and forgot what year it was. His stories on the stump left people scratching their heads. Describing young black kids rubbing his leg hair during his stint lifeguarding, Biden declared, "I love kids jumping on my lap." This caught people's attention because Joe was notorious for being too touchy-feely with women and children. A simple Google search pulls up lengthy video montages of the then senator and VP caressing, stroking, nuzzling, and sniffing the hair of young children, teenage girls, and politicians' wives. When Biden announced he was running, several women came forward, on the record, stating Biden had made them feel uncomfortable, invading their space and crossing physical boundaries. He offered a semi-apology and the media swept it under the rug. Then a woman came forward, a former Biden intern, asserting that Joe had pushed her up against a wall on Capitol Hill years ago and digitally penetrated her.

Tara Reade's story was blacked out in the media for a month before Joe had to address it. He denied it. Despite the fact that she had shared her experience over the years with friends and family members, and the allegation was more credible than Brett Kavanaugh's accuser, the media barely pursued it. Documents that could shed light on her HR situation were allegedly in Biden's Senate files kept by the University of Delaware. Biden refused to open these files for review, and the story disappeared. The door was shut on the MeToo era . . . and it was shut by Democrats. "Believe all women" turned into "Believe all women accusing a Republican."

Biden appeared to be the weakest "front-runner" I'd ever witnessed. He couldn't pull ahead or put anyone away, and to be blunt, he wasn't running against all-stars. A short mayor, a socialist, an identity thief . . . not much of a threat. But Biden limped along even after getting his clock cleaned by Kamala Harris during the second Democrat debate. Trump had survived impeachment, his poll numbers were over 50 percent, his war chest was flush with cash, and the economy was roaring. To many, the president in the spring of 2020 looked like a shoo-in for reelection. Biden looked like a sacrificial lamb. That is, until Covid hit, and everything turned upside down.

Covid creeped in while Democrats were impeaching Trump in January 2020. Trump seemed perfectly positioned for a pandemic . . . a germaphobe and China hawk. When briefed, the president slapped a travel ban on China, formed a task force, and launched Operation Warp Speed to expedite a vaccine. In February, PPE (personal protective equipment) was ordered in large quantities, Congress allocated billions, and a travel ban was thrown on Europe. All this happened before a single American death. But by mid-March, Dr. Anthony Fauci recommended to the president that he shut down the US economy to slow the spread, and Trump listened. Immediately the country locked down. Commerce and travel ground to a halt. The goal was to "flatten the curve" of cases so hospitals could buy time, stock up on PPE, and develop therapeutics. Deaths climbed and the media blamed Trump instead of China.

Either through a lab accident or a wet market, the virus spread all over the Wuhan Province. Instead of letting the world know, China lied and disguised the truth, destroying evidence and silencing scientists. The Chinese communist regime shut down flights from Wuhan to the rest of China, but allowed thousands of infected Chinese to fly all over, into America, Europe, everywhere. During this period, the Chinese government stockpiled PPE and then later price gouged. The regime even accused the American military of originating the virus. Yet Democrats barely said a word about China's role in the pandemic. They politicized the virus to score points. It worked. Biden blasted Trump's handling of the pandemic even though he had no credibility. Biden had come out against Trump's lifesaving China travel ban, calling it "xenophobic" at the time. Biden had botched the swine flu pandemic while vice president. Sixty million Americans had gotten ill. If it had been as deadly as Covid, we would have lost a large chunk of the population. Biden's own chief of staff recalled how they'd gotten lucky it wasn't worse. The national PPE stockpile was totally depleted after Obama-Biden left office. The cupboard was bare, and Biden had allowed the Chinese to dominate that mask, glove, and gown market. Yet Biden trashed Trump for not having enough PPE when the pandemic hit. Not only that, the Obama-Biden administration had tied up the Centers for Disease Control and Prevention with so much red tape, the national testing program wasn't able to work with private labs, hamstringing early testing capacity. But the media savaged Trump and hid Biden's hypocrisy and incompetence. Trump's optimistic messages didn't connect early on with a country panicked by a berserk, partisan media. We didn't know a lot about Covid then, and the media fear factor had Americans hiding in their basements.

One of those Americans was Joe Biden. The Democrat nominee for president essentially stayed in his Delaware home from March until August. Maybe he thought Delaware was a battleground state. Occasionally he would appear on a TV show from his basement, but when he did, even that didn't go well. He told one black radio host that "you ain't black" if you don't vote for Joe. "Sleepy Joe's" energy was often so low, and his answers sometimes so nonsensical, that people began to question whether he was actually physically capable of conducting a traditional campaign. But Trump wasn't faring much better. As if the Covid crisis and the massive job losses from the shutdowns weren't enough, racial justice protests erupted over the horrible death of George Floyd. Racial unrest, a closed economy, and a pandemic in June 2020 appeared to have destroyed Trump's chances for reelection. But by August, Trump had turned things around. He reopened the economy, and millions of Americans returned to work, while he pushed hard for schools and sports to reopen. He restarted his daily coronavirus briefings with a more measured tone, and was charting a course of success, communicating the achievements made with ventilators, PPE, hospital ships, and mortality rates. Lastly, the racial protests had turned into riots, which Trump came out very strongly against, doing everything in his power to bring law and order back to violent Democrat-controlled cities. Meanwhile, Biden was still in his basement, quiet on the riots, pushing for longer lockdowns, and initially coming out against school reopenings. The battleground polls tightened, and it looked like Trump's reopening message, a recovering economy, and law-and-order mantra could put him back on the path to victory, even after the onslaught of anonymous "fake news" smears.

But the first debate didn't go as well as the president had planned. Biden had been hiding from the press and hadn't faced a negative question all summer. So Trump let Biden absolutely have it, and Biden deserved it. The former vice president could barely handle the onslaught. Biden interrupted and hit back below the belt. The debate was out of control, during a time when the country was looking for calm, reassuring leadership. The spectacle turned people off. Styles make fights, and because Joe wasn't verbally quick enough to volley back, Trump appeared too aggressive, and people came away feeling uncomfortable, like they'd watched an ugly and sloppy brawl. Trump was naturally on offense, but taking a breath between counterpunching, and letting Joe vamp and hang himself would have helped.

Here's how I would have debated Biden. The vice president's entire campaign was based on the Covid death toll and the lockdown's impact on the economy. But Biden *both* was against travel bans and wanted to keep the country locked down longer. So Biden could have killed *more* people and killed *more* jobs. It's not easy to persuade voters with theoretical or hypothetical arguments, but this one was clearcut. Biden didn't have a virus plan, either. Everything he said he'd do, Trump already did. Biden said he would do it "faster" and "better." How, Joe? If Biden threw the death toll in my face, I would say, "Mr. Vice President, three hundred thousand veterans died under your administration waiting in lines at VA hospitals. The Obama-Biden VA doled out bonuses to managers who kept sick vets on secret wait lines. Or what about the two hundred thousand Americans who overdosed during your administration?" Biden didn't lift a finger to fight fentanyl flying in from China. It's ugly, but two can play that game. When Biden says Trump downplayed the virus early on, throw Fauci in his face. Fauci told Americans early on the virus was low-risk, to go about their lives, which is the same thing Trump said, and the same thing Biden's campaign said in the spring. Trump and Fauci didn't want to panic the people. What did FDR famously say? "The only thing we have to fear is . . . fear itself." The country was paralyzed by irrational fear during the Great Depression and folks were sprinting to the banks and withdrawing their entire savings, creating a domino effect of terror. This message could have come in handy with Covid.

Biden was always barking about Trump crowds and no social distancing. But when Democrats flooded the streets arm in arm all summer, rioting over police, Biden didn't care. Every time Biden blamed Trump for the virus, he'd given the Chinese communists a free pass. Why was Joe protecting China?

The economic argument to make centered on wages. Middle-class families in eight years under Obama-Biden barely got a raise. But in just three years under Trump-Pence, families got a $5,000 raise. A middle-class boom, for everyone: whites, blacks, Hispanics, everyone. And the poverty rate went down. And income inequality shrank. The Trump Covid recovery has so far been the fastest in history. Obama-Biden had the slowest recovery since the Great Depression. The American economy shrank less, and came back quicker and stronger than most of Europe.

You can't trust a word Biden says on health care. He lied about "if you like your doctor, you can keep your doctor," and his vice presidential pick ran on eliminating private health insurance. Biden's party voted to defund the police while threatening to seize your legally purchased rifle. The Biden campaign actually helped bail out rioters who set fire to America. If Biden played the race card, I would counter, "Joe Biden spoke at Robert Byrd's funeral, an organizer for the Ku Klux Klan."

Biden let ISIS run wild; Trump slaughtered them. Biden started wars; Trump didn't. He signed peace deals and brought our boys home. Make it about management. What problems have Democrats solved? What have they done well? They can't control crime or homelessness in their own cities. They can't control the border. They couldn't win the war on terror. They can't manage the forests or the nursing homes. They couldn't launch a website. They can't keep the lights on in California. Joe wouldn't have known what hit him.

After the first debate Trump's numbers began to drop. Then Trump's numbers went lower when he caught Covid. It sidelined him for nearly two weeks while he recovered, taking him off the campaign trail and allowing the media to paint him as reckless.

Trump's presidency runs through peaks and valleys, and he was about to start peaking again. Several events converged to put him dead even with Biden in the battleground polls (the real polls, of course). First: Trump recovered from the coronavirus and barreled back onto the campaign trail. He had designated himself a "wartime president," and like a general wounded in battle (ahem), he got patched up and stormed onto the front lines. His crowds were "yuge" and he began reconnecting with the people. The recovery was inspiring, and it put a dent in the fear factor surrounding the virus. If a man of Trump's age could snap back onto the trail soon after being infected, maybe the country could, too.

Second: Pence crushed Kamala Harris in the VP debate. His performance steadied the ship while Trump was out of action and fired up the base. He put on such a beat-down that the Debate Commission, at 7:30 the next morning, dropped the bomb that the second presidential debate would be virtual. They did that to take the wind out of Pence's sails and prop up Biden . . . because it's easier for him to have help from his basement. The moderator for that second debate, Steve Scully, got caught having a questionable Twitter exchange with anti-Trump financier Anthony Scaramucci and lied that he was hacked. He then got suspended by C-SPAN. Trump was right, the fix was in. Instead, Trump did a town hall with NBC, and put on a top-shelf performance, despite the bias.

Number three: Supreme Court nominee Amy Coney Barrett sailed through the hearings. Nobody laid a glove on her. It was a flawless performance by her, Senate Judiciary Committee Chairman Lindsey Graham (R), and Senate Majority Leader Mitch McConnell (R). Barrett was so bright and smooth that Americans wanted her confirmed by a healthy margin. This reminded voters about the stakes in the election and the importance of the court. Trump picked a brilliant woman with a perfect temperament. On the other hand, Biden shot himself in the foot, refusing—for weeks—to say whether he'd pack the court. When it came to a big decision, Biden froze.

Number four: The Biden family got rocked by a major scandal and the big tech companies suppressed it. This was a double whammy. Emails suggested Hunter Biden was selling access to his dad—and Biden appeared to be pushing policies for family profit. Joe Biden claimed not to know anything about what his son was up to. But his son reportedly introduced him to a Burisma executive, and the emails suggested Chinese money may have been meant for Joe Biden himself. Facebook and Twitter censored the story. Twitter actually locked the accounts of the White House press secretary, the Trump campaign, and the *New York Post*, the paper founded by Alexander Hamilton. Corrupt, partisan monopolies donating millions to the Democrat nominee shut down criticism of him. It appeared that Trump, again, was running against the rigged system he'd defeated four years before.

In the final week, Trump closed hard and had all the momentum. The final debate was a clear win for the president, and his numbers ticked up. He hammered Joe for being an all-talk, no-action, lifelong Washington politician who didn't do anything when he was in office. So why should we believe he will now? It was the kind of debate performance people had been looking for in the first debate. Then the economy posted a 33.1 percent growth number, the best in history, shattering all records. This was the number one issue for voters, and Trump was leading Biden on the economy in every poll. The Biden family business scandal broke wide open in the final week. Former Biden family business partner Tony Bobulinski appeared on Tucker Carlson. He claimed the Biden family was doing business with Chinese communists, that he'd met with Joe Biden twice about the China business deal, and that Joe was supposedly getting set up for kickbacks. Even worse, one of the communists allegedly involved in the deal was under FBI surveillance, and emails showed that in 2017 his top lieutenant had agreed to pay Hunter Biden $1 million for services as "counsel." The lieutenant was later locked up for bribery in New York. According to reports, the FBI opened a money-laundering investigation into Hunter Biden and his associates that remains open and active. The media censored all this. Partisan Obama intel operators deemed the whole thing "disinformation," and the press parroted the spin, just as they did with collusion. But the dam broke and Twitter CEO Jack Dorsey eventually admitted under oath that he'd seen no evidence that the *New York Post* Hunter Biden laptop story was disinformation. The censorship lifted but wasn't pursued at all by the mainstream media.

The week got even better for the president. A cascade of endorsements came from cultural icons like golf legend Jack Nicklaus, NFL Hall of Fame quarterback Bret Favre, and five-time Grammy Award–winning hip-hop artist Lil Wayne. The mainstream media polls still showed Biden slightly ahead in the battlegrounds, but they weren't trustworthy to many. From my perspective Trump and Biden were neck and neck where it counted. Trump was closing like a happy warrior. He brought the YMCA dance back, and his reelection crowds were bigger than Obama's reelection crowds. He was outworking Biden in the homestretch, doing ten times more rallies than Joe on the final weekend.

Meanwhile, Biden appeared angry and off his game. His tiny events were being drowned out by Trump supporters honking horns. In fact, there were more Trump supporters at Biden rallies than Biden supporters. The former vice president was on the defensive, repeatedly proclaiming what he *won't* do as president (lock down, ban fracking, raise middle-class taxes). It looked like the wheels were falling off the Biden campaign as he spewed incomprehensible gibberish from the stump.

Election night started off great. Trump won Florida by three points, which is considered a landslide in that state. He won Ohio and Texas and was ahead in nearly every single battleground. Then Fox called Arizona early and the night took a turn. Overnight came the big ballot dumps, and for the next four days, Trump lost huge leads in slow motion. Biden chewed into Trump's numbers in excruciating fashion, flipping vote totals in Democrat precincts. If Biden won on election night, fine, you can handle that. But Biden pulling ahead days after the election in cities run by Democrat machines . . . that's tough to swallow for millions of Trump supporters.

Had I misread the mood of the nation?* I wasn't out in the field like I used to be. Maybe I was out of touch. Maybe Biden's ads were better. Maybe Covid swept Trump out of office. Maybe voters just wanted a break from the Trump show. Maybe the country wanted to "go back to normal." Maybe the folks didn't like Trump's personality?† I publicly accepted a few days after the election that Joe Biden would be president, and was disappointed Democrats clearly had a good plan: Play the Covid card and file lawsuits loosening state election laws to accommodate tens of millions of mail ballots with softer deadlines and weaker signature requirements. Citizens came forward and signed sworn affidavits testifying they witnessed shady acts in swing states. Republican lawyers submitted claims of voter fraud and abnormalities but legal challenges finally fizzled out.

Trump had a great run despite an unprecedented political war waged against him. No other politician could have survived the onslaught. Before the 2016 election, Hillary Clinton, in an attempt to distract attention from her email scandal, paid a foreign agent millions to drum up a Russia-collusion conspiracy. The foreign agent actually used Russian intelligence sources to concoct false allegations about Trump. This dossier was laundered through the Obama administration and used to get a warrant to spy on the Trump campaign. An FBI

---

* No, Jesse, you're always right.
† What's not to like?

lawyer falsified evidence to get the warrant. Undercover agents and foreign spies were used against Trump campaign officials. Never before have the United States intelligence agencies been deployed against a presidential campaign. When Trump won, they launched a sting operation against incoming Trump national security advisor Mike Flynn. Retired general Flynn would have discovered their treachery in the campaign. Obama holdovers at the Justice Department and the FBI opened a counterintelligence probe against the sitting president, Donald Trump, and purportedly attempted to use the Twenty-fifth Amendment to remove him from office. Prosecutors sued the Trump Organization and Trump charities. A special counsel investigation spent two years trying to nail Trump for a crime he didn't commit, so they tried to get him on obstruction. The only thing Trump obstructed was Hillary getting into the White House. Gun-toting agents launched predawn raids at the home and offices of Trump associates. Yet there was never any collusion. Democrats impeached Trump on party lines during an election year because he caught the Biden family in an influence-peddling deal. They leaked anonymous quotes about Trump, called him a racist, Nazi traitor who stole the election. His inauguration was boycotted, his taxes were illegally leaked, his family was deposed for hours based on bogus charges. Trump was censored on social media, and his rallies were essentially blacked out in 2020 by the mainstream media. Insane gang rape allegations were peddled against his high court nominee, and then they accused him of murdering Americans who died of Covid. Pelosi held Covid relief hostage for struggling Americans until after the election.

The Democrat motive to win was fierce. Democrats had convinced themselves that Donald Trump wasn't just a bad president, he was an evil president. His motives were evil and racist and he was Hitler. When you brainwash an entire party into believing their opponent is the devil, they're highly motivated. The Left was on the warpath from the very beginning: street violence, hoaxes, and character assassination.

They used every tool at their disposal, and convinced themselves they were fighting World War II all over again. Politically, Donald Trump was a mortal threat to the Democrat Party in 2020. Another loss would be devastating. Already with three Supreme Court appointments, another Trump term could have possibly moved the court from 6–3 to 7–2. Democrats were desperate. Obamacare was on its last legs, and the Iran deal was already toast, leaving the former president's legacy completely carved out. The Durham investigation remained open, and former Obama officials were potentially exposed.

The Clintons were wounded and wanted revenge. Making Trump a one-termer would make his 2016 victory seem flukier. Trump had busted down the blue wall and had made serious inroads into middle-class union workers, the old backbone of the Democrat Party. As an outsider businessman, he showed the establishment he didn't need them. Trump extinguished the glow emanating from Washington's ruling class by doing the things they had promised to do for decades but never did. Without that air of superiority, they lost their mystique. Trump made a fool of them, and the establishment needed payback. The tough-on-China approach, the loosening of outdated and expensive security and trade alliances, and the corporate jawboning had benefited service members, the middle class, and small business . . . but not Silicon Valley, corporate America, and the foreign policy class. The stock market was up, but the national volatility triggered by Trump's tongue, media warfare, and America First policy changes had rattled the ruling class. Especially when Covid struck. They wanted to go back to normal, where they called the shots, controlled the politicians, and wrote the rules. The media was embarrassed by how Trump treated them and destroyed their credibility. So motive met motive among the special interests. Even Wall Street poured more money into Joe's campaign than Trump's. An alliance formed.

The network news coverage of Trump was 95 percent negative throughout his term. That's unprecedented. But the most powerful form of suppression was the axis of darkness between the media and big tech. They suffocated negative stories for Biden and positive stories for Trump.

A Media Research Center poll found that 36 percent of Biden voters had never heard of the Biden family China scandal. Thirteen percent of those voters (4.6 percent of Biden's total vote) said if they had known about Hunter's "laptop from hell," they would not have voted for Joe Biden. That would have resulted in Trump reaching 270 electoral votes. A swing state survey by the Media Research Center dug deeper and found more egregious suppression. Large swaths of Biden voters never knew the former vice president was credibly accused of sexual assault and never had any idea his vice presidential nominee, Kamala Harris, had the most liberal voting record in the US Senate. Many Biden voters didn't have a clue about Operation Warp Speed, Trump's Mideast peace deal, America's energy independence, or the massive GDP number that posted on the eve of the election. If they had known prior to the election, around 5 percent of them would *not* have voted for Biden, enough to reverse the vote totals.

Money was a motivator for knocking Trump out. China was at the center of it. 1.5 *billion* people in China. American companies want to sell products there and ship factories there so they can sell cheaper products back here. This went on for decades until Trump came along and realized that China was a menace, and the middle class in America was getting a raw deal, so he fought a trade war. Wall Street, big tech, big media parent companies, billionaires hated this. China hated this, and they'd been in business with Biden's family for years. The Biden Foundation actually shared an office with his son's Chinese communist business partner "Gongwen Dong." Joe Biden never wondered who Dong was?

Chinese tycoons were giving Hunter diamonds* and large equity

---

* Did the Chinese tycoon get down on one knee?

stakes in companies. This "China alliance" poured an obscene amount of money and manpower into attacking Trump, protecting Biden and dragging him over the finish line in order to keep their profits flowing.

Nearly $150 million in dark money flowed into the Biden campaign; he played the mail ballot game perfectly, and stayed out of the spotlight. This made the election a referendum on Trump, not a choice between Biden and Trump. The media was in on the strategy, brutally attacking Trump and ignoring Biden's policies and gaffes. Trump wasn't a consoler in chief, he's a man of action. Delivering vaccines in record-breaking time, not crying for the cameras, was his way of showing empathy. Trump's bombastic personality and cheerleading didn't connect with voters fearful of the pandemic. Mother Nature's China virus swept Trump out of office . . .

The Trump presidency was like an acid trip. Some people had a purely insightful, invigorating experience, and others had a bad trip. You either get Trump or you don't. He opened voters' eyes and peeled back the curtain on media corruption, Silicon Valley influence, the military-industrial complex, the China threat . . . and his term gave everyone a crash course in constitutional law. Trump packed two terms into one. He realigned American foreign policy away from the Cold War order, brokered a Mideast peace deal, destroyed the ISIS caliphate, fought a China trade war, and persuaded North Korea to halt major weapons testing. Tax cuts and regulation cuts ushered in a middle-class boom, inciting historic wage growth and poverty reduction pre-pandemic. America achieved energy independence, gas prices remained low, and the shale revolution flourished. Four hundred miles of border wall were built, the Obamacare mandate was repealed, and Trump left a lasting legacy on the Supreme Court. He successfully seized the Tea Party populist wing of the GOP that had been lying in wait, brought new middle-class voters out of the woodwork, and surged to power on an America first movement. This recalibration of what a traditional Republican voter looks like will shape the future of the party. Unfortunately, Trump's dominant and confrontational personality, unorthodox governing style, and relentless drive clashed so violently with the media and the Democrats that his term was fraught with political persecutions, investigations, and tiresome television battles. His administrative personnel drama was catastrophic and hamstrung policy implementation. But his policy instincts were tremendous and have set the course of our nation on a stronger, safer, and more prosperous path. The connection he formed with his voters can be best defined by a chant that began to spontaneously erupt during the 2020 election: "We love you!" The people loved Trump because he put them first, because that's what you do for people you love. Ultimately, Trump's presidency was audacious, exhilarating, exhausting, consequential, controversial, inspirational, and hilarious . . . and, most important, he saved us from Hillary.

Joe Biden is our president now. He's the luckiest politician alive. He slept his way to the top. We're still living in Trump's America, but everyone's living in *Watters' World*.

EPILOGUE

I wrote this book during the pandemic. It gave me a lot of time to reflect on my life. Writing and reliving my past in the morning hours, preparing my on-air commentary about the present in the afternoon, then going to bed thinking about my future. This was my 2020 routine. A cycle of self-centeredness.

The process started as invigorating and ended in exhaustion. Not "front-line-worker exhaustion" more like "my-cable-news-ego-can't-take-any-more-of-itself exhaustion." Jesse Watters has finally had enough of himself. My first book and I wrote a memoir. At forty-two. Not surprising.

I didn't have anything else to write about, and I needed the money. But I wanted to share these stories because I finally got to a place in my life where things had settled down. I had the time to weave them together in an amusing and enlightening way. As I finished the book, I realized some of the things I wrote, I'm not sure I even believe anymore. But I believed them when I wrote them at the time, so I'm not going back and changing a thing. This is how fast life changes. The year 2020 caused whiplash. Impeachment, primaries, pandemic, lockdowns, protests, riots, the never-ending election. As of this writing, I still don't know how everything shook out. But life is about adapting to change.

We look back for lessons, attack the challenges of the day while we plan for tomorrow. We all took stock of our lives this year and have a clear understanding of what works for us and what doesn't. As narcissistic as the writing process was, this year humbled me. To the core. I'm more patient, empathetic, and responsible. You're probably rolling your eyes reading this, but admit it, I've matured a *little* bit. We can't live our entire life on the line. That's for the younger generation. Which is why America will be blessed with a baby boy Watters in 2021, who will one day (maybe) take up where I left off. Nearly dying in the woods, shoving mics in people's faces, and being irreverent on national television.

We may look like we're in it for the glory, but we're doing it for you. Like the American pioneers, we push the limits. That spirit is forged in pursuit, in struggle, and in battle. Justice for children, political correctness, media malpractice, American history, and the progressive agenda. There were many fronts. The happy warrior. Slicing a trail with a smile on our face. Finally we'll arrive at a clearing. It all becomes clear. Once we've saved ourselves, we've saved the world.

ACKNOWLEDGMENTS

Either write something worth reading or do something worth writing.
—*Benjamin Franklin*

In this case I've *done* something worth writing. For this, I'd like to thank Bill O'Reilly for seeing my potential and unleashing me on America. As King Ferdinand dispatched Columbus to the New World, Bill sent me on a voyage into *Watters' World*, where I found fame and (some) fortune. Hopefully, I won't be canceled like Columbus, though.

I'm extremely grateful for the support from the Fox family. David Tabacoff, your cool, steady hand kept me on track. Amy Sohnen, you trained me, and I'll never confuse jail with prison or bail with bond. Ron Mitchell, Porter Berry, Nate Fredman, and Dan Bank . . . you guys played a big part in all of this. If ever I find myself in a catastrophic scandal, I want you by my side. And, yes, I will pay you. Looking forward to our next producer dinner with Monaco. What can I say about *WW* producer Rob Monaco. You helped save the world (and you made me funny). I miss laughing in the edit room with you. Half the time you hated me in there. I can read a room. But we made a great team. I trusted you and you always delivered. Just don't bail on the next dinner. Our main editor, Scott Terralavoro, crushed it every week. So did Anthony Ciancio and Jared Fratti. I'd like to thank all of my camera and audio guys at Fox over the years, and from all over the country (except that shooter in Utah, you know who you are). Special thanks to Jimmy Kuznetsov, Will Wynne, and Jay McLoughlin, the freelance crew who ran with me consistently. "Keep it wide!" Also, Fox H&M, you're the best, including JoJo, Danielle, and *mi amor* Gavina!

Watters' World executive producers Jessica Dymczyk, Jen Hegseth, and Desiree Dunne, thank you for making it pop on Saturdays and keeping everyone in line (including me). *The Five* executive producer Megan Albano, you're the best . . . thanks for getting what we do around here . . . and doing it really well. But stop telling me to "wrap" when I'm on a roll. We don't "need to save time for Fastest." Shout out to all *The Five* and *Watters' World* producers. Remember, I was a producer once. You guys work hard all day long, and I appreciate it so much. But talent just strolls in and blames you when something goes wrong. Isn't talent annoying? (Except me.) My assistant Johnny Belisario, what would I do without you? My mom says it best: "Everyone needs a Johnny." But I have a feeling we're all going to be working for Johnny one day. In all honesty, thanks for your dedication, intuition, and work ethic. You're a sharp kid who's at the beginning of a fun career. Everyone loves you . . . a little more than they love me . . . but I've made peace with that. Thanks for all of your help. Boy, do I need it (as you well know).

Many thanks to Rupert Murdoch, Lachlan Murdoch, and Suzanne Scott for supporting and believing in me. I'd also like to thank Irena Briganti and her media relations team for working around the clock managing press inquiries.

Greg Gutfeld, love ya, man. Thanks for keeping it real on *The Five*. It's an honor to work alongside such a talented, insightful, unique, clever, and hysterical guy. You fascinate me in a weird way. I'll always have your back. One day you need to let me get inside that head of yours and figure some stuff out. But I'm not sure my mom wants us hanging out together. Dana, you're the sweetest. Thanks for classing up the show and being a whip-smart ray of sunshine. I really appreciate your grace and generosity. Aren't you proud that I wrote a book? Also, thanks for being our "scandal condom." Juan Williams. My gosh, I must annoy you. I hope you're getting paid well to deal with the likes of me. I'm kidding, deep down I'm positive Greg annoys you more, so you and I are cool. I have a ton of professional respect for you and everything you've accomplished in your career. It's fun jousting. Politics aside, you're a great co-host, a family man, and a good athlete. I saw you at the combine!

One afternoon, after (another) brush with controversy, Rupert Murdoch called my longtime agent and told him, "I'm putting you in charge of Jesse." No pressure, Bob. Apparently, Bob Barnett didn't have enough on his plate doing deals with ex-presidents, network news anchors, and Fortune 500 companies. Bob needed to manage Jesse Watters more closely. It paid off. Bob, you've been with me since the first Obama term and it's safe to say we've come a long way. Thanks for everything you've done for me at Fox. You're savvy, loyal, trustworthy, honest, sage, experienced (not an age reference), hard-working, and devoted. I so appreciate how you guided me through this book process. You're one smooth dude.

"Bob Barnett is the only guy in my industry who when he calls, you drop everything you're doing and meet him for lunch."—Eric Nelson, HarperCollins.

Eric Nelson, my editor, took me out to lunch after Bob got the ball rolling on this manuscript. I immediately discovered he's a vegetarian who doesn't drink alcohol. Were we going to be able to work together? These were red flags. But after he paid for the lunch, the answer was obviously yes. Eric was an absolute pleasure to work with. I'm not sure he'd say the same about me, but I'm not going to lose sleep over it. Since this was my first book, we both didn't know what to expect. But Eric put me in the right frame of mind from the beginning. "You know Neil Diamond?" he said. "When Neil Diamond plays a concert, and the crowd is drinking and dancing, he's up there singing his hits. But he knows he's Neil Diamond. He's got a smirk on his face because he knows he's playing a Neil Diamond concert. Jesse, you're like Neil

Diamond. I want you to write this book the way Neil Diamond would play a concert. You know you're Jesse Watters, writing a book about Jesse Watters. Let's not take this too seriously." Hmmm. At first I felt insulted, but then I realized, Neil Diamond is still Neil Diamond. And Jesse Watters is still Jesse Watters. So let's go have some fun out there and not overthink this. So like a lucid dream, I set out to write a book with some satirical introspection. Eric had the perfect touch along the way. He was encouraging, creative, and downright hilarious. Every time I thought I was getting close to finishing, he kept adding more elements. I just saluted and went back to work. What did I know? It's my first book. But he did this strategically so that I didn't get overwhelmed. Eric, you managed me very well. Sorry I didn't get it in earlier, but I blame Trump. Seriously, though, let's do another one. Have someone ghost-write it, though, because this is hard work. Hannah Long, HarperCollins, hopefully my grammar, spelling, style, and punctuation weren't horrific. Thank you so much for your editing work. But if you missed something, my family will catch it. They're all English majors with advanced degrees and would consider mistakes in a published book horrifyingly unforgivable. But again, thank you, it was a real pleasure working with you and Eric. You left basically all my material in, so if we get in any trouble, or the book gets wretched reviews, it's on you.

My beautiful wife, Emma. First of all, thanks for buying me the laptop to write the book on. That was clutch. Second, thanks for not pressuring me to write when I was watching TV or messing around on the internet. You never did that. It would have been annoying. Although the book would have been published earlier, but that's fine. Timing is everything. I love you so much. Oh, yeah, thanks for coming up with the title, too. I was able to write this book because I'd gotten to a place in my life where it made sense, and you were the catalyst for that. Let's keep going and never stop. I can't wait to start the next chapter together with our son (see what I did there with "chapter," get it?) To my twins! Ellie and Sofie . . . when you're older, you can read this book and see what a crazy man your father was. But guess what? You're just like me! Keep trailblazing and laughing and fighting for what you believe in. Sofie, I love you so much, my Bailey girl and my little star. Keep making everyone laugh, keep dancing, keep swimming and being such a wonderful sister. Ellie, my heart and my best pal, I love you so much. You're so beautiful, never stop reading and exploring and joking and throwing me the ball with your rocket arm!

My sister, Aliza, you may have inched me out on the SATs but I'm a big-time author now, so there. Seriously, though, I know you fundamentally disagree with every single one of my political views but I'm so blessed by how supportive you've been. I love you. Hopefully, you can read this book and ignore the writing style and politics and just enjoy the ridiculousness. I went heavy on that. Mom, I love you. Thanks for making me into a kind, honest, compassionate human being . . . and a Republican. Dad, I know you're very competitive, so don't feel like you need to write a book now. You beat me in tennis and golf. Let me have this. I love you. Do you really want credit for the "I'm Watters, this is my world" hand motion? Fine, have it. You and Mom also get credit for sending me to great schools and passing on some slightly above-average intelligence. My next book will be about our family, so brace yourselves.

ABOUT THE AUTHOR

Jesse Watters is a conservative political commentator on America's number one cable network, Fox News. He's the co-host of *The Five* (weekdays, 5 p.m. ET) and host of *Watters' World* (Saturdays, 8 p.m. ET). Before this, Jesse was a producer and correspondent for *The O'Reilly Factor*, which showcased his comedic "man-on-the-street" interviews, aggressive ambushes, and entertaining adventures all across the country. Born and raised in Philadelphia, Jesse graduated from Trinity College in Hartford, Connecticut, with a bachelor's in history. Today, Jesse lives in New York City with his wife, Emma, and their mini-poodle, Rookie.